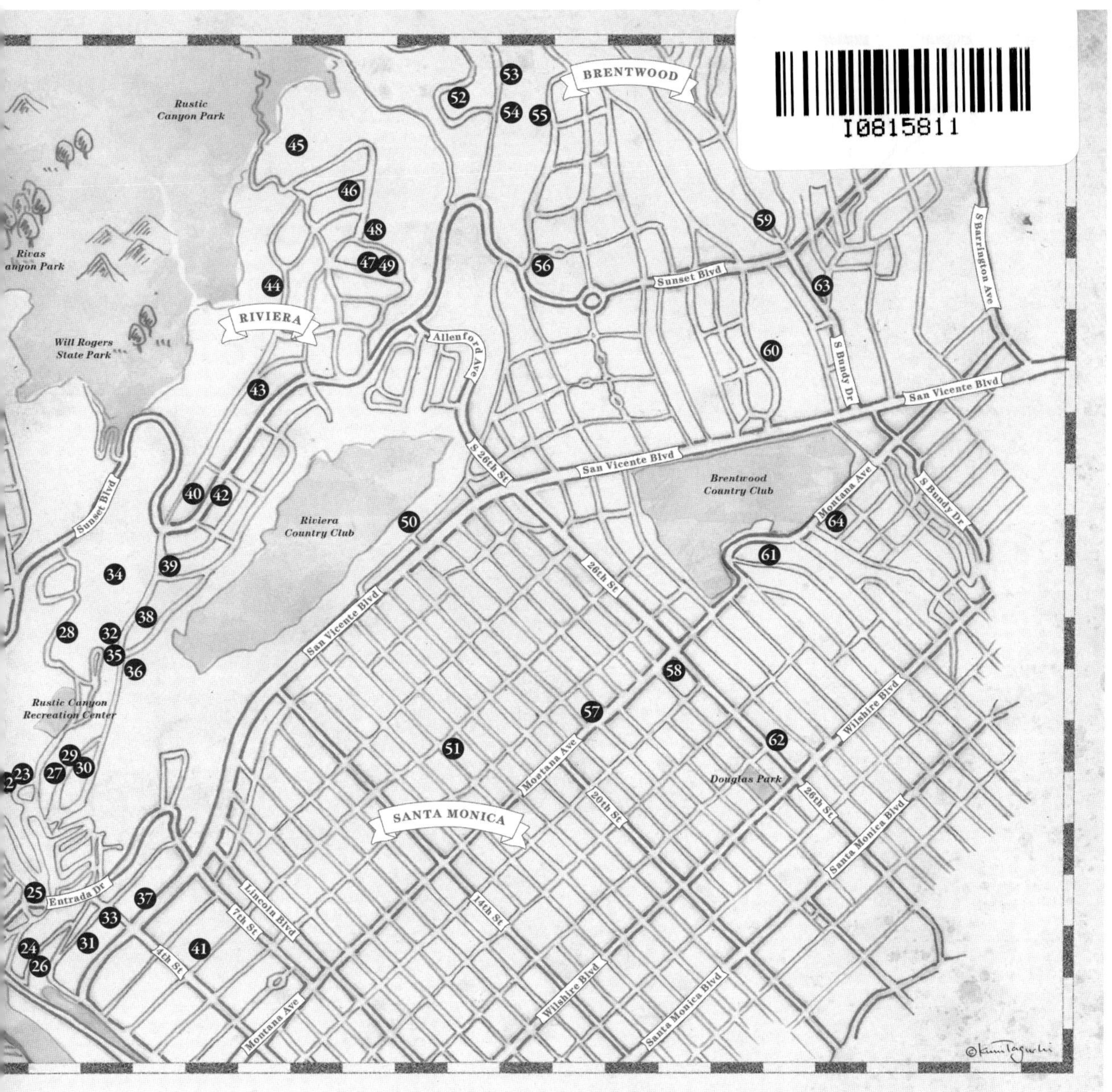

Laughton, Charles: *14954 Corona del Mar* 17
Lorre, Peter: *326 Adelaide Drive* 33, *1670 Mandeville Canyon* 54
Ludwig, Emil: *701 Amalfi Drive* 32, *303 Grenola Street* 9
Malcolmson, David S.: *533 Mount Holyoke Avenue* 11, *544 Rustic Road* 22, *491 Mesa Road* 23
Mann, Heinrich and Nelly: *2145 Montana Avenue* 57
Mann, Thomas and Katia: *441 North Rockingham Avenue* 55, *740 Amalfi Drive* 38, *1550 San Remo Drive* 48
Marcuse, Ludwig: *451 San Vicente Boulevard* 37
von Mendelssohn, Francesco: *515 Radcliffe Avenue* 10
Miller, Henry: *444 Ocampo Drive* 19
Niven, David: *1525 Amalfi Drive* 44
Preminger, Ingo: *14949 Corona del Mar* 18
Rainer, Luise: *740 Amalfi Drive* 38
Reagan, Ronald and Nancy: *1258 Amalfi Drive* 43, *1669 San Onofre Drive* 45
Reichenbach, Hans: *496 17th Street* 51
Reinhardt, Gottfried: *12324 Montana Avenue* 64
Reinhardt, Max ad Helene Thimig: *15000 Corona del Mar* 16
Reinhardt, Wolfgang: *415 Marguerita Avenue* 41
Scott, Charles Holmes: *631 Via de la Paz* 14
Schönberg, Arnold: *116 North Rockingham Avenue* 56
Selznick, David: *1525 Amalfi Drive* 44
Sommer, Hans and Ann: *569 Mount Holyoke Avenue* 13
Spielberg, Steven: *1525 Amalfi Drive* 44
Stradner, Rose and Joseph L. Mankiewicz: *694 Amalfi Drive* 36
Tabori, George: *165 Mabery Road* 24
Toch, Ernst and Lilly: *601 Toyopa Drive* 20, *811 Franklin Street* 61
Toller, Ernst: *413 West Channel Road* 30
Viertel, Salka and Berthold: *165 Mabery Road* 24
Weil, Felix: *533 Spoleto Drive* 27
Whale, James: *1048 Amalfi Drive* 40
Zaser, Gertrud: *13525 D'Este Drive* 47
Zinneman, Fred: *132 Mabery Road* 16, *1766 Westridge Road* 33

WEIMAR UNDER THE PALMS

WEIMAR UNDER THE PALMS

Pacific Palisades, German Exiles, and the Invention of Hollywood

THOMAS BLUBACHER

Translated by Elisabeth Lauffer

BRANDEIS UNIVERSITY PRESS WALTHAM, MA

Brandeis University Press

First published in German as *Weimar unter Palmen – Pacific Palisades: Die Erfindung Hollywoods und das Erbe des Exils* by Piper Verlag GmbH, 2022

Manufactured in the United States of America
Designed by and composed in Garamond Premier Pro
and Fonseca by Mindy Basinger Hill

The translation of this work was supported
by a grant from the Goethe-Institut

BRANDEIS UNIVERSITY PRESS acknowledges the generous support of the Center for German and European Studies at Brandeis University, which is supported by the German Academic Exchange Service (DAAD) with funds from the German Federal Foreign Office (Auswärtiges Amt).

Library of Congress Cataloging-in-Publication Data
available at https://catalog.loc.gov/
cloth ISBN 978-1-68458-287-7
e-book ISBN 978-1-68458-288-4

5 4 3 2 1

CONTENTS

PREFACE

PLANNING WAS UNDERWAY for presenting this book at Villa Aurora in Pacific Palisades when the first ghastly images appeared in the news on January 7, 2025. Multiple wildfires were ravaging Southern California, fueled by a combination of powerful Santa Ana winds and unusually dry conditions exacerbated by human-caused climate change. The Palisades Fire proved most grievous, spreading across 23,700 acres, from the hills of Pacific Palisades to the beaches of Malibu. Over the following weeks, it claimed twelve human lives and destroyed more than 6,800 structures, representing the vast majority of a truly beloved community. From the Alphabet Streets to the "Village," the fire left nothing but destruction, with much of the Palisades commercial center burned to the ground. Village School and Palisades Charter Elementary, Pierson Playhouse, and the ranch home that once belonged to vaudeville performer, philanthropist, and radio personality Will Rogers were reduced to ash. Other landmark structures were saved, including the Getty Villa and modernist icon the Eames House. As flames threatened to consume the Thomas Mann House and Villa Aurora, German federal commissioner for culture and the media, Claudia Roth, told the German news agency dpa, "The destruction of these important cultural sites would be a cultural catastrophe. They are symbols of exile and the freedom of art."[1] Miraculously, the buildings were spared the Armageddon's wrath. At a time when the values these places represent come under threat on both sides of the Atlantic, their continued existence is more important than ever.

Thomas Blubacher | MARCH 2025

WEIMAR UNDER THE PALMS

"A REAL CASTLE ON THE SEA"

IT'S A MILD, springlike seventy-two degrees, and the air smells of bougainvillea and fresh-cut grass. Hummingbirds zip about the lush gardens at Villa Aurora. Back home in Basel, that January 2002, the mercury hovers at just fourteen degrees. And in New York, where I spent a few days at the public library doing research for my project—the first-ever biography of siblings Eleonora and Francesco von Mendelssohn, who fled to the United States in 1935—temperatures haven't been much warmer. From my window I gaze past a shady eucalyptus tree and spindly pair of palms, those hallmarks of the LA streetscape, to Santa Monica Bay, where the lights glitter at night, and the still, glassy ocean. Here, in the seaside neighborhood of Pacific Palisades, there is no sign of the infamous smog shrouding the City of Angels.

The Spanish colonial revival villa, where I have been invited to reside (in the toniest sense of the word) for three months, doesn't look like much from Paseo Miramar, which snakes up a steep, overgrown hill to the right, off Sunset, just before the boulevard hits the coast. From the narrow gate at number 520, stairs lead down to an Azulejo-tiled patio. Only once you're inside and facing the villa from the south do its imposing dimensions reveal themselves: nearly seven thousand square feet spread over fourteen rooms on three floors, the property itself just shy of half an acre. "A real castle on the sea," Thomas Mann marveled, whereas Hermann Kesten sniped, "Would that all writers lived that way . . . with twenty rooms, eleven thousand books . . . , a hilly two-acre property, a secretary, and a woman to cook, garden, bake, drive, and dutifully serve the great man of letters. What a life."[1] That's where I am now, along with two other artists-in-residence, a Kazakh composer and an Austrian filmmaker. We have neither the secretary nor the "woman," of course, but Juan tends the gardens and the marvelous Betty keeps our rooms shipshape—the two immigrated from Mexico and Guatemala, respectively. During the week Joachim and Claudia in the office take care of our needs. Truly, truly: what a life.

Sixty years ago Villa Aurora was one of the most important gathering places for European and US intellectuals. Marta and Lion Feuchtwanger's regular guests included Thomas Mann and his brother Heinrich, Bertolt Brecht, Alfred Döblin, Bruno Frank, Arnold Schoenberg and Kurt Weill, Ludwig Marcuse and Max Horkheimer, Charles Laughton, Peter Lorre, Ingrid Bergman, Charlie Chaplin, and Franz Werfel and his wife, Alma Mahler-Werfel. I currently sleep in Lion Feuchtwanger's bed. I work at the desk that once belonged to Franz Werfel. He was sitting at this desk when his heart stopped beating, and he slumped to the floor from his swivel chair. Many years later Werfel's furniture was moved to Villa Aurora, as was a reasonably comfortable couch of Hanns Eisler's. My coresident, celebrated in the press for her uncompromising artistic integrity, plays easy-listening Mariah Carey tunes on Ernst Toch's Blüthner just for us, in performances closed to the public. Toch himself—or his bust, anyway, crafted by Gustav Mahler's daughter Anna—watches from his perch atop the grand piano. To one side white lettering on a green background indicates the "exile route." Heiner Müller—who in 1995 was the first guest at the newly renovated retreat, the paint scarcely dried—employed a bit of adhesive tape to change the "EXIT" sign to read "EXIL": exile as an emergency exit; an emergency exit into exile. The thirty-four–stop organ, which needs some work done, has always been here. (Organs used to symbolize status the way swimming pools later would.) Eisler intoned "Üb' immer Treu' und Redlichkeit" on the instrument when the Feuchtwangers moved in.

Twenty-two thousand volumes from the Feuchtwangers' library are still housed at Villa Aurora, only eight thousand of the most valuable works—including a 1493 *Nuremberg Chronicle*—having been entrusted to the University of Southern California. Memorabilia are displayed in a glass case: a medicine vial, letter opener, pair of scissors, an ink pot and blotter, a lacquer box and small tin, and the Commander's Cross of the Order of Merit of the Federal Republic of Germany conferred on Marta in 1966. A slip of paper bears Lion's handwritten words: "I am a German writer, / The beat of my heart is Jewish, / My thinking belongs to the world." Villa Aurora never feels like a museum, though. Only once, when a timeworn shot glass slips and breaks, are we jolted by the thought that it had likely belonged to Marta and may have been used by Albert Einstein or Bertolt Brecht.

THEIR SPIRITS LEAVE US BE. The big names we encounter are different. Pacific Palisades, population twenty-seven thousand, has the placid feel of a small city. Its downtown, a contained area fittingly known as the "Village," comprises three grocery stores, seven gas stations, and a bookstore that stays open late, which helps make up for the fact that there's no movie theater. The neighborhood is home to the rich and famous. Michael Douglas, Nicole Kidman, and Arnold Schwarzenegger live here, I'm told, as do Anthony Hopkins, Sylvester Stallone, and Whoopi Goldberg. Sure enough, Tom Hanks can be found sitting at the Starbucks where I get my Americano, and waiting in line at Gelson's is none other than Steven Spielberg. Because it's off the beaten path, Pacific Palisades affords greater privacy than areas like Beverly Hills. There are no stargazing tours, no buses packed with oglers eager to snap photos of celebrity mansions who mistake every landscaper they see for a star; paparazzi rarely lie in wait here either. As it is, residents routinely engage with people most of us know only from the silver screen, whether professionally or at parent-teacher conferences.

One evening my cohorts and I are invited next door to take in the priceless view of Los Angeles' sparkling sea of lights, while a young Mexican woman doles out what for us are equally unpayable quantities of caviar—rather a surreal experience. I do my best to make requisite small talk with the young woman installed beside me on the sofa, who introduces herself as Constance. I comment on the Balinese décor in every furnishing and fitting, down to the coffee-table books. She thanks me, as though I had praised her personally; then it turns out she was the interior designer. This room, Constance tells me, was still new; many homes were redecorated, the furniture swapped out, every few months, and she was currently doing Sharon Stone's estate. On another occasion talk turns to Tom Cruise, and Doug—a successful young playwright penning a piece about Vladimir Horowitz, the concert pianist and friend of Francesco von Mendelssohn's—asks crisply if I would like to meet the superstar: "Shall I call him?" (It is through Doug that I will meet some of the most interesting artists in Los Angeles, most of them liberal, Jewish, and gay.) My heart, though, is set on meeting Mickey Rooney, who played Puck in Max Reinhardt's *A Midsummer Night's Dream* nearly a lifetime—some sixty-seven years—ago.

Long before I arrived here, I read that Alfred Döblin had groused about the "dreadful garden city," and Vicki Baum had complained that a person couldn't walk anywhere without raising suspicion—not that it stopped Thomas Mann from strolling about the Palisades.[2] I rent a tomato-red Mitsubishi, and before long I get used to the multilane traffic that felt so scary at first and start driving more in a day than I would in weeks back home. Driving is a way of life in Los Angeles. Hanging my left arm out the window, opened with the press of a button (my car in Switzerland still has a manual crank), listening to smooth jazz on 94.7 The Wave, I cruise down Paseo Miramar and stop at Vons, on the corner of Sunset and Route 1, to grab bagels, some shrimp, or a bottle of cabernet sauvignon. I continue on to Santa Monica, where I have discovered a Thai restaurant with the best *panang nua* on Earth, or meander along Sunset Boulevard through Beverly Hills, toward Hollywood or downtown to visit a library or attend a play. The very first week I'm here, I stumble upon a performance of *Mephisto*, based on Klaus Mann's novel, that blows all my preconceptions about commercial US repertoire out of the water. The show is staged by Hollywood star Tim Robbins at the Actors' Gang. Afterward I have a long exchange about Germany and emigration with Bill Cusack, John's and Joan's younger brother, who stars in the role of Sebastian Bruckner, essentially a stand-in for Klaus Mann.

I am astounded by how close the relationship is between Hollywood and exile, the two main topics of my research and reason for my stay. It's on full display, and not only on the eve of the Oscars, when the who's who of German film and culture flock to Villa Aurora—in the garden, on the vast terrace, and in the parlor, which by now feels like our own living room—to celebrate German nominees. The same stone bench that once appeared in a famous photo of Feuchtwanger and Brecht in conversation is now occupied by Udo Kier and hippie icon Uschi Obermaier, while Jürgen Prochnow and muscleman Ralf

Moeller have ensconced themselves on Marta's couch. And something tells me Lion would have been amused by one particular scene: after telling the partner of a Hollywood star that I am from Switzerland, she bared her breasts, stretched out on the floor, and announced, "Here are the mountains!" Ever since I started sleeping in Lion's bed, I like to think we're on familiar terms.

As a theater director, I am anxious to learn more about acting techniques developed in the United States. And as a Villa Aurora resident, with Claudia and Joachim pulling some strings, otherwise locked doors now open. Ron Gilbert, né Ronald Goldstein—an actor whose father, it practically goes without saying, was a Jewish emigrant—gets me into the legendary Actors Studio West. This nonprofit organization is not an acting school but rather a place for members to hone their craft in an experimental setting. Anywhere from thirty to forty of these professionals—some well into old age, their drive to improve undiminished—gather biweekly to watch one another perform scenes and then share their notes. In typical American fashion, with charm and chutzpah to spare, Ron makes sure everyone gives me some of their time. I recognize Frances Fisher as Rose's mother from *Titanic* and Bruno Kirby from such films as *Birdy*, *When Harry Met Sally*, *City Slickers*, and *The Godfather Part II*, of course, in which he plays Vito Corleone's friend Peter Clemenza. Ron provides discreet hints whenever I draw a blank, as when I meet Terry Moore, who as a girl played alongside Shirley Temple, Judy Garland, and émigrés such as Albert Bassermann; she was later cast opposite Burt Lancaster and Fred Astaire. By her own account, she married Howard Hughes in secret in 1949, a detail Ron naturally mentions, coaxing a smile from her.

Every Wednesday and Friday, I drive about twenty miles to 8341 De Longpre Avenue, the former residence of western star William S. Hart, whose significance in the history of Pacific Palisades is not yet clear to me. As a "foreign observer," I am welcome to attend as many sessions as I like, though I am not allowed to chime in. I will later see how differently things are done in New York, where the Actors Studio moderators Ellen Burstyn, Lee Grant, and Estelle Parsons run a tight ship. On the West Coast it's far more relaxed, from the coffee and cookies served beforehand to the breaks. Yet again I'm stunned by the tremendous interest in German culture. What surprises me most is how many people here, of all places, ask about Bertolt Brecht and the alienation effect—here, the mecca of method acting, the technique that exemplifies American dramatic realism and defines Hollywood productions to this day.

Brecht is of interest to Academy Award–winner Martin Landau, whose Austrian-born father tried to rescue relatives back home from the Shoah. As a young man, Marty was active at the Actors Studio in New York with fellow aspirants James Dean and Steve McQueen, and today he runs Studio West with Mark Rydell, who directed *On Golden Pond* with Katharine Hepburn and Henry Fonda and *For the Boys* with Bette Midler. Like Marty, Mark descends from Jewish immigrants: his grandfathers Abraham Rubinstein and Michael Cohen came to New York from Russia in the 1880s. In the weeks to come, it is from him I will learn the most.

OMNIPRESENT AS THE TOPIC of emigration seems to be in Los Angeles, I'm writing the biography of a brother and sister who came here from Berlin in the 1930s, so what interests me most is the period when Pacific Palisades became "Weimar under the palms," in both senses. Some of the Weimar Republic's most prominent cultural figures found their way here, to a community wedged between the mountains and Santa Monica Bay, an area as compact as the German city of Weimar, home to so many great minds in the late eighteenth and early nineteenth centuries. People say that Marta Feuchtwanger's death in 1987 marked the end of German exile in Los Angeles. Indeed, she was the final member of the august inner circle of that very sun-drenched, palm-shaded Weimar. Its legacy feels vital, though, and I meet several witnesses to that period who, despite their advanced years, prove incredibly vivacious.

Just up the street from my interim home, at 540 Paseo Miramar, lives Konrad Kellen, who is nearly ninety and once served as Thomas Mann's private secretary. He was in the revered author's employ for just two years, almost six decades ago, and yet the "magician's" presence in his life is palpable. "Back then he worked from nine to noon every day on the fourth part of *Joseph* [*and His Brothers*], all hand-written, and passed it to me to transcribe," Konrad recalls.[3] In his library he proudly shows me a framed photo of the writer, made out to "Konrad Katzenellenbogen—grateful for his help."

He was born Konrad Moritz Adolf Katzenellenbogen in Berlin in 1913, his family German Jewish upper class. His father, Ludwig, had built a business empire and was the director of the Schultheiss-Patzenhofer brewery. The cream of society would gather at the family's city manse or their grand estate outside Oranienburg, which bore the lovely name Freienhagen. Albert Einstein was a relative. Art and culture were integral to everyday life. Konrad's mother owned a major collection of French impressionist works, and his father underwrote the leftist theater run by avant-garde director Erwin Piscator. In 1930 Ludwig married a second time, his bride the Austrian actor Tilla Durieux, who sat for more portraits in her day than any other woman, her likeness captured on canvas by Lovis Corinth, Oskar Kokoschka, Max Liebermann, Pierre-Auguste Renoir, Max Slevogt, and Franz von Stuck.

At Ludwig's insistence, as he hoped his son would take over the family business, Konrad began studying law in Heidelberg but transferred to the University of Munich after his first semester. At a memorial event, the head of the university delivered a "stirring speech about the glorious Battle of Langemarck" of 1914, which German propagandists upheld as an emblem of the younger generation's bellicosity. To this day Konrad's agitation is unmistakable: "No sooner had he finished than, to my surprise and horror, the student body erupted into cheers. And I said, 'For the love of God, you can't stay here, especially not as a law student. I've got to get out of here.'" He relocated to Paris, spent time in the Netherlands and Yugoslavia, started planning his move to Indonesia—and ultimately emigrated to New York. "Since I didn't achieve fame or fortune in New York, I figured I'd try my luck in Los Angeles."

Erika Mann told Konrad that her father was hiring a secretary, so he applied. "Like many German boys and girls, I admired his books, especially [*Confessions of*] *Felix Krull*." Thomas Mann took a shine to "Konny," who started working for him in 1941, typing up two or three manuscript pages a day and helping with his wide correspondence. Naturally Konrad met such exiles as Bruno Frank, Lion Feuchtwanger, and the conductor Bruno Walter, but their interactions were fleeting. "The emigrants were all earnest gentlemen who had big conversations about the future of the world, whereas I was a young fellow in my twenties." Konrad is still fascinated by the writer. "He was more of a listener than a storyteller. People didn't realize that when they tried to discuss world matters with him. He was happy listening but didn't issue any grand statements himself. People would get frustrated, because they thought that talking to the great man meant his wisdom would bubble over and into their heads. Thomas Mann was more interested in hearing about a person's flat tire than their thoughts on Goethe."

In August 1943 Konrad—who had changed his last name to Kellen, after a brief attempt to shorten Katzenellenbogen to Bogen—was drafted for service in a propaganda unit. "They had to lob me, as a soldier, against Fortress Europe to win the war," he jokes. Stationed as an officer in occupied Germany after the war, Konrad was part of the slackening denazification process and later worked in the United States for the RAND Corporation. Konrad always kept in touch with Thomas Mann, even after the writer had left Pacific Palisades for Kilchberg, on Lake Zurich. "He felt good in Switzerland, which he never did in Germany after the war. He was extremely disappointed in the Germans. He was most rattled by how many weren't actual anti-Nazis but always gave the Nazis a pass on one thing or the other. He spoke of them as 'people with befouled brains.' And the Germans' obsession with apologizing for Nazism and dragging him into it alienated him terribly from them."

When Heinrich Breloer's acclaimed three-part TV miniseries and companion publications about the Mann family were releasedin 2001, Konrad observed "all that fanfare" with skepticism. Breloer had shot footage for *Die Manns: Ein Jahrhundertroman* (*The Manns: Novel of a Century*) at Villa Aurora and interviewed Konrad about his former employer: "I didn't know what those people wanted to hear about Mann. For a while they all hated him, and now he's being celebrated. He wouldn't have liked that. I can't speak for him, but of that I'm certain. The Germans want to co-opt Thomas Mann, but ultimately he became a global citizen, which is why he was so content living in neutral Switzerland."

Going back to Germany was never in the cards for Konrad either: "Nothing in the world, all the way to the moon, was further from my mind than ever returning to Germany. It's unimaginable to me. That doesn't mean I hate the Germans, but living among them would be like living among the Hottentots."[4]

The polite, modest old man says this softly, without getting worked up; he formulates his sentences deliberately, sometimes tentatively. "It's too bad I've lost everyday ease in my mother tongue," he says in unaccented German as I'm leaving, the sporty old gent standing outside his long, low house, whose flower gardens glow in the California sun. "But maybe I could try writing something in German for a Swiss newspaper?"

AT A VILLA AURORA EVENT I strike up conversation with Walter Arlen, born Walter Aptowitzer in Vienna in 1920. His father was deported to a concentration camp in 1938, and his mother was institutionalized, so in March 1939 Walter made his own way to Chicago, where he had relatives; he next saw his family in London in 1946. He first worked for a furrier, studying composition on the side. From 1952 to 1980, he was a music critic for the *Los Angeles Times*, and in 1969 he founded the music department at Loyola Marymount University, which he chaired until 1990. When I mention the Mendelssohns, he tells me about the Max Reinhardt production of *Maria Stuart* with Eleonora in the title role, which he saw around age fourteen at the Theater in der Josefstadt in Vienna. Like Walter, many involved in the play later escaped to the United States, including twenty-four-year-old Herbert Berghof, who played Maria Stuart's lover, Mortimer; he would go on to train such stars as Al Pacino, Robert De Niro, and Liza Minnelli in acting.

A woman in her early sixties introduces herself as Barbara Zeisl Schoenberg. She is the daughter of the late-romantic Austrian composer Eric(h) Zeisl, who died in Los Angeles in 1959 and worked as a film composer for Metro-Goldwyn-Mayer in the *Schein-Heiligenstadt*, as he referred to Hollywood, in a rather involved play on words.[5] Zeisl also instructed composition at City College, a role Igor Stravinsky had helped him land. Barbara's father-in-law, meanwhile, was the rather more famous inventor of twelve-tone technique, Arnold Schoenberg.[6] Barbara herself exudes a mix of faded Viennese charm and evergreen Jewish humor. She wrote her dissertation on Peter Altenberg, the fin-de-siècle coffeehouse man of letters; fittingly, she invites me over for coffee and takes my impertinence in stride when I request a homemade Sacher torte.

A few days later, I ring the bell at 116 North Rockingham Avenue, the Spanish revival mansion in Brentwood, where Schoenberg lived from May 1936 until his death in 1951. His neighbors included the composer Cole Porter and movie stars Shirley Temple, Tyrone Power, Johnny Weissmuller, Paul Henreid, and Bette Davis. Temple, who lived at number 231, made $307,014 in 1938, or around sixty times Schoenberg's income. The tour buses used to inch by their house, Barbara tells me, because Temple's erstwhile estate was just across the street. More recently, interest had shifted to 360 North Rockingham, though O. J. Simpson's former home there has since been demolished.

Inside the Schoenbergs' house, one can feel the famed composer's presence. (Barbara's husband, Ronald, the spitting image of his father, says just a quick hello.) The living room seems untouched; a photograph of Schoenberg at the grand piano sits atop the same, with another hung over the sofa. Barbara tells me about her son Randol, a brilliant attorney fighting for the return of several Klimt paintings to Maria Altmann, the niece and heir of Ferdinand Bloch-Bauer, a Viennese sugar manufacturer and art collector who died in exile in Switzerland in 1945. The Republic of Austria restituted the artworks in 2006, and four were sold through Christie's for $192.7 million. The most famous of these paintings, *Portrait of Adele Bloch-Bauer I*, also known as the "Woman in Gold," depicts Ferdinand's wife and sold to the cosmetics tycoon Ronald S. Lauder for $135 million. (Randol Schoenberg purportedly received 40 percent of proceeds.) The 2015 film *Woman in Gold* tells the story of the restitution case, starring Helen Mirren as Maria Altmann, Ryan Reynolds as Randol, and Frances Fisher, whom I met at the Actors Studio, as Barbara.

Real-life Barbara in January 2002 takes visible pride in sharing her boy's exploits, but she is also very curious about my work. When I tell her that Francesco von Mendelssohn performed for years as a concert cellist, she grabs the phone, calls a friend from the tennis club, and tells her we'll be right over. On the short drive to 400 South Bundy Drive, all Barbara says is that her friend's late husband was also a cellist, so there was a chance she might have something I could use in my book.

The door is opened by a ninety-year-old woman in coveralls, who has clearly been busy in her sculpture studio. She, too, displays pride in showing us some of her creations, abstracted birds of alabaster and nonfigurative pieces wrought in Carrara marble, then invites us into the sitting room. Her tone friendly but firm, she informs me that she will not be of much help, as she was never very interested in her husband's line of work. Her husband, I now learn, was Gregor Piatigorsky, and, although I know he was one of the twentieth century's great cellists, what I don't realize is that "Grischa" was also one of "Cesco's" great friends. Sadly, because I fail to probe, I won't discover this fact until a later date. There is one thing I will never forget from that visit, though: hanging on the wall above our elderly host is a Modigliani, and, in response to my praise, she asks if I like art: "*Vous vous intéressez pour l'art*?" (She speaks to me exclusively in French.) I say yes—and I'm not just being polite—and she leads me through a collection of paintings by Chagall, Degas, Manet, Pechstein, Soutine, and Toulouse-Lautrec, a trove of impressionist and expressionist works that puts many museums to shame.

It's on our drive back that Barbara finally clues me in, laughing, "Didn't I tell you Jacqueline was a Rothschild?" The banker Édouard de Rothschild's daughter fled from France to the United States with her husband shortly after the war began; they were regular guests of the Feuchtwangers' at Villa Aurora as well. The mansion where I visited Jacqueline Rebecca Louise de Rothschild Piatigorsky was designed by none other than Frank Lloyd Wright. It was torn down after her death at age one hundred, and of the many artworks I had admired there, several were ruined in Hurricane Sandy, after Christie's was accused of mismanaging their storage at a Brooklyn warehouse.

MY ACQUAINTANCE with Ann Sommer, who at ninety-one is even older than Jacqueline Piatigorsky, will prove the most edifying. She is the widow of the film composer Hans Sommer, who died in 2000. We meet at another Villa Aurora event, and I start visiting regularly, driving exactly eight minutes from Paseo Miramar to her bungalow at 569 North Mount Holyoke Drive. Ann herself is fearless behind the wheel, with a lead foot to boot, and I breathe a sigh of relief whenever we reach our destination, usually the Chinese spot she loves for its cheap all-you-can-eat buffet. Over time the native Berliner opens up about her family, escape, and experiences in exile. Her stories rival Marta Feuchtwanger's reflections or Thomas Mann's diaries but are more immediate and moving.

Her daughter-in-law Veronika also tells me that "Moppi," who has not touched German soil since 1939, has never shared so candidly.

"I was a high society girl," Ann says with a laugh.[7] She grew up in the kind of luxury it's hard to imagine these days, but she does not mourn her lost riches. There is just one thing she misses: a large-scale drawing by Max Liebermann of her grandfather, Oscar Huldschinsky, which adorned her parents' parlor until their emigration in 1939. Beyond her obvious tie to the sitter, Ann was also distantly related to the artist: as a child Liebermann received his first paint box from his uncle Ferdinand Reichenheim, who was Ann's great-great-uncle. Her grandfather was a major figure representing Silesian heavy manufacturing in Berlin; the 1913 *Jahrbuch des Vermögens und Einkommens der Millionäre in Berlin* (Yearbook of assets and income of millionaires in Berlin) lists him as the city's twelfth-wealthiest resident, with a fortune of twenty-seven million marks. In addition to their town house, Oscar and his wife, Ida—who came from Vienna's Brandeis-Weikersheim banking family—owned an imposing summer residence on the eastern banks of Wannsee, its rooms adorned with a collection of Old Masters, paintings by Frans Hals, Rembrandt, Rubens, Botticelli, Tiepolo, and Sebastiano del Piombo as well as the only Raphael in a German private collection. Oscar's youngest daughter, Susanne, married the physicist Otto Reichenheim, a friend of Albert Einstein's and future colleague of Otto Hahn's and Lise Meitner's; he, too, hailed from one of the best-known Jewish families in Berlin and was related by marriage to many other influential houses. His cousin Charlotte (known in the family as Tante Lotte Fettgenick, or Aunt Lotte Fat-Neck), for instance, had married the banker Paul von Mendelssohn-Bartholdy in 1902 and amassed an impressive art collection of her own that by as early as 1910 included works of Pablo Picasso.

My ears perk up—not because of Picasso, but at the mention of Mendelssohn. Yes, Ann says, she spent time with Eleonora and Francesco. She was also pals with Anthony Goldschmidt, who as a child had encountered Francesco at his grandfather Jakob Goldschmidt's house and who made a name for himself as a "fabulously successful film producer." I simply had to meet Anthony, she insisted; there was a "truly delightful anecdote" I just had to hear from him.[8]

Otto and Susanne Reichenheim, Ann's parents, lived more modestly than

Grandfather Oscar or the Mendelssohns. Even so, their household included a cook, kitchen maid, chamber maid, gardener, driver, and two other maids; when hosting larger groups, the Reichenheims simply borrowed servants from Oscar. Countless scions courted young Anna-Susanne, born around 1910, but, to her grandfather's horror, she fell in love with the pianist, composer, and conductor Hans Sommer. At the tender age of fourteen, she delighted in listening to his jazz pieces on the radio. Oscar, a man so proud of his station he would not condescend to accept the emperor's offer of a title of nobility, disdained this mésalliance with an artist—who, to make matters worse, was not Jewish. "Some people marry their coachman," he is said to have spat, threatening to disinherit his granddaughter.[9] Five weeks after Oscar's death, in 1931, Anna-Susanne married Hans Sommer, whom her grandfather had reviled as a "traveling entertainer." From 1933 Hans worked primarily in film. His biggest hit was a high-spirited tune called "Jawohl, meine Herr'n," which Hans Albers and Heinz Rühmann sang in the 1937 crime film parody *Two Merry Adventurers*. To be able to continue working in Germany, after "duly furnishing proof of Aryan descent back to [his] grandparents," Hans joined the Reichsfachschaft Film, a division of the Reich Chamber of Film.[10]

In December 1937 Sommer was arrested in the middle of a theater production and taken to Gestapo headquarters on Wilhelmstrassein Berlin. There authorities pressured him to agree in writing to divorce his Jewish wife. (Until the Nazis came to power, Anna-Susanne was barely aware of her own Jewishness, not once having stepped inside a synagogue.) Hans refused, resulting in his expulsion from the Reich Chamber of Music in January 1938. According to the Reich Chamber of Culture Act of November 1, 1933, as a *jüdisch Versippter* (a person married to a Jew), Hans lacked the "necessary aptitude for the purpose of National Socialist state leadership."[11] Just six months later, however, Joseph Goebbels—who, like Hermann Göring and Adolf Hitler, was taken with a march Hans had composed for the film *Dr. Engel: Child Specialist*—extended a "special permit, subject to revocation," as he wanted Hans to write more "children's marches."[12]

During the Kristallnacht pogrom of November 9–10, 1938, Anna-Susanne's uncle Paul Huldschinsky—who had emigrated to the United States the year before but returned to Berlin for his family—was apprehended in a hotel and sent to the Sachsenhausen concentration camp. Using his connections, Hans secured Paul's release and retrieved him from the site on November 22. Paul Huldschinsky, his wife, their daughter, and his stepdaughter boarded the SS *President Roosevelt* in Hamburg and made their way to New York.

Hans was acutely aware of the threat to his wife's safety and that of their son, Michael, born in 1935, who was considered a first-degree *Mischling* (a pejorative Nazi term for persons of mixed Aryan and non-Aryan parentage) under the Nuremberg Laws. Hans pushed for their emigration, and, between his connections—whom even he described as "gangsters"—and fifteen thousand reichsmarks, he managed to obtain passports for his family on January 9, 1939. Shortly before their planned departure, Hans received a call from an old flame, who was now seeing a high-ranking SS dignitary and warned the Sommers of their imminent arrest. The family fled Berlin in a hurry, leaving the lights on so the neighbors would think they were still at home. Friends had finagled a monthlong visa for them in Denmark. Harry Warner, one of the four Warner brothers, and Louis B. Mayer of Metro-Goldwyn-Mayer issued affidavits for them. On February 10, 1939, the family embarked on the SS *Erria* in Copenhagen, traveling by way of Jamaica and the Panama Canal to Los Angeles, where the ocean liner arrived on March 18. The Sommers had an impressive amount of luggage—thirty-eight pieces in total—and Ann recalls how Americans laughed themselves silly when they saw the monogram "ASS" embroidered on her bed linens. Anna-Susanne Sommer's mother Susanne Reichenheim died of pneumonia in February 1939, her father escaped the Shoah in England, and her four siblings fled to Brazil, England, and Switzerland.

The Sommers stayed with Paul Huldschinsky, at 310 Rodeo Drive in Hollywood, when they first got to America. Hans was received at Warner Studios by Harry Warner himself; Warner was fascinated by Anna-Susanne's passport, to which the telling middle name "Sara" had been added, and offered Hans a five-year contract at one hundred dollars per week. The family was in the country on tourist visas, though, meaning they had to leave again. Like so many in this situation, the Sommers traveled to Mexico and resided in Nogales, just across the border from Arizona. Hans gigged in bars to pay the bills. Despite the support of Warner Brothers and MGM, the Sommers were issued another set of tourist visas. They returned to the United States by way of El Paso on June 12, stayed with Huldschinsky again, who had since moved to 370 Via Florence in Pacific Palisades, then went back to Mexico, hoping they would finally make the immigrant quota and be allowed to relocate to the United States once and for all. This time they made their way to Cuernavaca, about fifty miles south of Mexico City, where Nazis and Jews joined hands at breakfast, lunch, and dinner at Muellers' Guesthouse. I can see how painful it is for Ann to talk about that year and a half in Mexico. All she tells me is that her husband nearly died of dysentery, while she herself contracted meningitis and almost went blind.

On May 31, 1941, the Sommers boarded a flight from Mexico City to Los Angeles, where they would finally settle down. Huldschinsky, who at the time was managing the interior decoration of the house Thomas Mann was building on San Remo Drive, hosted the family until they moved to 2271 Cheremoya Avenue, a modest home in Hollywood. After the United States joined the war on December 8, 1941, the Sommers—like all Germans over the age of fourteen—were declared "enemy aliens." They had an 8:00 p.m. curfew, their movement restricted to a five-mile radius around their residence. Although Hans was working for Warner Studios in Burbank, he was not allowed to draw on his earlier success in Germany and faced stiff competition from other composers, including many émigrés. He later wrote the soundtrack for Douglas Sirk's 1951 drama *The First Legion*, and in 1953 he conducted Bronisław Kaper's score for the musical romance *Lili*; Hans arranged the Academy Award–winning music, parts of which he also helped compose.

Hans Sommer applied for reparations from the Federal Republic of Germany but did not do the same on Ann's behalf. (She had since adopted this more American-sounding name.) He did this partly out of pride, because he wished to provide for his family, and partly because he had suffered persecution his whole life and wanted as little to do with German bureaucracy as possible and certainly did not want to bring his wife's Jewish heritage into the equation—at least, that's what Ann tells me. In 1979 Hans finally sought royalty back payments for his prewar compositions and submitted a complete list of titles, many of which were still played, to GEMA, the German performing rights organization, but was compensated for just two. By the time Ann—who had worked as a real estate agent to keep their family afloat—could legally submit her own application without her husband's consent, the statute of limitations for reparations had expired. When I ask how she survived the hardships of emigration, Ann smiles: "I was so loved as a child, showered with so many gifts from the heart; it gave me the strength I needed my whole life." I stay in touch with Ann, even after my residency at Villa Aurora concludes. She is the final resident of Pacific Palisades who can speak from experience about the "nervous terrors of homelessness" or the "cardiac asthma of exile," as Thomas Mann once put it.[13] I see her again the very next year, when I return to Los Angeles to direct a play.

The last time I see Ann—who was killed in a car accident in 2009—is February 25, 2007. I have no trouble pinpointing the date, as we got together for our own private little Oscars party. The previous day I had attended the annual reception for German nominees at Villa Aurora, feeling a bit wistful to be back, five years after my stint there. Now Ann, who is pushing ninety-seven, and I are sitting on the couch in her weathered little house in Pacific Palisades, sipping champagne, eating canapés, and watching the live broadcast of the ceremony, which lasts for hours. It all seems terribly glamorous to me, whereas Ann registers disappointment: "The dresses used to be much nicer." We have never discussed Hollywood or movie stars, but now she uses the commercial breaks (there are certainly enough of them) to fill me in on everyone she met in the 1940s, gushing about Greta Garbo and MGM head costume designer Adrian and his elegant creations and about the 1945 Oscars, which she attended at Grauman's Chinese Theater: "Uncle Paul won an Academy Award for the sets used in George Cukor's film *Gaslight*, with Ingrid Bergman. And when they asked where he got the brilliant idea for the design, he said, 'I simply built the set to look like our home in Berlin.'"

FRITZ DIVES OFF A CLIFF, THE LAKOTA DANCE, AND CHRIST RETURNS TO EARTH

THE FIRST CELEBRITY to settle down in Pacific Palisades—or the area that would eventually come to be known as such—went by Fritz. The year was 1911, and, like many who followed, Fritz represented the worlds of both film and literature. He wasn't just the area's first movie star; in 1922, the year Pacific Palisades was formally founded, he also became the first author to live there with the publication of *Told under a White Oak Tree*. As has long been the case for celebrity memoirs (no one expects athletes or reality TV stars to write their own books, after all), a ghostwriter penned the slim, fifty-one-page volume, which was published in Boston and sold for one dollar. In Fritz's case there was no way around it: first of all, he was only fourteen, and, more importantly, despite what the German name might suggest, he was a pinto pony from Nevada. Fritz was not just any horse. He was the most famous animal actor of his time, the first to be named in the title sequence alongside his rider, William S. Hart, and presumably the only one to receive fan mail, which often included a sugar cube or two.[1]

Fritz was equally famous for his beautiful piebald coat—brown with a white muzzle, white blazes down either flank, and white legs—as for his moxie. He performed all his own stunts—plunging across raging rivers, crashing through windows, and leaping over fire—with a lone exception in a scene in his final film, *Singer Jim McKee* (1924), in which horse and rider dive off a cliff. In his place a lifelike dummy, constructed over five weeks, was set at the edge of the precipice. Hart mounted the prop, held upright with piano wire, and, with cameras rolling, the wires were cut, the pair tumbled down the hillside, and Hart rolled off to safety with just a few scratches.

WHEN FRITZ ARRIVED in Santa Ynez Canyon, his master was not yet the former Shakespearean actor William S. Hart, who had risen (or perhaps fallen) to stardom in the early westerns. At the time the horse belonged to the film producer Thomas Harper Ince.[2] Born in 1880 (though he would tell people 1882), Ince had started his own career in the theater at the age of six, practically a given for the child of thespians. After a few years' touring with second-rate companies, he made his Broadway debut while still in his teens, and in 1908 he appeared on camera for the first time. Thirteen years after moving pictures had first begun captivating audiences, the European film industry was in crisis, with attendance dwindling. Meanwhile, business was booming in the United States, where moviegoers had an insatiable appetite for new adventures on the silver screen.

It was a man originally from Swabia in southern Germany who offered Ince the chance to step behind the camera in 1911. Carl Laemmle was born in the town of Laupheim before immigrating to the United States in 1884, as a penniless seventeen-year-old. He would found the Universal Film Manufacturing Company in 1912, which in time became Universal Pictures, one of the biggest film production companies in the world. Laemmle went on to open Universal City Studios in 1915 on the site of an old chicken farm south of Los Angeles, and two decades later he helped upward of three hundred people flee the Third Reich for the United States, with several landing in Pacific Palisades. Back in 1911, however, when a fresh-faced Ince crossed his path, Laemmle was still running the Independent Motion Pictures Company, founded two years earlier. Although based in New York City, the company shot most of its films in Cuba, beyond the jurisdiction of the Motion Pictures Patent Company, also known as the Edison Trust. Formed in 1908 by the Edison Manufacturing Company and the Biograph Company (established in 1894 and 1895, respectively), the trust that held Thomas Edison's patents did not shy away from enlisting thugs to target competitors, destroying cinemas, confiscating or smashing unlicensed cameras, or going after film crews. These goons acted with impunity until the Supreme Court revoked the patent on raw film in 1912, followed by the company's remaining patents in 1915.

This is how Ince landed in Cuba, a formally sovereign nation that in fact relied heavily on the United States. He cut his directorial teeth there on sundry projects, including a short starring "America's sweetheart" Mary Pickford, who was on her way to becoming the most beloved actor of the day. Later the same year, 1911, he was hired by the New York Motion Picture Company (NYMPC) to direct a western, this time in Los Angeles. Like Cuba, the Pacific coast seemed a safe distance from the internecine battles in New York, and shooting there was both cheaper and easier: because early filmed images appeared so dark, filmmakers depended on the sun, which happens to shine more brightly in California than on the East Coast. Real estate was affordable, there were workers aplenty, and the landscapes ranged from deserts to snow-capped peaks. In 1911 alone, sixteen companies relocated from the Hudson to Hollywood, at the time a backwater with just five hundred residents that had been incorporated by Los Angeles in 1910. Within a few years it would emerge as the undisputed home of the nation's dream factories, its film studios, with the place-name "Hollywood" soon symbolizing the industry as a whole. By the 1930s 60 percent of all California-produced films were shot in Culver City; the local chamber of commerce adopted the slogan, "Culver City, where Hollywood Movies are made."[3]

After a brief stint at NYMPC's Bison Studios in Edendale, a standalone neighborhood that has since been absorbed by Echo Park and Silver Lake, Ince leased a 460-acre tract of land near the present-day junction of Sunset Boulevard and the Pacific Coast Highway. He dubbed it Bison Ranch, though the area would soon become known as Inceville. It seemed an ideal location, the surroundings suited to all manner of film sets, from the nearby ocean and sandy beaches to vertiginous bluffs, photogenic rolling hills, and the foothills of the Santa Monica Mountains. Transit to and from the city, however, left much to be desired. Just over a mile from the newly christened Bison Ranch was Long Wharf, built in 1894 to the south of Potrero Canyon. Extending almost a mile into the Pacific, the pier was the world's longest at the time of its construction. It served as the cargo and passenger port for the region until 1907, when San Pedro Harbor opened on the LA waterfront.

The new port was much larger and rendered Long Wharf obsolete; the latter was razed in 1920. Between the hours of 6:35 a.m. and 10:40 p.m., an electric tramway ran between the harbor and downtown Los Angeles: a 331-foot tunnel connected the coastal terminal to the intersection of Ocean Avenue and Colorado Avenue in Santa Monica, from which point the Santa Monica Air Line continued into the city. Employees who neither lived on-site (many did) nor owned a vehicle (most did not) were thus compelled to take one of the so-called Red Cars to Long Wharf, then walk or ride a horse the rest of the way to Bison Ranch if the studio failed to send a car.

Ince had workshops and wardrobes built, though most important were the extensive frontier town sets. At the time artificial lighting was not yet up to snuff, and interiors were shot outdoors: two, very occasionally three, but often no more than a single wall would be erected on a wooden platform. Some sets were on casters that could be moved to follow the sunlight. No one minded when tablecloths or long skirts flapped in the breeze passing through supposedly indoor spaces or when bugs buzzed about the actors' faces. Production teams could at least count on temperatures never dipping lower than the midforties, even in January. Male actors filming in winter on the East Coast meanwhile had to smoke throughout their scenes to disguise the plumes of their breath, whereas female actors were instructed to keep their mouths shut whenever they weren't delivering lines. Glass stages were slow to become established.

California crews were not entirely safe from the Edison trustees' Motion Pictures Patent Company either. Ince was allegedly one of the last to duke it out with the monopolists: legend has it he spotted company toughs approaching his studio along the coastal highway and fired a cannon at them, using props from a Civil War film, sending the men running and thus saving the future of Hollywood. *Se non* è *vero . . .*

Ince established new standards for verisimilitude. As Bison Ranch expanded, he hired performers from the "Miller Brothers' 101 Ranch Real Wild West Show," which wintered in Venice, five miles to the southeast. The troupe included 150 cowboys and cowgirls, horses (Fritz among them), bison, cows, and notably a 100-member Lakota tribe, who set up their tepees on the studio grounds. Ince betrayed his own prejudices when he reflected on the experience years later, in 1924:

> When I took [the tribe] over, I had to sign an agreement with the Indian commissioner in Washington, according to which the Indians were to have certain hours of schooling. I furthermore had to assume full responsibility for their well being and care. I was soon to realize the importance of what I had voluntarily taken upon my shoulders, for they were difficult to handle. They were stolid and non-communicative and had a strong dislike for doing anything that did not happen to appeal to them at the moment. . . . They were peaceable and preferred loafing to the type of action which was necessary in the making of pictures. . . . Arousing their anger sufficiently to attack the enemy with any semblance of reality was one of the hardest things I have ever had to tackle in my whole career in motion pictures.[4]

In 1912 Ince purchased the plot outright, while the success of his western *War on the Plains* enabled him to lease another eighteen thousand acres, covering nearly eight miles through Santa Ynez Canyon into the Santa Monica Mountains. That same year more than one thousand white bit players and as many Lakota people reenacted the Battle of the Little Bighorn, fought on June 25–26, 1876, in *Custer's Last Fight*, directed by and starring Francis Ford—the elder brother of John Ford, who to this day holds the record for winning the most Academy Awards for best director. In the early 1900s westerns weren't considered period pieces by any means; rather, most moviegoers retained vivid memories from the pioneer era, though even then it was romanticized as a wild and lawless time. After all, the US Army's notorious massacre of more than three hundred Lakota people at Wounded Knee in December 1890, an event that provided a symbolic end to the "Wild West," was still a recent occurrence. Geronimo (Goyaałé, the "one who yawns") had died as recently as 1909; after witnessing the white trader James Johnson slaughter and scalp four hundred Apache people as an eight-year-old in 1837, the famed Chiricahua Apache medicine man had written a new chapter in US history with his struggle against white oppression, carried out through 1886. And the legendary gunslinger Wyatt Earp—known as a buffalo hunter, gambler, and lawman at the center of the 1881 shootout at the O. K. Corral in Tombstone, Arizona—lived until 1929.

IN THE EARLY DAYS of his career, Ince was turning out one "two-reel picture" per week, each thousand-foot roll of film good for about fifteen minutes on screen, though before long he increased weekly production to two, then three thirty-minute films. The films were shot and edited concurrently, meaning an actor like Francis Ford might play a chieftain in the morning and Abraham Lincoln after lunch; diligent organization was critical to the process. However widespread the practice of cast and crew improvising plotlines based on a rough outline presented by the director, Ince required scripts with details on the characters, sets, and props appearing in each scene, all of which enabled meticulous planning. Production was modeled on the assembly line. As it happens, another man by the name of Ford—the automobile manufacturer Henry, who introduced the assembly line to his plants in 1913—paid courtesy calls to the studios alongside Thomas Edison. Mishaps inevitably slowed things down and drove up costs, as in April 1915, when more than one hundred pounds of rice intended for a wedding scene in *The Italian* were destroyed by heavy rainfall after the prop master accidentally left the bags outside overnight. *The Italian* was a "five-reeler": by this point studios' feature films were at least seventy minutes long and presented the main attraction in theaters, shown together with a short, cartoon, travelogue film, and/or newsreel, a weekly roundup of reporting on current events, society, sports, and culture.

Among Ince's greatest contributions were the hierarchies and processes he established in film production, innovations that today go without saying. Informed by his background as an actor and his expertise behind the camera, he divided up the tasks of screenwriter, director, and editor, which in the past had fallen to a single person. He also redefined the role of producer, who now wielded total control over the film, from soup to nuts; to this day only a handful of Hollywood's most influential directors are contractually allowed to approve the final cut, or final edited version of the film. Ince himself tended to every last detail, including writing the intertitles to his silent films and dictating the typeface and layout. The press celebrated his assiduity, and Ince—who relished the attention and cultivated the image of an indefatigable, "cyclonic" workaholic—was more than happy to inform the public that he had whittled his lunch break down from five minutes to three by drinking a glass of milk in lieu of eating a sandwich.[5] To save time on the sprawling grounds, he rode on horseback from set to set and directed from the saddle, often accompanied by his wife, Elinor, who played an active role in running the studio, despite having three sons, born in 1909, 1912, and 1915. In 1913, a year in which he produced 150 films alone, Ince pioneered the role of unit production manager, a position from which to coordinate all the organizational, financial, and technical details of a given project—taking cues directly from the producer, of course.

A diminutive figure, dubbed the "Napoleon of Inceville," today Ince is considered the first true film tycoon; his posts also included the official vice president of the New York Motion Picture Company and the general manager of a production group that included Broncho Pictures, Domino Pictures, and Kay-Bee Pictures. Inceville was the prototype of the modern Hollywood studio and, some said, the biggest studio in the world. At its height it was home to seven hundred permanent residents, among them different tribes of Lakota and Blackfeet. The US government had approved a local post office on-site, and there was serious talk of establishing Inceville as a town. The premises housed three hundred dressing rooms: luxurious bungalows for the stars, simpler accommodations for white employees, and tent cities for Native people, often treated as an afterthought. The list goes on. There was a cafeteria that served one thousand, a swimming pool, stables for three hundred horses (and at times elephants and camels), corrals for bison and cattle, and an extensive fleet of covered wagons, coaches, and the latest Ford automobiles. Massive warehouses held sets and props, costumes, production offices, and workshops to produce everything a shoot might need, from house keys to castles. There were also vegetable gardens and greenhouses, as well as eight glass stages.

Everything at Inceville expanded over time, especially the exterior sets, with construction crews recreating a Puritan settlement straight out of seventeenth-century New England for one film. There was a lighthouse, mission station, wooden church, full-fledged fort, and "Oriental" bazaar. There were also several villages (Malay, Scottish, and Dutch, complete with windmill and canal); entire streets plucked from London and New York; Swiss chalets; and an Aztec temple that featured in *The Captive God* (1915). A pirate ship anchored close to shore. A Japanese village was also built: in 1913 Ince hired the California-based Japanese actor Tsuru Aoki and her stage partner, Sessue Hayakawa, for a series of films, whose popularity reached new heights after the on-screen couple fell in love in real life and married in 1914. Extras for the films set in Japan were fairly easy to come by—about three hundred Japanese families (and a few Russians) lived in a nearby fishing village located between Long Wharf and the end of Temescal Canyon, today the site of Will Rogers Beach State Park. The village was destroyed in a fire in 1916. Many of its former residents, who had made a living fishing in Santa Monica Bay, subsequently sought work as gardeners or in laundries.

In 1914 Ince engaged eight hundred extras for *The Battle of Gettysburg*, shot simultaneously on eight cameras set at different angles. That same year he began to elevate William S. Hart, already in his late forties, to stardom. Hart's fame extended beyond his stature at the studio to make him one of the biggest stars in Hollywood, placing him in the same echelons as Mary Pickford, Douglas Fairbanks, and Charlie Chaplin. Ince knew the actor from their early days on the stage; the two had appeared together on Broadway, even sharing a room for a spell when money was tight. Hart's acting was considered authentic, the standard for male leads in westerns well into the 1950s. After all, as a teenager in the Wild West, he had not only encountered cowboys and ranchers, Blackfeet and Lakota, gold prospectors and Civil War veterans but learned how to ride, hunt, and speak Lakȟótiyapi, the Lakota language. Hart was stone-faced on camera, his features chiseled granite. He played not effulgent heroes but broken outsiders, a character type he had created and christened the "good bad man." Though this lawless antihero is reformed by religion, a crisis of conscience, or love for a young woman he has rescued, the path of righteousness is one of vengeance, littered with the bodies of those who wronged him. Hart's films aimed at realism. The blonde starlet does not sink into the arms of the ambivalent hero at the end; instead, the hardened desperado rides off or dies tragically in atonement, sooner recalling Greek drama or Shakespearean tragedy. Within a few years, such endings would become unthinkable.

Hart starred in six westerns alongside Louise Glaum, who usually played the vamp, a stock character of a beautiful, enigmatic, and treacherous woman out to seduce and entrap men. His favorite on-screen partner, however, was Fritz. He first worked with the pony in 1915 on *The Taking of Luke McVain*, presented by Hart's own W. H. Productions Company, though it may be more apt to call it a group, since the opening credits read, "Produced by Thos H. Ince." Hart finally managed to purchase Fritz in 1917; Ince had long refused the sale in the belief that, as long as he owned Fritz, Hart would not work with competitors. Ultimately, Fritz was at the center of the rift between the movie mogul and his loyal star: Ince was irked by the fact that when six-foot-two Hart rode little Fritz (himself not quite fourteen hands high, or four foot six), the actor's feet almost reached the ground. Ince thought it looked ridiculous and made Hart ride horses better suited to his size. The moment he could, Hart dissolved his contract and brought the pony home to live on his ranch. He commissioned several portraits of himself and Fritz and held a solemn ceremony upon Fritz's death in 1938. A stone monument marks the grave site, with a bronze plaque that reads, "To Bill Hart's Pinto Pony Fritz / Age 31 Years / A Loyal Comrade."

In 1915, with moving pictures getting longer (five-reelers with a running time of around seventy-five minutes were soon the norm) and production growing more expensive, the "king of the western" Thomas H. Ince joined the Triangle Motion Picture Company. There he presided over a number of prestige productions, as did his colleagues D. W. Griffith, the director of *Birth of a Nation* and hailed for his contributions to narrative cinema; and the "father of slapstick comedy" Mack Sennett, who had collaborated a year earlier with Charlie Chaplin as the actor was developing his signature tramp character. They scored a first major success with the romantic comedy *Peggy*, starring Billie Burke, who was married to the theater producer Florenz Ziegfeld and is best known for playing Glinda, the Good Witch of the North in 1939's *The Wizard of Oz*. Burke came by private motor coach to Los Angeles, maid in tow. Burke was chauffeured to Inceville, wined and dined and even treated to a lavish vacation on the island of Catalina off the coast of California, all of which Ince hoped would induce her to sign on with Triangle—which it did. The picture was a hit for the nascent production company and made a lasting impact on the world of fashion as well, with scenes of Burke in pajamas shown on screen. Conservative media were scandalized, while countless women mimicked the look.

TRIANGLE'S GROWING PRODUCTION demands soon outstripped what Inceville had to offer. The company invested half a million dollars in the construction of a new studio in Culver City, equipped with the latest technology and conveniently located near downtown Los Angeles. It was also less susceptible to the coastal fog that routinely enveloped Inceville in murk and forced hundreds of people to stop what they were doing and wait for it to lift. This cost the studio scads of money, evidently despite the efforts of the resident Native Americans, who must have been intent on keeping their jobs: in February 1916 the *Los Angeles Times* reported on a nightly drum circle, led by the medicine men Lone Bear and Good Voice Crow, with more than one hundred participants dancing to drive off the fog.[6] Nevertheless, the company held on to Triangle Ranch, as Inceville was now known, for exterior shots and westerns in particular, as a tribe of Lakota still made its home there under the leadership of Chief Eagle Eye.

In the late afternoon of January 11, 1916, a few days before operations moved to Culver City, a fire broke out in an editing room at Inceville. Fourteen people were hurt, including Ince, who was hampered by a leg injury and trapped in his office by the flames. He lost consciousness and was rescued by a Lakota man. Ince was badly burned but survived and reported for work at the usual hour the next morning, his head bandaged and arm in a sling. The fire destroyed two completed and six half-finished films, thirty-five screenplays, and three hundred more manuscripts. The press reported damages between $111,000 and $250,000, equivalent to between $2.7 and $6.3 million in 2022.

Three months later a mudslide blocked access to Inceville for several weeks and halted all production. Thankfully, *Civilization*, Ince's final codirecting effort and his most challenging project was complete—a film that took a good year to make, with sixty set builders toiling for three months to the tune of $80,000 to erect a cityscape that appears for no longer than a minute in the final cut. *Civilization* premiered on April 17, 1916. The king of Wredpryd, whose people are manifestly Teutonic but whose palace resembles the US Capitol, orders Count Ferdinand, a religious man who has invented a new submarine, to torpedo the *Pro Patria*, a ship with civilians on board. The count disobeys ("We are not butchers!"), sinks the submarine, and drowns. Surrounded by suffering, naked people in purgatory, Ferdinand encounters Jesus Christ (George Fisher was the first actor to play the son of God on camera). Christ returns to earth in the count's body and pleads with the *Pickelhaube*-behelmed king for peace, but he is tried and sentenced to death for treason. Thousands of nuns and mothers storm the palace, beseeching the king to end the war, when he announces that the count has escaped punishment, having died in custody. When the king visits the cell, Jesus rises from the dead body and guides the king through the battlefields, on which the reformed monarch signs a peace treaty. Children dance merrily in the streets, sheep graze serenely, and the shepherd blows his horn. The End.

Civilization was brazenly marketed as a million-dollar production, though in reality it cost one tenth that sum; promotional materials further claim the involvement of forty thousand people, ten thousand horses, and forty airplanes. Ince inundated the press with tales of triumph; he was proud to report that President Woodrow Wilson had seen the film and that the German emperor, kings of England and Spain, and Pope Benedict XV had expressed their interest in the project. The pacifist film grossed an impressive $800,000, until it was pulled from screens in April 1917, after the United States entered World War I.

In a modest ceremony on June 27, 1917, the day after Ince signed on with Paramount and left Triangle, the latter production company rechristened Inceville "Hartville," in honor of William S. Hart. A foundation stone was set and a massive sign bearing the new name erected, though the effort was in vain: Hart remained loyal to Ince and continued to work with him. By the next year the Triangle Motion Picture Company had dissolved, and Samuel Goldwyn took over its Culver City studio, where such MGM classics as *The Wizard of Oz*, with Judy Garland; *Singin' in the Rain*, with Gene Kelly; and *Ben-Hur*, with Charlton Heston were subsequently filmed. Hartville was sold to the US branch of the British import-export and film distribution company Robertson-Cole, which renamed the property R. C. Ranch and put it to occasional use. Ince built a new studio in Culver City in 1918, used by David O. Selznick in 1939 for *Gone with the Wind* and Steven Spielberg for *E.T.* in 1982.

In late May 1921, Ince returned to his former studio for the first time since he left Triangle and for the last time in his life. Things had deteriorated after his departure; the media were already talking about Inceville as the "Pompeii of the ghost towns." The sets were in varying states of decay, and a solitary equestrian statue was all that remained of the royal capital city constructed for *Civilization*; a large cross from the same film stood atop another hill. "There was never a studio like it," Ince was reported to have cried at the sight of the ruins.[7] On October 13, 1923, a brushfire that progressed from the mountains to the coast by way of Santa Ynez Canyon consumed what was left of Inceville—around one hundred buildings. The stone church, constructed in 1915 for *Peggy*, was all that survived. It stood for another several years, the final relic of the illustrious studio.[8]

Ince's achievements were epochal. He produced eight hundred films, established the US studio system, and defined roles and processes in film production that remain standard in Hollywood and around the globe, yet they would be overshadowed by the circumstances of his death. He was allegedly shot by William Randolph Hearst on board the *Oneida*, the media mogul's yacht, after a wild party celebrating Ince's forty-fourth birthday on November 16, 1924. The bullet, issued from a diamond-studded revolver, was intended for Charlie Chaplin, who had been making advances on Hearst's lover, Marion Davies. Although ample evidence points to a far less cinematic demise, this was the version of events filmed a lifetime later in Peter Bogdanovich's 2002 film, *The Cat's Meow*. The real cause of death for Ince was heart failure, the place of death Beverly Hills, the date November 19, 1924.

Part of the land where Inceville once stood was acquired in 1950 by the Self-Realization Fellowship (SRF), founded three decades earlier by Paramahansa Yogananda, né Mukunda Lal Ghosh and known as the father of Western yoga. Born into a prosperous Bengali family in Gorakhpur in 1893, at age seventeen he became a student of Swami Sri Yukteswar. In 1920, while meditating, Yogananda had a divine vision that directed him to teach in the West. He founded his first meditation center in Boston and in 1925 established

SRF international headquarters in Los Angeles. The fellowship emphasizes the fundamental unity of all major belief systems in the world. The SRF was legally designated a charitable religious organization in 1935; that same year, during a trip to India, Sri Yukteswar accorded Yogananda (whom the guru described as an incarnation of divine love) the Sanskrit honorific title of paramahamsa, which translates literally as "supreme swan."

On August 20, 1950, less than two years before his death, Yogananda dedicated Lake Shrine as a ten-acre meditation garden located at 17190 Sunset Boulevard in Pacific Palisades. At its heart is Lake Santa Ynez, a spring-fed body of water formed in 1927 during an earthmoving project. With several temples and pavilions as well as a huge white archway crowned by golden lotus blossoms, Lake Shrine also features a replica sixteenth-century Dutch windmill, built in 1940 by then-owner H. Everett "Big Mac" McElroy, who worked at Twentieth-Century Fox and lived with his wife, Adeline, on a Mississippi houseboat that still sits in the lake. A sarcophagus in the Mahatma Gandhi World Peace Memorial contains the only mortal remains outside India of Gandhi, an icon of nonviolent resistance whom many revere as a saint. Today the Self-Realization Fellowship Lake Shrine is regarded as one of California's most important spiritual sites.

METHODISTS CAMP OUT, AND A LONESOME SWABIAN CONSTRUCTS A JAPANESE PALACE

IT WAS PURE COINCIDENCE that the "world's greatest Christian educational center" was built at the very location Jesus Christ had returned to earth just a few years prior.[1] As it was, movies were of little concern to Methodists, especially one like *Civilization*, which the *Los Angeles Times* had panned as a "violation of good taste." The critic wrote that Christians were likely to be offended and find it "irreverent," Jewish viewers would probably think it "mystical and exaggerated," and the "non-church-goer" would find it "absurd and undramatic." The film's appeal, in other words, would extend only to people who did not belong to any of these three groups.[2]

Inceville's decline was well underway when the Huntington Beach Assembly of the Methodist Episcopal Church, founded in 1784, entered the scene. Residential development was gaining momentum around Huntington Beach, where summer camps had been held for the past ten years, and, on top of all that, the church hoped to drill for oil there, which seemed a more lucrative pursuit than drilling into questions of faith alone. The town of Huntington Beach would block these plans, prompting the black-gold–obsessed church to sue (unsuccessfully) in late 1922—but, first, the bishop of San Francisco, Adna W. Leonard, instructed the Huntington Beach Assembly superintendent, Rev. Charles Holmes Scott, to widen the search for a permanent alternative in 1920. Scott landed on a large tract within the bounds of Rancho Boca de Santa Monica, an erstwhile Mexican land grant near Santa Monica.

Now home to nearly one hundred thousand, at the time the city, named after Saint Monica of Tagaste, the mother of Augustine of Hippo, had a population of around fifteen thousand and was built on Chumash and Tongva land. In 1839 Juan Bautista Valentín Alvarado y Vallejo, the governor of Alta California (as the Mexican territory was named after independence in 1821), gave more than thirty thousand acres of land to the colonial military officer Francisco Sepulveda, who named it Rancho San Vicente y Santa Monica. The same year Ysidro Reyes and Francisco Marquez each received half of the 6,656-acre Rancho Boca de Santa Monica to the south and west of Sepulveda's land. Marquez, a blacksmith, built an adobe house—the first in the canyon—where San Lorenzo Street runs today. The Marquez family's small graveyard can still be found at 637 San Lorenzo Street. Reyes had a business selling tar and owned one of the largest vineyards in the area; he lived on a ranch located around the modern-day intersection of Adelaide Drive and Entrada Drive.

California came under US control following the Mexican-American War (1846–48), eventually becoming the thirty-first state on September 9, 1850. In 1872 Col. Robert Symington Baker, who had arrived in California during the gold rush in 1849, acquired Rancho San Vicente y Santa Monica from Sepulveda's heirs for $50,000, as well as property in Rancho Boca de Santa Monica that he bought from Reyes's widow, Maria, for an additional $6,000. Shortly after selling two-thirds of the land in 1874 to John Percival Jones, the English-born Republican senator from Nevada, Baker married the widow Arcadia Stearns, née Bandini, the highest of high-society ladies in Los Angeles. Their union merged two of California's largest fortunes. In 1875 Baker and Jones built a rail line to Los Angeles. On July 15 they auctioned off the first plots of land for anywhere between $75 and $500, earning a grand total of $85,000. Their efforts brought explosive growth to Santa Monica—twenty-one wood-frame houses had been built by the end of July. According to the census, the town had 417 residents in 1880, but by 1886 it was declared a city, continuing to develop into a beach and entertainment destination for greater Los Angeles, with seasonal spots such as hotels, restaurants, bath houses, and a dance pavilion. Since 1909 the main attraction has been Santa Monica Pier.

The City of Angels was relatively young itself in those days, founded in 1781 as El Pueblo de Nuestra Señora la Reina de los Ángeles by a group of forty-four *pobladores* (settlers) from the Mexican province of Sonora—twenty-two adults and twenty-two children, to be precise, almost half of whom were of African

American or Native descent. In 1821 El Pueblo became Mexican until the Americans took control in 1847. When Los Angeles was incorporated as a US city on April 4, 1850, it had a population of 1,610. Half a century later, that number had grown to one hundred thousand. According to the most recent US census count, from 2023, nearly four million people live in Los Angeles, with another thirteen million in the greater metropolitan area, including the city of Santa Monica, of course.

BACK TO THE METHODISTS: on April 30, 1921, Reverend Scott acquired a relatively modest thirty-seven acres in Rustic Canyon. The University of California had been using the area primarily as a forestry research station focused on the use of invasive plants such as the eucalyptus tree, launched in 1893 by none other than Senator John Jones, Arcadia Bandini de Baker, and Abbot Kinney, whom we will spend more time getting to know. Scott had already purchased about seventeen acres bordering the plot and was involved in further negotiations; on May 17, 1921, he signed a purchase contract for a 1,100-acre site in Temescal Canyon and an adjacent mesa to the east. The area occupied today by Pacific Palisades—a part of the city of Los Angeles since the "Westgate annexation" on June 14, 1916—features several mesas, separated by Santa Monica Canyon, Rustic Canyon, Temescal Canyon, and Santa Ynez Canyon, among others.[3] The church had big plans: $4 million (equivalent to around $55 million in 2022) was earmarked for residential construction to accommodate ten thousand within five years. Residents did not need to be Methodist, but they did need to share Christian ideals. The prominent city planner and landscape designer Clarence Parkman Day, who, like Reverend Scott, lived in Pasadena, was commissioned to lay out the street networks and overall site.

One major model for the grand endeavor was the Chautauqua, a kind of educational assembly that achieved popularity in the United States in the late nineteenth and early twentieth centuries. *Chautauqua* is an Iroquois term that translates as "two moccasins tied together," although the literal meaning was irrelevant in this instance. Instead, the Chautauqua was named after Chautauqua Lake in western New York State, not far from Lake Erie, where the first such gathering was held, in 1874. Originally conceived as a summer enrichment program for Methodist Sunday School teachers, the assemblies soon expanded to include educational offerings and events aimed at spreading culture and learning. In the first decade alone, more than one hundred thousand people enrolled in its reading groups, and in 1883 Chautauqua University opened its doors as the first institution to offer correspondence courses in the United States. To this day the Chautauqua Institution hosts more than two thousand events over its nine-week summer season.

From that first Chautauqua, the idea spread across the country. There were "independent" Chautauquas constructed and run like summer camps, with permanent assembly and community spaces, as well as "circuit" Chautauquas, at which lectures, plays and operas, and forums on political, social, and cultural topics were held in large tents. At the height of the movement around 1915, there were one thousand independent and more than ten thousand traveling Chautauquas; the Chautauqua in Boulder, Colorado, attracted upward of one hundred thousand people each summer. The biggest Chautauqua hub on the West Coast would soon emerge just outside Santa Monica, in a place newly dubbed Pacific Palisades. Among other things, the term *palisade* refers to a series of cliffs along a body of water, in this case the Pacific Ocean, a geological formation that resembles the palisades of a fort.

Reverend Scott, born in Lapeer, Michigan, in 1877, might well be considered the father of Pacific Palisades. He was elected president of the Pacific Palisades Association, founded on August 9, 1921, for the purpose of creating a pedagogical and religious site, and, on June 17 of that year, Scott presented his ambitious plans at an extravagant banquet. Four hundred people were invited to the event, held at the rooftop café of the colossal Broadway Department Store, located on the southwest corner of Broadway and Fourth Street in downtown Los Angeles. The guests represented religious, political, and business factions, including California governor William D. Stephens and LA mayor-elect George Edward Cryer, along with a host of influential businesspeople: Robert Conran Gillis, who since 1906 had owned a good forty-six square miles of land once part of the Santa Monica Land and Water Company (founded in 1897 by Senator John Jones and Arcadia Bandini de Baker); Harry Chandler, the publisher of the *Los Angeles Times* and soon the largest real estate mogul in the United States;

the streetcar pioneer Moses Hazeltine Sherman, another of California's most successful property developers; Paul Shoup, the vice president of the Southern Pacific Railroad; the "Orange King" Charles Clarke Chapman, and the banker Andrew M. Chaffey.

Financing for the project would come through the sale of thousand-dollar certificates that entitled holders (also known as "founders") to select a personal plot before Pacific Palisades' official founding date, then use it over a ninety-nine-year leasehold contract in return for ground rent; the certificates also gave them free access to all Chautauqua events. The policy allowed the church to retain ownership of the land and ensure over the long term that only those who abided by the Methodists' moral standards were permitted to live there. The sale of tobacco and alcohol, for instance, was strictly prohibited. The plan proved short-lived; by 1924 the principle of leaseholds was abandoned, and lots were listed for sale. One quarter of the money generated by the sale of certificates was intended for the construction of Chautauqua community spaces: there would be an auditorium and rooms for Bible study as well as a school, administrative buildings, a library, and an art gallery; it was generally agreed that a small commercial strip would develop on its own.

In early August 1921, in the cool dappled light of Temescal Canyon (just north of Palisades High School today at the intersection of Temescal Canyon Road and Sunset Boulevard, near the Temescal Canyon Trail), 225 tents were pitched for a church summer camp. The operation was headed by Charles Hoss, a former teller at First National Bank in Earlville, who had rented out his house and moved to the area with his wife to manage the finances for the planned settlement. By November he had sold $30,000 worth of certificates. It was announced that the new colony would open at the start of the new year.

THE MORNING OF JANUARY 14, 1922—still celebrated in Pacific Palisades as Founders' Day—nearly 200 of the 275 founders gathered in a verdant meadow under a majestic oak tree. Today a commemorative park bench invites a moment of reflection where the tree once stood in Founders' Oak Island, a pocket park on Haverford Avenue, situated between Pierson Playhouse (Pacific Palisades' modest 125-seat theater) to the west and the pretentiously named

Chateau Paliset condominiums at 15510 Sunset Boulevard to the east. Once the founders had picked out properties and committed to building homes there within three years, the three hundred people who did not count as founders but who had made partial payments were allowed to select plots. The official opening of Pacific Palisades took place on February 22, 1922, at 10:30 a.m., with a number of speeches by various religious leaders and a free picnic for attendees. It goes without saying that other investors were sniffing around the project. Frank E. Bundy from Santa Monica, for instance, bought a neighboring piece of land from the Santa Monica Canyon Land and Water Company, with space for more than six hundred building plots. He would soon acquire more property along Mesa Road, remove the perimeter fencing, and build Bundy Ranch, the family seat.

The first major event in Pacific Palisades, known as the "Chautauqua of the Pacific Coast," was a mammoth Easter sunrise service on April 16, 1922.[4] It was held on a hillside where the million-dollar construction of a church was slated to begin soon. If contemporary accounts are to be believed, five thousand people flocked to the Palisades to hear Rev. Edgar Fay Daugherty of Los Angeles sermonize. Santa Monica judge William R. Garrett recited the Henry Van Dyke poem "God of the Open Air," and fifty musicians from the First Methodist Church of Los Angeles accompanied a five-hundred-member mixed choir, led by the Santa Monica Bay Women's Club.

In the month of May alone, the Pacific Palisades Association raised $182,000. The association acted in trust for the Huntington Beach Methodist Assembly. Its board was chaired by former lieutenant governor Albert Joseph Wallace, a Republican, devout Methodist, and avowed teetotaler. By early June 1922, association president Scott was proud to announce that the association had passed the million-dollar mark on May 30; of the 1,600 plots across 350 acres, 725 were taken. The City Club hosted a lavish "Million Dollar Dinner" in celebration. Via de la Paz and about six miles of side streets had been paved, the first four houses were under construction, plans for eight more had been approved, and optimistic estimates put the population at five hundred, at least, by year's end.

The first residence was built on "Founders Tract No. 1," located on one of the Alphabet Streets, at the time simply named by letter, though later renamed after famous Methodists, starting with Albright Street and Bestor Boulevard. Located today at 819 Hartzell Street, the 1,130-square-foot house was built on a lot just over 5,200 square feet as a single-story, two-bedroom, one-bath affair. It's still there and, for all the renovations and modernizations over the years, there have not been any additions. This makes it something of an oddity in a place where homes ten times its size are commonplace; in 2019 the ex-boxer Sugar Ray Leonard listed his nearly 17,000-square-foot villa at 1550 Amalfi Drive for $52 million. Two years later the twenty-six-year-old tech entrepreneur Austin Russell paid $83 million for a mansion at 1601 San Onofre Drive, which is more than 3,000 square feet larger.

If Founders Tract No. 1 was a latticework of narrow streets and manageable plots of land intended for affordable bungalows for retired church people and widows, the plots on Founders Tract No. 2 were much larger and located south of Beverly Boulevard, which was first paved in 1925 and integrated into Sunset Boulevard in July 1934. Though by no means a luxury residence, Reverend Scott's 3,875-square-foot house was lavish in size compared to the homes that came before. True to Genesis 1:28, he and his deeply pious wife, Anna, had been fruitful and multiplied. After living in a cottage in Temescal Canyon for a year, the family of eight moved to Via de la Paz—today number 631—on an otherwise undeveloped plot between the planned commercial center of Pacific Palisades and the ocean. The bedrooms were upstairs, one for the four boys and the other for the girls. It would be a stretch to call them loving parents, the reverend and his wife, who monitored the children through holes in their bedroom walls.

The Pacific Young People's Conference kicked off the inaugural Chautauqua summer program on June 29, 1922, originally intended to run until August 19 but then extended by popular acclaim until September 2. Groups from the Bible Institute of Los Angeles and the United Presbyterian Synod made the journey. On July 11 Gov. William D. Stephens officially opened Pacific Palisades as "the Great Permanent Chautauqua on the Pacific Coast."[5] More than two hundred carpenters had built a dining hall and cafeteria to accommodate seven hundred each, a temporary 1,500-seat church, a 2,000-seat auditorium, a grocery store, playgrounds and tennis courts, adequate sanitary facilities, and 250 cabins as dormitories. Another 250 two-person tents were rented out for six bucks a week.

Twenty thousand participants were expected. Chautauqua programming ranged from conferences and informal gatherings to a July 18 concert by the "World's Greatest Contralto," Ernestine Schumann-Heink.[6] Since 1878 the singer had dazzled crowds in Dresden, Berlin, London, Paris, Bayreuth, and in New York City at the Met. She had defined the role of Clytemnestra in the premiere of Richard Strauss's opera *Elektra* in Dresden in 1909—and on this occasion refused to perform in the Christian tent village accompanied by anything less than a Steinway grand piano. There was a staging of Shakespeare's comedy *As You Like It*, directed by Eleanor Miller from Pasadena's School of Expression and Music, along with a host of chamber ensemble and orchestral performances. Well-known writers James Foley and Frieda Peycke read from their works; Charles Wakefield Cadman performed original compositions based on melodies from the Omaha tribe; Rev. Benjamin Sherwood Haywood shared an account of his trip to Palestine; and University of Southern California president Rufus Bernhard von KleinSmid—yet to disgrace himself with his endorsement of eugenics and sterilization—delivered a lecture. Certain days were reserved for Presbyterian, Baptist, or Congregationalist events. There were sports, arts and crafts, and courses on a broad range of topics, from literature to the Bolshevik threat to nutrition, a pet interest of Reverend Scott's wife, Anna.

BY THE TIME A POST OFFICE OPENED at the corner of Marquez Avenue and Terminal Avenue on September 14, 1923, the church and the Pacific Palisades Association had invested millions. (The association had purchased the 1.7-square-mile site from the Methodists on July 1 and raised substantial further funds through the sale of bonds.) The money went toward purchasing more land, valued at $1,575,000, and constructing nearly seven miles of concrete sidewalks, gutters, and paved roads; installing electricity, gas, and telephone lines; and building a high-pressure water line almost fourteen inches in diameter. By 1925 the first hundred houses had been built in the Palisades, with nearly all residents bearing close ties to the Methodist Episcopal Church. Overall association earnings were approaching $4,780,000.

In 1923 the renowned Olmstead Brothers landscape architectural firm from Brookline, Massachusetts, was hired as a successor to Clarence Parkman Day in designing the town center, known as the "Village." The Business Block, also financed by the Pacific Palisades Association, was built opposite what is today known as the Village Green, a snug privately owned park located at 15290 Sunset Boulevard. Designed by architect Clifton Nourse, the Business Block offered thirty thousand square feet of retail and office space and from 1928 onward housed the Santa Monica Land and Water Company. The Spanish colonial revival building—brick with stucco flourishes, dark-green window awnings, and a pale-pink exterior—opened in 1924, and, when a shopping mall threatened to replace it in 1983, many Palisadians protested, including such famous residents as Peter Graves and Walter Matthau. The Business Block still stands, today home to a Starbucks and a Bank of America. Since 2018 the biggest draw in the area has been Palisades Village, an outdoor shopping center.

When the Methodist Episcopal Church attempted to restation him in Hawaii in 1924, Reverend Scott, emboldened by his connections to big investors, relinquished his role as servant of God and parish to pursue a full-time career as a property developer and real estate agent. In 1927 he and his family left Pacific Palisades for neighboring Brentwood, then later moved into Los Angeles proper.

With most significant pieces of infrastructure in place, Pacific Palisades quickly developed as a small community. On May 4, 1928, the first issue of the *Palisadian* came out, an eight-page weekly newspaper that sold for five cents and kept locals informed of the latest goings-on. A firehouse and police station opened on July 1, 1929, followed on August 18 (at which point the Palisades boasted a good 350 homes and one thousand residents) by the first cornerstone being laid at the northwest corner of Via de la Paz and Bowdoin Street for the 350-seat United Methodist Episcopal Church, at the time the area's only house of worship. The cross topping the steeple today is the same erected on Peace Hill, above Via de la Paz, where worshippers once gathered for services. Palisades Elementary School opened across the street from the church on June 12, 1931.

BY THIS TIME Pacific Palisades' transformation from a community based on shared religious beliefs into a refuge for the rich was well underway. In 1923 the millionaire oilman Alphonzo E. Bell, who had founded the swank neighborhood of Bel Air the year before, purchased more than fifty-four thousand acres from the Santa Monica Mountain Park Company and the Santa Monica Land and Water Company and began developing the Riviera, an area bounded by Amalfi Drive to the west and north, San Remo Drive to the east, and Sunset Boulevard to the south. Starting in 1927, the Riviera was marketed by Frank L. Meline, a one-time window dresser who had worked his way up to architect and real estate developer. The same year the 250-acre Riviera Country Club opened at 1250 Capri Drive, with an eighteen-hole golf course, twenty-six tennis courts, and an equestrian center; a Spanish colonial clubhouse went up the following year. In 2022 the club's reported initiation fee—should one wish to join the ranks of Charlie Chaplin, Walt Disney, Howard Hughes, Humphrey Bogart, Katharine Hepburn, and Spencer Tracy—was around $300,000.

In just a few years Vicki Baum would move to the Riviera, followed in time by Hanns Eisler, Emil Ludwig, Max Horkheimer, and many other exiles. Thomas Mann would deem it a worthy place to settle down. Much later Tom Cruise, Tom Hanks, and Steven Spielberg would live there too, to list just three of the countless Hollywood greats to have resided on the neighborhood's wide and winding streets, with names such as Capri Drive, Napoli Drive, or Sorrento Drive.

By 1924 Pacific Palisades was home to one of the most popular and highest-paid entertainers in the United States. Will Rogers was a syndicated newspaper columnist—his writing appeared in the *New York Times* and many other publications—whose waggish pieces about politics and society made him the best-known humorist since Mark Twain. Although largely forgotten as a comedic actor and writer, Rogers is the namesake of the Will Rogers phenomenon, which describes an effect of averages in groups: when an element migrates from one group to another, the average of both groups rises. Or, in the words attributed to Rogers, who was from Oklahoma: "When the Okies left Oklahoma and moved to California, they raised the average intelligence level in both states." In 1924 Rogers paid an impressive $400,000 for a lot just shy of two hundred acres, situated between the Palisades and the Los Angeles Athletic Club. He built a thirty-one-room ranch, complete with guesthouses and stables, polo grounds and a golf course. He rounded off the property over time, reaching nearly 360 acres by 1935, when he was killed in a plane crash. Rogers's widow, Betty, donated the family ranch to California State Parks in 1944. To this day the Will Rogers State Historic Park is one of the most beautiful recreational areas in Pacific Palisades.

In late 1925 the Pacific Palisades Association purchased 230 acres of coastline between Rustic Creek and Potrero Canyon for $1,625,000. The plan was allegedly to prevent the construction of Mount Saint Mary's College, a Catholic girls' school, but the real aim was far more ambitious. In 1887 Abbot Kinney—who would develop Venice in 1905—had bought land on the mesa west of Santa Monica Canyon from the Marquez family. His intention had been to found Santa Monica Heights there, but decades passed, and the land remained undeveloped. Known as Huntington Palisades—named after the railroad tycoon and previous owner Collis Potter-Huntington—the area overlooked the ocean and seemed the perfect place for extravagant villas. The Pacific Palisades Association enlisted the Santa Monica Land and Water Company to manage the sale; the company was appointed the association's exclusive agent and paid a commission of 25 percent, a model that similar agreements for other areas used.

Before long, however, strife arose between the involved parties. On April 30, 1928, Robert Conran Gillis transferred the contract and associated rights to the Pacific Land Corporation. It would be too much to go into detail here about disputes over interest payments and bonds or about which company sold or leased which properties to whom at what price and who owed what commission to whom. Suffice it to say, there was no end to the lawsuits, counterclaims, and court rulings. The days of the area serving as a modest home for devout Methodists were long gone. In early January 1929, the Santa Monica Land and Water Company announced that it would be selling lots in Pacific

Palisades, Huntington Palisades, and Beverly Boulevard with price tags pushing $80,000 and finished houses for upward of $3 million.

The stock market crash of 1929 and the Great Depression caused development in the Palisades to stagnate and contributed indirectly to the decline of the Pacific Palisades Association, which by spring of 1934 was no longer liquid but in fact bankrupt. On May 15, 1934, the Palisades Corporation took over hundreds of building plots—the association's primary assets—along with the Temescal Canyon site, which the association received permission to use for summer camps until September 30. As it was, for years the Scouts, YMCA, and YWCA had used the campgrounds, which war veteran groups and a private military academy for children had also leased. The Pacific Palisades Assembly Camps were run by the Palisades Corporation, which decided in September to turn over all marketing and sales of its properties in Huntington and Pacific Palisades to the Santa Monica Land and Water Company. The Presbyterian Church purchased the former Chautauqua site in 1943 and sold it to the Santa Monica Mountains Conservancy in 1994. Temescal Gateway Park, with its oak and sycamore forests, is one of the most popular destinations in the Santa Monica Mountains.

HUNTINGTON PALISADES had been inaugurated on January 20, 1926, as an exclusive neighborhood that saw its first house completed by the end of the year, a twelve-room colonial-style mansion at 601 Ocampo Drive. Such palatial estates sprang up like mushrooms and still characterize Pacific Palisades today. One need look no further than Miramar Estates, on the western slope of Santa Ynez Canyon, where the *Los Angeles Times* "demonstration home" was built—"one of the most important steps ever taken in Southern California to disseminate authoritative information on all phases of homebuilding"—and eventually sold to Lion Feuchtwanger in 1943 for a ridiculously low price or in the Castellammare district west of the former Inceville Studios, developed by Frank L. Meline in 1926.[7] One of the first houses to be built there at 17948 Porto Marina Way was Villa de Leon. The imposing residence was modeled after the Petit Trianon in Versailles and cost around $1 million. It belonged to the Russian wool merchant Leon Kauffman, who was naturalized in 1894.

The twelve-thousand-square foot villa has thirty-five rooms, including a parlor almost thirty-three by sixty-six feet, a circular dining room, a library, nine bedrooms, and ten bathrooms, whose imported Italian tiles were grouted with gold. Elsewhere in the house, the mahogany wood paneling came straight from Thailand. The garage fit seven cars, while a private funicular provided beach access.

In 1928 a commercial building for the neighborhood went up at what is now 17575 Pacific Coast Highway. It was there that Thelma Todd, known for playing the blonde opposite the Marx Brothers and Laurel and Hardy, opened Thelma Todd's Sidewalk Café in 1934. Producer Hal Roach created the so-called potato clause specifically for Todd: if she gained more than five pounds, her contract would be terminated without notice. On December 16, 1935, she was found dead in the driver's seat of her chocolate-brown Lincoln Phaeton, parked in her lover's garage at nearby 17531 Posetano Road. She was wearing a sequined blue evening gown, mink coat, and $20,000 worth of jewelry. The circumstances of her death—suicide, accident, or murder—remain a mystery, making the building that once housed her restaurant and hosted so many Hollywood parties one of the biggest tourist attractions in Pacific Palisades.

Kauffman's villa can still be admired from a distance; an equally spectacular building, however, was demolished in the early 1950s: the Japanese palace of a Swabian art collector. In 1883 sixteen-year-old Adolf Bernheimer followed his brother Eugen to New York, a year after Eugen left home to join another sibling. The young men came from a large family that belonged to a small, rural Jewish community in the Württemberg village of Buttenhausen, outside Ulm. Their relatives included the Bernheimers in Munich, whose firm decorated the palaces of the Fairy Tale King, Ludwig II of Bavaria, as well as the private residences of Thomas Mann, the Krupp family, and Hermann Göring.

The Bernheimer brothers—urbane, lifelong bachelors who had anglicized the spellings of their names and now went by Adolph and Eugene—had a penchant for art and antiques themselves. They made their fortune as co-owners of the New York–based Bear Mill Manufacturing Company, which neither milled nor manufactured anything but rather imported goods like silk. In

1911 they relocated to Los Angeles. In want of an appropriate space to display the Asian art and artifacts Adolph had collected over seventeen trips, the brothers hired the New York architect Franklin M. Small to design a house modeled after a temple near Kyoto, move-in ready by November 1914. During World War I, the Bernheimers fell under suspicion of being German spies or at least of aiding and abetting espionage. Exasperated by the accusations and growing antisemitism, they sold their estate at 1999 North Sycamore Avenue in Hollywood in 1924, at which point it became a clubhouse as singular as it was inviting for an exclusive group of film stars and directors known as the "400 Club." Since 1948 the building has housed a restaurant called Yamashiro and occasionally served as a film set for cult hits including *Sayonara*, starring Marlon Brando, or Quentin Tarantino's *Kill Bill*, with Uma Thurman. Anyone who can afford it is welcome to dine there today.

After Eugene died unexpectedly in late 1924, Adolph retreated to Pacific Palisades, where he purchased a seven-and-a-half-acre plot with a view of the ocean from Alphonzo E. Bell. The property was located at 16980 Sunset Boulevard (today occupied by the Pacific Garden Apartments), just above the Pacific Coast Highway, originally named Roosevelt Highway at its 1929 opening ceremony. Adolph again engaged Franklin M. Small, this time to design a Sino-Japanese–style manor house surrounded by the Bernheimer Oriental Gardens, sweeping grounds filled with rare plantings from Japan, China, and Tibet; pagodas; and little Japanese cottages painted in black, mauve, and gold. The precious sculptures adorning the property included a herd of bronze elephants, which for some reason routinely attracted real-life mountain lions. Adolph reportedly spent around $4 million to realize his Japanese dream atop the bluffs of Pacific Palisades.

The gardens opened to the public in 1928 and drew more than two million visitors, until the attack on Pearl Harbor extinguished US enthusiasm for Japanese garden culture, particularly when those gardens were owned by a German with the same first name as the führer, even if this Adolph was Jewish. The gardens fell further (and literally) into ruin in 1944, with parts of the estate tumbling down the cliffside. This would have come as little surprise to many

Palisadians; after all, the Chumash people had always believed that evil spirits lurked beneath the hill, which would occasionally emit smoke and sulfur fumes. Adolph succumbed to pneumonia the same year, surrounded by his prized pieces, including life-size statues of Lao Tzu and Confucius, which went under the hammer in 1951. The auction was more than a commercial occasion, the *Los Angeles Times* wrote; it was "the funeral dirge for a lovely vision that died."[8]

"GIVE IN TO THEIR 'TAKE IT EASY'"

THE DECLINE of Inceville Studios and the founding of Pacific Palisades were simultaneous if separate phenomena. Without the film industry, though, the Palisades are unlikely ever to have become the unspoken center of German and Austrian exile culture, or "Weimar on the Pacific," a phrase still occasionally applied to Greater Los Angeles, though the exiles never used it themselves. There is a reason the *New Yorker* titled a snarky 1941 profile of Thomas Mann "Goethe in Hollywood."

The dream factory that was Hollywood and drove Los Angeles' rapid growth was largely built on the backs of poor Jewish immigrants, many of them the children of refugees who had fled the pogroms of eastern Europe in the late nineteenth century. The film industry was new, with neither establishment structures nor social barriers in place, and attracted people who saw few, if any, opportunities for themselves elsewhere. They did, however, know what audiences wanted, since they shared in those dreams and desires: the America they conjured and projected onto screens was often characterized by kitschy ideals and naive patriotism.

The founder of Universal Studios, Carl Laemmle, had emigrated from Laupheim, in southern Germany; Adolph Zukor, who founded Paramount Pictures, came from Ricse, in the Hungarian wine region of Tokaj. Harry Warner—who entered the annals of film as one of the four Warner Brothers, alongside Albert, Samuel, and Jack—was born Hirsch Moses Wonsal in Krasnosielc, a village in Poland that at the time belonged to the Russian Empire. Harry Cohn, a cofounder of Columbia Pictures, was the son of a German tailor. William Fox, a.k.a. Vilmos Fuchs, who started Fox Film Corporation, was part of a German-speaking family from the Hungarian village of Tolcsva. Joseph Schenck, whose Twentieth-Century Pictures would merge with Fox in 1935, was born Ossip Schenker in the Russian city of Rybinsk. Marcus Loew, the son of an immigrant from Vienna, and Louis B. Mayer, of Minsk, created Metro-Goldwyn-Mayer, the studio with a lion in the logo; the middle part of the name came from Samuel Goldwyn, born Szmuel Gelbfisz in Warsaw. MGM was derisively referred to as "*Mayers ganze Mischpoche*" ("Mayer's whole mishpocha," the latter a Yiddish term for one's entire family network, sometimes including close friends), as the cofounder was in the habit of employing his relatives, including the Swiss filmmaker William Wyler, who for three decades would reign as a top director in Hollywood with twelve best-director nominations to his name.

It was an era in which many Germans were immigrating to the United States—361,000 between 1923 and 1929 alone—and film studios naturally drew talent from the pool of newcomers. One such "discovery" in 1923 was Ernst Lubitsch, who would become one of the most influential Germans in Hollywood, known for directing lighthearted, spirited comedies in a signature style dubbed the "Lubitsch Touch." His colleague Friedrich Wilhelm Murnau, born in 1888 as Friedrich Wilhelm Plumpe, had swapped out his rather unfortunate surname following a love affair with the expressionist poet Hans Ehrenbaum-Degele in the city of Murnau, in Upper Bavaria. Murnau achieved international fame with the first vampire film in history, *Nosferatu: A Symphony of Horror*, and directed *Sunrise* for Fox Films in 1926–27.

In 1931, one week before the premiere of his film *Tabu: A Story of the South Seas*, shot in the South Pacific, Murnau's life met a tragic end when his car swerved to avoid a collision and went off the road. Rumors quickly spread that it had not been Murnau but his fourteen-year-old Filipino lover at the wheel. The director's body was embalmed, made up, and laid out on white silk in a glass coffin. Eleven people attended his funeral in Hollywood, before Murnau's remains were transported to Berlin and interred. His death mask, which Greta Garbo had made, was found decades later, caked in dust, in the attic of 165 Mabery Road in Pacific Palisades, where the "divine" Garbo's best friend, Salka Viertel, once lived.

MURNAU HAD BEEN THE ONE to help Salka's husband, the director Berthold Viertel, secure a three-year contract with Hollywood in 1927. Born in 1885, Viertel had displayed talent for literature and theater alike. Before turning to film direction in the mid-1920s, he wrote for *Die Fackel* (The torch), the Austrian journalist Karl Kraus's magazine in Vienna. He was also a theater critic for the Prague daily newspaper *Prager Tageblatt*, while producing theater pieces in his native Vienna as well as in Dresden, Munich, Düsseldorf, and Berlin. His wife, Salka, was born Salomea Sara Steuermann in 1889 in Sambor, Galicia—then part of the Austro-Hungarian Empire, today the Ukrainian city of Sambir, located at the foot of the Carpathian Mountains. She appeared on stage in Germany and Austria but never advanced to the top ranks, not because she lacked talent but presumably because her looks did not correspond to the "classic" beauty standards of the time.

The couple was warmly welcomed to Hollywood in late March 1928 by German friends who were already established. Emil Jannings, who would soon become the first actor in film history to receive an Academy Award for Best Actor (thirteen Oscars were presented at a drab ceremony at Hotel Roosevelt that lasted all of five minutes), and his wife, Gussy Holl, threw a party for the new arrivals at their splendid twenty-room mansion on Hollywood Boulevard. The directors Ernst Lubitsch and Ludwig Berger attended, as did the film star Conrad Veidt. Other prominent European guests included Thomas Mann's children, Erika and Klaus, who reflected that, "however boring, [there was] something fascinating" about Hollywood, that it "pulls you in, sucks you up, holds you captive. One loses a sense of time, like in *The Magic Mountain*. It passes without one's knowing what substance it might have had."[1]

Berthold's collaboration with Murnau proved rocky. Murnau was three years younger and prone to arrogant, seigneurial airs, and their plan to coauthor the screenplay for *City Girl* failed, a turn of events that dampened the relationship between "Murr" and Salka as well. Salka was lonely and depressed. Her marriage was in ruins and the arrival in May of their three sons—Hans, Peter, and Thomas, who were raised primarily by their nanny, Nena, born Helene Gnichwitz in Wrocław—did as little to fulfill her as domestic matters. The household was run by Elisabeth Hanelik, from the town of Hamborn in North Rhine-Westphalia, and included a Black housekeeper named Emma and a Black chauffeur from Kansas named De Witt Fuller. The children "adored Emma and De Witt, who reciprocated with great warmth."[2]

Most challenging to Salka was adapting to the social life, "the lunches and parties getting [her] down."[3] Alcohol flowed freely despite Prohibition. Bootleggers supplied the stars with wine and liquor, though good beer was hard to come by, much to the Germans' dismay. The Viertels had met Murnau in 1926 through Salka's friend Francesco von Mendelssohn, a flamboyant and multitalented scion, who tried to mediate:

> Murr . . . told me explicitly how deeply he regrets all the disturbances caused by professional troubles, which at times prevent him from "speaking his mind," which in all of America he can do only with you. . . . Look at Americans. Give in to their "Take it easy." It's good, even if *obviously* only useful to you as a passing thing, it would *certainly* be useful as a way to take a break, then dig deep again, only you know those depths are *not* a place one should permanently reside!! The way you were behaving yesterday and today, you'll never survive that in your skin. *Tu m'as fait pitié*—I can't even express how sorry I feel for you.[4]

The Viertels initially lived in an inexpensive house on Fairfax Avenue in a predominantly Jewish neighborhood west of Hollywood. Salka, who still felt like she was in "exile," asserted her desire to be closer to the ocean, over her husband's objections.[5] Berthold had no interest in moving to Santa Monica Canyon, which was considered damp and foggy and far from the studios. In June 1929 they rented a Tudor-style house in Pacific Palisades—white with painted green wooden beams and a roof to match—for three months, at $300 a month. This made them the first of the residents who would eventually form the German-speaking émigré community in the Palisades, one in which Salka was a key figure, her home its epicenter.

At the end of their lease, the Viertels renegotiated terms and extended the rental agreement at half the price. In April 1933 they bought the thirty-eight-hundred-square-foot house for a reasonable $7,500. On the ground floor, a spacious living room with a fireplace opened into a garden filled with hibiscus bushes; two pines; pittosporum, apricot, and fig trees; and a massive magnolia, all bordered by a fence festooned with honeysuckle and pink and white hedge roses. Adjacent to the dining room was the large kitchen, while upstairs were the bathrooms, three bedrooms overlooking the ocean and a fourth that faced the street. Salka had some earthquake damage repaired, central heating and comfortable servants' quarters installed, a guest apartment put in above the garage, and everything repainted and refurnished. A pedestrian underpass a stone's throw from the house led down to the beach.

Before long 165 Mabery Road was frequented by such luminaries as the Russian film pioneer Sergei Eisenstein and Greta Garbo, whom Salka initially met at a party thrown by Ernst Lubitsch. Every Sunday, at regular gatherings later glorified as "salons," guests would come for an afternoon of table tennis, serious discussion, or a bit of banter over tea and Gugelhupf cake; regular customers included *Tarzan* star Johnny Weissmuller; playwright Marcel Achard; conductor Otto Klemperer; French actor Françoise Rosay and her husband, Jacques Feyder; and the famous American screenwriter Oliver Garrett, who lived a few doors down at 49 Mabery Road and carried on an affair with Salka from 1931 to 1934.

Though he would go down in history as the director of such classics as *High Noon* and *From Here to Eternity*, Fred Zinnemann started out as Berthold Viertel's assistant director after leaving Vienna for Hollywood in October 1929. At the time interactions with stars like Charlie Chaplin left him "speechless and paralyzed."[6] Salka's house—Berthold was often absent and soon rarely ever there—also served as more than Greta Garbo's preferred hideaway. As Berthold articulated in a letter to his wife, after 1933 theirs became a legendary address, "165 Mabery Road" synonymous with "a place of refuge, a place of heartfelt help, and a kind of oasis in the ever-expanding desert of spiritual and emotional desolation, of impotent and sadly all-too potent hatred."[7] Salka's house was better known than later hubs, like the Feuchtwangers' palatial estate on Paseo Miramar or the Mann residence on San Remo Drive.

Salka appeared in several films using her maiden name of Steuermann, including a supporting role as a speaking wax figure of Catherine the Great in *Seven Faces*, under her husband's direction. In the spring of 1930, she acted in Jacques Feyder's German-language remake of *Anna Christie*, based on the Eugene O'Neill play; it was Greta Garbo's first sound film, in which she played an embittered, alcoholic, Swedish-born prostitute.

The advent of sound films put an end to many Europeans' Hollywood careers, as actors such as Emil Jannings and Pola Negri (but unlike Garbo) struggled with English. It also severely limited international marketability, as audiences abroad could not follow the English dialogues and rejected subtitles. Until effective dubbing processes were developed, the industry experimented with multiple-language version (MLV) films shot in various languages, whether concurrently or one after the other, and sometimes with new actors, permitting the films to be exported to different countries. Garbo mostly had Salka to thank for appearing more relaxed in the German version of *Anna Christie* than in its English counterpart—which, unlike other MLVs, was produced and released with some delay; Salka had coached her friend, and her own exaggerated style, still reminiscent of German expressionist film, complemented Garbo's sparing gestures. The women were close friends by then, and it was Garbo who encouraged Salka to start writing. Salka came up with the idea for Garbo's film *Queen Christina* and soon became the in-house expert at Metro-Goldwyn-Mayer for all things related to the enigmatic Swedish film star. She was Garbo's closest confidante, a position not to be underestimated.

Back in Europe since the early summer of 1932, Berthold Viertel traveled to Berlin on January 30, 1933, to start preproduction on a new film. That very morning, shortly after eleven o'clock, Adolf Hitler was appointed Reich chancellor by Reich president Paul von Hindenburg; that evening uniformed supporters of the Nazis and civilians alike bore torches and took to the streets to celebrate their führer. In his diary Joseph Goebbels described the "spontaneous explosion of the *Volk*" as nothing more than "senseless frenzy," though it was a highly choreographed demonstration of Germany's new power structure.[8] Within two days Hitler urged Hindenburg to dissolve the Reichstag and schedule new parliamentary elections for March 5. Demonstrations were banned; on February 4, 1933, the Decree for the Protection of the German People docked freedom of speech and constrained the press. Jewish and politically willful stage performers were dismissed from Prussian state theaters in Berlin on February 27, just hours before the Reichstag went up in flames. The arrests began that night, and the next day the Ordinance for the Protection of the People and the State suspended the basic democratic rights outlined in the Weimar Constitution. Berthold Viertel fled to London by way of Prague, Vienna, and Paris. On July 14 he arrived in the United States.

The National Socialists received 43.9 percent of votes in the March 5 parliamentary election, giving the Nazis an absolute majority in the Reichstag with their coalition partner, the German National People's Party. Within days planned attacks on German Jews began along Berlin's Kurfürstendamm, one of the city's grand boulevards. In a display of premature capitulation, large parts of the film industry were "Aryanized." On March 29 the board of directors of Ufa, the country's top production studio, resolved that "[as] a result of the national revolution taking place in Germany, the question of continuing the employment of Jewish staff members has become pressing. It will henceforth be our policy, where possible, to terminate contracts with Jewish employees."[9] The Ufa policy even applied to heavyweights like Erich Pommer, the producer of such seminal films as *The Cabinet of Dr. Caligari*, *Metropolis*, and *The Blue Angel*.

On April 1, 1933, Jewish businesses, medical practices, and law firms became the target of boycotts. Shops were destroyed and people terrorized in arbitrary, pogrom-like attacks. In utter disregard for constitutional safeguards, the Law for the Restoration of the Professional Civil Service, enacted on April 7, 1933, granted the state the right to dismiss civil servants who were critical of the regime or "non-Aryan." In the first few weeks after the National Socialists came to power, it was mostly political opponents who fled the Reich for fear of reprisals and persecution; between thirty and forty thousand exiles initially sought refuge in France, Switzerland, and Czechoslovakia. Later many Jewish Germans fled as well, first to neighboring countries and Great Britain. In 1933 alone nearly thirty-seven thousand Jews left their homes.

That year Hedwig "Vicki" Baum took up residence in Pacific Palisades. Baum was born in 1888, her family part of Vienna's Jewish bourgeoisie. She was one of the first media sweethearts of the German literary scene, the Weimar

Republic's prize writer. Baum wrote in her memoir, which she never got around to finishing before her death in 1960,

> Sometimes I get a trifle sentimental when I remember what this insatiable octopus of a town was thirty years ago. Now that we live in an ill-smelling, khaki-colored tent of smog, it's hard to believe that there ever was a gentian-blue sky above us, filled with glittering stars and the perfume of jasmine in the cold nights; hillsides and gardens sparkling with dew each morning, with all the colors of a wild Van Gogh palette as the sun rose, the air so clear you didn't want to breathe but drink it. I think I stayed drunk for weeks with this sun and air and the beauty of the hills.[10]

Baum grew up wealthy and had begun a career as a harpist when her first novel, *Frühe Schatten: Die Geschichte einer Kindheit* (Early shadows: The story of a childhood), was published in 1919. From 1926 to 1931, the author worked as a magazine editor at the Berlin publishing house Ullstein. Her 1928 novel, *Stud. chem. Helene Willfüer* (Helene Willfüer, student of chemistry), was celebrated by critics and readers alike. The following year Ullstein published *Menschen im Hotel* (*The Grand Hotel*), first as a serial in the weekly illustrated magazine *Berliner Illustrirte Zeitung*, then as a book. It would become the most popular of Baum's thirty-plus titles. The novel's mix of melodrama, romance, and crime struck a chord at the time. The theatrical version, directed by Gustaf Gründgens, premiered in Berlin in 1930 and was eventually performed on more than 120 other stages. MGM acquired the film rights in 1930 and was involved in the Broadway production as well. At a time when interminably long-running shows like *The Phantom of the Opera* or *Chicago* were unthinkable, *Grand Hotel* was performed an impressive 459 times.

Made famous the world round by *Grand Hotel* and adored by the public, if summarily dismissed as a literary lightweight by some critics, Baum went to the United States in 1931 to draft two screenplays for Paramount. She was paid $2,500 weekly, the equivalent of $45,000 today. Her work did not find much favor with the studio bosses, though, and she was fired—only to be hired by MGM to collaborate on the screenplay for *Grand Hotel*. Her pay there was $2,000 per week, which, although less than what she had made at Paramount, was equal to what she had earned in selling the film rights. In a departure from standard studio practice, not two but five Hollywood stars were cast in *Grand Hotel*: Greta Garbo played alongside Joan Crawford, Lionel and John Barrymore, and Wallace Beery.

Baum returned to Berlin without the faintest sense of how successful the film would turn out to be; it would earn the studio almost $1 million. She had, however, decided to emigrate permanently to the United States and applied within the quota system for visas for herself; her second husband, the conductor Richard Lert; and their two sons, which in 1932 was still fairly straightforward. Baum embarked on the SS *Europa* in late March, a plush contract with MGM in her pocket that guaranteed her $3,500 a week. On April 12 she attended the world premiere of *Grand Hotel* in New York City. The rest of her family arrived later, and on July 12 they all moved to California, to the same neighborhood as the Viertels. In February 1933 Baum purchased property at 1461 Amalfi Drive in the Riviera section of Pacific Palisades, where she had a Spanish colonial villa constructed.

By late summer Baum and family—her husband had directed his final concert in Germany on March 6, 1933—moved into the two-story, whitewashed brick house with a red tiled roof, viewings of which the builder had promoted in large-format ads. The seven-thousand-square-foot, five-bed, five-bath villa was situated on a half-acre plot with gardens and a large swimming pool. The master bath was clad in onyx, and most of the downstairs rooms featured black-and-white marble checkerboard floors. A ten-foot-wide window in Baum's raspberry-pink, gray-furnished study overlooked the canyon, while the adjoining library was dominated by a black Bauhaus three-seater and decorated with statues of the Buddha and a Bavarian Madonna. The enormous kitchen was also on the ground floor. The household staff changed over time, but it always consisted of people of color, whether Mattie, who had worked as a host at an upscale Hollywood brothel, and her husband, Alex; Velma, a cook from Mississippi; or Leola, who came from Louisiana and worked as the Baums' maid.

While Amalfi Drive was mostly undeveloped at the time, another Austrian author lived three plots down at 1515 Amalfi Drive, bordering Baum's property to the northwest. Before marrying an Italian count, the somewhat shifty Countess Caroline Zanardi Landi had worked as a cook, shop girl, and language teacher. In her book *The Secret of an Empress*, she claimed to be the secret daughter of Empress Elisabeth (Sisi) of Austria. Her Spanish colonial house, dubbed "The Cloisters," was built in 1925, designed by Mark Daniels, the architect behind the Villa Aurora. After the countess and her beautiful daughter, the actor Elissa Landi, moved out, the director David O. Selznick lived there while he was shooting *Gone with the Wind*. Douglas Fairbanks Jr. bought it in 1939, had a few additions built, and in 1942 rented it for $600 a month to Cary Grant and his second wife, the Woolworth heir Barbara Hutton. Yet another famous owner was the singer Bobby Vinton, known for songs such as "Blue Velvet" and "Mr. Lonely," who in 1985 sold it to Steven Spielberg, the only director in history to be nominated for an Academy Award in six different decades.

There was no lack of money in Baum and Lert's household in the 1930s either. Baum had, however, insisted on a clause in her MGM contract that allowed her to devote six months of the year to writing, effectively halving her annual earnings: "I had been taken down another notch and now belonged to the seventeen-hundred-fifty-a-week crowd." The average US family earned around $1,500 annually, meaning Baum was making about sixty times that, plus her husband's income:

> In Hollywood you had to swim with your crowd or sink. That was one of the many new difficulties I had to face: spending those huge earnings on the all-pervading conspicuous consumption, on show, prestige, status. . . .
>
> Invitations were an eye-for-an-eye, tooth-for-a-tooth affair, and I was constantly invited. This meant a large open house, servants, gardeners, auxiliary butlers and waitresses and bartenders for the frequent parties I was more or less forced to give. In Hollywood, if you invited sixty guests they would bring another forty uninvited ones. Being my pixilated Grandma's true offspring, naturally I'd prepare food for

> a hundred and fifty. Neither I nor my husband drink or smoke, but rivers of alcohol were poured incessantly into my guests' dry gullets—and bootlegged drinks of good quality were ridiculously expensive.[11]

It bears mentioning that Baum had a speakeasy-style bar built in the basement of their house, the entrance concealed behind a bookcase that pivoted open.

Writing for film did not bring Baum any great pleasure. "My career in Hollywood is and was nothing but a series of disappointments and annoyances," she declared by late 1933.[12] In the spring of 1934 she signed a contract with the producer Samuel Goldwyn and returned ruefully to MGM, where she now earned just $1,000 a week. Her income was of course supplemented by magazine pieces and book royalties; Baum was certainly still rich and could maintain her upper-class existence. The year 1935 saw her fulfill a long-cherished dream of traveling to Bali, where she sought out Walter Spies, Friedrich Wilhelm Murnau's ex-partner. Spies was a gifted painter and musician, fervid ethnographer, archaeologist, and naturalist; he was also a museum curator who helped steer Balinese art in a new direction with painting classes, marketing, and advocacy efforts for local artists. Last but not least, Spies was known as a charming host and travel guide to the rich and famous. The trip made a real impression on Baum, who returned a year later, this time with her 16-mm camera. She photographed ceremonies, cockfights, and dances, images she shared proudly with guests back home in Pacific Palisades. Thomas Mann was taken with the "lads in ritualistic trance" and with one "beautiful young Indian dancer" in particular.[13]

It was during her visit with Spies that Baum wrote her second international bestseller, *Love and Death in Bali*, whose main character, Doctor Fabius, bears a striking resemblance to her host. She focused more and more on her writing, and in 1940, at age fifty-two and two years after becoming a US citizen, Baum wrote her first novel in the language of her new home country. She continued to earn hefty sums through film-licensing agreements, selling the rights to her novel *Hotel Berlin '43* to Warner Brothers for $50,000 in November 1943, for instance. Writing the screenplays herself, however, had lost its appeal around 1941:

> Speaking for myself, once I realized that I had no talent for movie writing, I withdrew from it. To have nothing to do with the studios is my one great luxury. If my agents, and it happens rarely enough, succeed in selling a story of mine to the industry, I am pleased but by no means elated; it's not my property any longer, I don't care what happens to it, and I avoid seeing the picture. That's part of my simple method of needing neither drinks, nor dope, nor tranquilizers.[14]

Baum largely kept her distance from exile circles. Her teas and dinner parties were, however, frequented by a number of prominent émigrés, including two-time Oscar winner Luise Rainer, who lived down the street; Peter Lorre, who lived on Adelaide Drive in neighboring Santa Monica; the directors Otto Preminger and Fritz Lang; and Gina Kaus, a fellow writer and close friend of Baum's.

In 1942 Baum and Lert rented out their house and moved to Pasadena, where Lert led the symphony orchestra. Three years later they relocated again, this time to a less imposing residence in Hollywood. The English actor David Niven owned the art deco villa on Amalfi Drive for a time before Whoopi Goldberg, who had gained recent fame through her roles in *Sister Act* and *Ghost*, purchased the estate in 1993 for $2,547,500. She lived there for twenty-five years, then sold her home for $8,795,000; the listing explicitly mentioned that the estate was "[originally] built for famed author Vicki Baum."[15] A year and a half later, shortly after Goldberg had sparked outrage in January 2022 by stating on television that the Holocaust had nothing to do with racism, the house built for "the Jewess Vicky Baum-Levy"—a Jewish woman who escaped the Shoah and was once defamed in Nazi Germany as a writer of "shallow, amoral, sensationalist novels"—again went up for sale, this time as a teardown.[16]

"WHAT WATCH?" "TEN WATCH." "SUCH MUCH?"

"SO MUCH GERMAN IS SPOKEN THERE" that he could have sworn he was on Berlin's fabled shopping boulevard Kurfürstendamm, the film journalist Rolf Nürnberg wrote in 1932 after returning from Hollywood.[1] The fact that several fellow Germans had settled down in Hollywood before Adolf Hitler came into power—Marlene Dietrich, who signed a seven-year contract with Paramount Pictures in 1930, the most famous among them—benefited a good number of creatives exiled from the Reich, which included around 5,000 film and theater professionals and 1,500 writers. Of the 105,000 Germans who emigrated to the United States between 1933 and 1941 (almost three-quarters of whom came between 1938 and 1941), about 15,000 landed in southern California, and 70 percent of these had Jewish roots. By 1945, 25,000 more Germans had resettled in the United States. Many tried in vain to establish themselves in the film industry, but a good 1,500 did manage to find work in Hollywood, which was booming: in 1939, for instance, there were more cinemas in the United States than banks, with upward of 50 million moviegoers weekly; the studios were producing more than four hundred new films every year. German and Austrian filmmakers who had fled the Nazi regime became some of the greatest architects of Hollywood's golden age: "Don't you guys know you're in Hollywood? Speak German," Otto Preminger once reprimanded some people he overheard conversing in Hungarian.[2]

These filmmakers were grouped among those known as "émigrés," Europeans who tended to be highly educated and enrich the cultural and intellectual life of the United States. They were distinguished clearly from "immigrants," those people who had come from all over the world in search of a better life. Many who worked in the film industry did not want to be seen as seeking protection in exile but instead as transplants to the promised land, which they considered their new home and extoled with ardent patriotism. Unlike the philosopher Ludwig Marcuse, for instance, who carried on as though he still lived in Europe, writing in German and fraternizing almost exclusively with other exiles, most of the émigrés Americanized their names and worked hard at integrating. A good number avoided emigrant circles and made fun of the "backhomesters" who remarked constantly on how much better things were "back home" in Vienna or Berlin.

Nearly all who came to Los Angeles did so on temporary tourist visas. What they required to remain long-term was an immigrant visa. In 1924 the US government had set an upper annual limit of 164,667 immigrants and capped the number of those allowed to immigrate from each country to 2 percent of the US population according to the 1890 census. With 51,227 possible immigrants, Germans represented the largest group, exceeding those born in Great Britain and northern Ireland. The law aimed at barring entry to people from Asia as well as southern Europe. Italy, for instance, was granted a contingent of 3,845, whereas Greece, China, and India were permitted no more than 100, the absolute minimum. In 1929 Washington lowered its annual cap to 153,879. Germany was limited to 25,957, though it barely reached half: by 1937 only 10,895 Germans were resettling permanently in the United States. In the years immediately following 1933, the United States was not a top choice for people fleeing or expelled from the Third Reich, as many hoped for the political situation in Germany to improve and thought they might wait it out in neighboring countries.

After the annexation of Austria in March 1938, the United States combined the visa quotas for Germany and Austria for a total of 27,370. The quota was met in 1939, with 240,748 people on the waiting list. In 1940, 27,355 visas were issued, 15 fewer than the upper limit—though the waiting list had swelled to 301,935 names—and in 1941 only 16,994 Germans were granted visas. In June of that year, all US diplomatic missions in Germany and occupied Europe were closed. The Third Reich imposed an emigration ban starting October 23, 1941, and on November 25 Germany withdrew the citizenship of any and all Jewish Germans who had not yet been expatriated and lived outside the territory of the Reich, which further hindered their admission to potential countries of asylum.

For those entering the United States on tourist visas, the only way—however tortuous—to attain an immigrant visa that guaranteed permanent residence and that had to be applied for abroad, was to leave and reenter the country. This sent many to Mexico. Berthold and Salka Viertel, for instance, had crossed the border from Tijuana to San Ysidro back on March 4, 1932. Most headed for the border city of Mexicali and booked a room at a spot like the Hotel Comercial. After a visit to the US consulate, where they collected their visas, they set foot back on US soil in Calexico, quite literally—as immigrants they were required to enter the United States on foot. The process required all manner of documentation, some of which had to be requested from Nazi Germany, as well as an affidavit of support from a US citizen, disclosing personal finances and pledging readiness to cover the living expenses of the visa applicant, should such support be needed. Authorities also required an affidavit of sponsorship and a moral affidavit from a US citizen, guaranteeing that the sponsored individuals would not act in any manner harmful to the United States during their time there and that they would not overstay their visa.

IN THOSE EARLY YEARS, Pacific Palisades played a marginal role as a place for these émigré film professionals to settle down. This had less to do with the fact that the neighborhood was steadily becoming one of the pricier parts of town, in a league with Beverly Hills or the Hollywood Hills, than with the length of the commute to the studios; for those who did not work from home or have a chauffeured car, like writers Salka Viertel or Vicki Baum, the distance was simply too great. In many cases exiles living across Los Angeles belonged to "Weimar on the Pacific" as well.

The scene included directors such as Wilhelm Dieterle from Ludwigshafen am Rhein, who arrived in Hollywood in 1930; Vienna-born Fritz Lang; Bukovina-born Otto Preminger; and Robert Siodmak, who hailed from Dresden. These men sometimes found themselves walking a tightrope between art and commerce. There was master of melodrama Douglas Sirk, né Detlev Sierck, from Hamburg; king of comedy Samuel "Billy" Wilder, from Galicia; and Fred

Zinnemann, born in the foothills of the Carpathian Mountains, whose films debuted such future stars as Marlon Brando, Grace Kelly, and Meryl Streep. One mustn't forget Henry Koster, born Hermann Kosterlitz in Berlin, who relocated to 1216 Lachman Lane in Pacific Palisades long after the war; or Kurt Bernhardt, rechristened Curtis Bernhardt, from Worms, who spent his later years at 1350 Berea Place. Their industry colleagues Reginald Gröbel (who inverted the spelling of his last name to become Le Borg), John Brahm, and Edgar G. Ulmer lived comfortably enough as B-movie men.

Film technicians, cameramen, and editors found as much success in Hollywood as the composers Erich Wolfgang Korngold, Ernst Toch, Werner Richard Heymann (who had provided the music for such Ufa blockbusters as *Die Drei von der Tankstelle*, or *Three Good Friends*), and Friedrich Hollaender, who composed "Ich bin von Kopf bis Fuss auf Liebe eingestellt" ("Falling in Love Again [Can't Help It]") for Marlene Dietrich in *The Blue Angel*. Franz Wachsmann (who now went by Waxman), once a member of the Berlin jazz ensemble Weintraubs Syncopators, scored more than two hundred films and received Oscars in 1940 and 1941. The Viennese composer Hans Salter, who was behind the music for around three hundred films, including many horror films, was considered the "master of terror and suspense" and netted six Academy Award nominations.[3] Another Vienna-born composer was Ernest Gold (or rather, Ernst Siegmund Goldner), who had to wait a bit longer for his breakthrough, which came in 1961, when he won an Oscar for the music in *Exodus*. He was the first film composer to be honored with a star on the Hollywood Walk of Fame. He lived in Pacific Palisades after the war too, first at 500 Paseo Miramar, next door to Villa Aurora, and ultimately at 269 Bellino Drive. His wife, Marni Nixon, lent her singing voice to many a film actor, including Salka Viertel, daughter-in-law Deborah Kerr in *The King and I*, Natalie Wood in *West Side Story*, and Audrey Hepburn in *My Fair Lady*. Successful screenwriters included Walter Reisch, one of Germany's top writers for film until he emigrated; Robert Siodmak's younger brother, Curt Siodmak, who specialized in science fiction and horror writing; and George Froeschel. This cohort was a far cry from screenplay neophytes such as Alfred Döblin or

Heinrich Mann, whom the European Film Fund hired in 1940 only to facilitate their immigration.

Securing the studio spotlight was often tough going for actors in exile, which the Austrian composer Georg Kreisler described as a "sunshine prison . . . with oranges outside the window."[4] They were stuck playing accent roles and often portrayed Nazi henchmen, thus making a performance "of the bestiality one has fallen victim to," as Alfred Polgar put it.[5] Their style was too theatrical for American tastes, and they also battled the typecasting so common in Hollywood—rather than landing roles based on their acting skills, they were cast according to the "type" they represented. The fame these screen actors had attained back home did not count for anything.

Take Fritzi Massary: a director at Twentieth-Century Fox once asked her—Massary, the uncrowned queen of operetta in Berlin in the 1920s, whose erotic aura, graceful femininity, and irresistible charm made her an idol of the era—if she had any stage experience. Although she was financially stable and did not need to work, Massary felt a void in her new life and terribly depressed at the loss of her status. She took walks and gardened to pass the time and attempted to preserve some remnant of the upper-class lifestyle she had known in Berlin. Massary, whose daughter was married to the writer Bruno Frank, was friendly with Franz Werfel and his wife, Alma; the director Bruno Walter; Salka Viertel; Ludwig Marcuse; and Thomas Mann, who sensed an "atmosphere of operetta" at her sixty-fifth birthday party at Ernst Lubitsch's villa in Bel Air.[6] The celebratory spread featured aspic with onions, meatballs, and smoked pork—Berlin home cooking in the shade of the palm trees. There was a reason Theodor Adorno groused, "In the recollection of emigration each German venison roast tastes as if it had been felled with the charmed bullets of the *Freischütz*."[7]

There was little Hollywood could offer Ernst Deutsch either, earlier in his career the expressionist actor par excellence. Credited under the stage name Ernest Dorian, from 1942 on his roles were limited mostly to Nazis and military officers. Fritz Kortner, meanwhile, had been celebrated in the Weimar Republic as a prototypical modern republican theater man, slandered by the National Socialists as "probably the sleaziest and nastiest Jewish type ever to stand on a

German stage."[8] He came to discover that jobs were not necessarily given "on merit and ability" in Tinseltown: "It was more like professional success doled out roulette-style. To get ahead in film in America, one's social graces tended to carry more weight than talent. Tennis players, cardplayers, or simply fun party guests were among the privileged."[9] Brecht, however, attributed Kortner's failure to his accent and acting style: "kortner can't land any roles. eisler tells me the people at RKO laughed out loud during his audition: he was rolling his eyes. actual acting is frowned upon here, only negroes permitted to do so. stars don't perform roles, they're placed in 'situations.'"[10]

Only a handful had successful careers. Albert Bassermann, the leading realist performer of the early twentieth century, had left his home in 1933 because of his beloved wife's Jewish heritage; she was the actor Else Schiff, whom he considered a better actor than himself, though he may have been alone in this view. When in 1939 the couple reached the United States on tourist visas with just eight hundred marks between them, Bassermann spoke barely any English, a fact that did little to dampen the seventy-two-year old's pluck. "There must be a film for me in the lead role of a foreigner in unfamiliar surroundings, given my noticeable accent," he wrote to Paul Kohner, originally from Teplitz-Schönau, who had founded a talent agency on Sunset Boulevard in 1938. The agency became a hub for emigrants, and Kohner himself sponsored around sixty people to enable their entry into the United States.[11]

Bassermann was an overnight success. He first played Robert Koch in William Dieterle's *Dr. Ehrlich's Magic Bullet*, a role for which he learned his lines phonetically; this was a star in the making, everyone agreed. He was nominated for an Academy Award for Best Supporting Actor for his performance as Van Meer in Alfred Hitchcock's *Foreign Correspondent*, whereas the National Socialists deemed his involvement in the film reason enough to revoke Bassermann's citizenship in 1942. The doyen of German actors appeared in twenty-five US pictures over seven years, working his way up from $250 weekly pay to $2,000.

The actor Walter Weinlaub, now Walter Wicclair, earned his keep as a dishwasher, gardener, and airline worker. His cohort Manfred Fürst started out as a door-to-door hairbrush salesman, then drove taxis for nine hours a day, six days a week, for around sixty to seventy bucks weekly. He stressed that "the willingness of Hollywood emigrants to help each other out financially is tremendous. . . . Nevertheless, a strange dynamic exists: the understandable desire for life to continue within the sphere of one's old profession is met with considerable resistance. Everywhere one turns are open doors, helping hands, money—but any mention of one's beloved old occupation falls on deaf ears."[12]

Fürst's wife, Margarete Hruby, whose credits include runs at Vienna's Burgtheater and collaborations with Max Reinhardt, ran a doggie salon. Trude Berliner, who had appeared in thirty talking pictures in Germany between 1929 and 1933 but was cast in just five bit roles in Hollywood, worked glazing ceramics in her sister-in-law Hedi Schoop's factory and later ran an animal shelter. Leopoldine Konstantin, who in 1907 made her stage debut at the Deutsches Theater in Berlin under the direction of Max Reinhardt and four years later played *Buhlschaft* (Paramour), in the world premiere of Hugo von Hofmannsthal's *Jedermann* (*Everyman*), struggled for years and worked in factories to get by. It was only in 1946 that she landed a major role, playing the possessive mother of a Nazi sympathizer in Alfred Hitchcock's *Notorious*; the acclaim was significant but did not lead anywhere.

Helene Weigel was slated to play the vegetable peddler Dvorak in Fritz Lang's *Hangmen Also Die!* It was an arrangement her husband, Bertolt Brecht, had made with Lang. Brecht had helped write the screenplay and craft the role, which was mostly nonspeaking. One of Lang's crew, however, added "a few superfluous lines," and Lang brought Weigel in for "a quick sound recording, [and] promised a complete screen test but kept her waiting and working on it, then simply shot the film with someone else without even telling her." Outraged, Brecht questioned whether "the old duty to respond violently to private immorality" had "expired."[13] Between Weigel's thick German accent and a face hardly made for Hollywood, over the six years spent in California, she appeared on camera just once, in Fred Zinnemann's production of Anna Seghers's novel *The Seventh Cross*, in which she did not have a single line and enjoyed a scant thirty seconds' screentime.

"My humble life's purpose shrinks by the day. And I am finding it impossible to take myself seriously," Weigel lamented to her friend, the Danish writer Karin

Michaelis.[14] In exile in California, she had little to do beyond housework and gardening. She made orange, fig, and apricot preserves and occasionally hopped in Salka Viertel's "brave little convertible" to buy groceries at Los Angeles' inexpensive Grand Central Market, where "for ten or twelve dollars, we could buy food for a whole week," as Viertel recalled. "At the stalls previously owned by Japanese, Mexicans and Filipinos now stood behind mounds of fruit and vegetables. If only one could send some of it to Europe."[15]

Lotte Mosbacher is remembered for her performance in John Schlesinger's 1976 film *Marathon Man*, in which she plays an aged Holocaust survivor who recognizes the Nazi war criminal Dr. Christian Szell (Laurence Olivier) and chases him, screaming, down Forty-Seventh Street in Manhattan. In their early days in the United States, however, she and her first husband, Viktor Palfi, kept their heads above water employed as a cook and butler. That said, she did play in eleven films during the war, initially using the screen name Jean Brooks and later Lotte Andor. She titled her 1983 memoir *Ich war nie ein Bernhardiner* (I never was a Saint Bernard). In it she wrote, "Whereas most emigrants spoke about their past with proper truthfulness, there were also those who—knowingly or not—embellished the circumstances of the past or adorned them with invented successes. Thus the tale emerged: One émigré dachshund asks another, 'So, were you a Saint Bernard once too?'"[16]

Among the steadily employed character actors were Siegfried Arno—who from 1939 on appeared in such films as William Dieterle's *The Hunchback of Notre Dame* alongside Charles Laughton—and Curt Bois, one of the first child stars in history, who emigrated to the United States in 1934 and made his Hollywood debut in 1937. Bois would go on to make more than forty films and ultimately earn $1,250 per week. His friend Felix Bressart, a comedic actor, signed a contract with MGM in 1938 to appear in substantial supporting roles. He played an insecure Soviet commissar in Ernst Lubitsch's *Ninotchka*; a nervous sales clerk in *The Shop around the Corner*; and, in the masterpiece *To Be or Not to Be*, an unsuccessful bit actor who yearns to play Shylock.

Peter Lorre was born Ladislav Löwenstein in 1904 in what was then the Hungarian city of Rosenberg and is today Ružomberok, Slovakia. Unmistakable in his physicality—his diminutive height, round baby face, and bulging eyes in particular—Lorre rose to fame as a stage actor in Berlin in the late 1920s, then gained international renown playing a compulsive child murderer in Fritz Lang's 1931 film *M*. Forced to leave Germany in 1933, Lorre shot films in Vienna, Paris, and London until Columbia Pictures brought him to Hollywood in 1934; for the first few years, he lived with his wife, the actor Cäcile Lvovsky, at 326 Adelaide Drive, directly on the border between Pacific Palisades and Santa Monica.[17] He gained popularity for his portrayal of the Japanese detective Mr. Moto in eight crime movies as well as for supporting roles such as Joel Cairo in John Huston's *The Maltese Falcon*; Dr. Einstein in Frank Capra's dark comedy *Arsenic and Old Lace*; and the crooked Guillermo Ugarte in Michael Curtiz's *Casablanca*. Lorre's second wife was the actor Kaaren Verne, whom he met in 1941 on the set of *All through the Night*, the spy film starring Humphrey Bogart; Verne was an emigrant too, born in 1918 in Berlin, her father, Erich Klinckerfuss, the director of C. Bechstein. Her great uncle, Edwin Bechstein, and his wife, Helene, had been among Hitler's most ardent supporters since 1921 and donated tremendous sums to the Nazi cause. Once one of the highest-grossing character actors in Hollywood, Lorre—who became addicted to morphine—ultimately fell into financial ruin and spent his final years, until his death in 1964, in a two-room apartment, picking up jobs in television and trashy movies to get by.

The Bohemian-born Franz Lederer, on the other hand, celebrated his hundredth birthday in style, though his later wealth could scarcely be attributed to his auspicious start in Hollywood in 1934. Following a dazzling career in theater and film in Germany, where he had starred alongside Elisabeth Bergner, Henny Porten, and Louise Brooks, it would seem everything was in place for him to play the European heartthrob in Hollywood. Cast opposite the likes of Ginger Rogers, Ida Lupino, and Claudette Colbert, Lederer gained widespread popularity and in 1939 played the German spy Kurt Schneider in Anatole Litvak's thriller *Confessions of a Nazi Spy*, the first anti-Nazi film produced in Hollywood, after which he was increasingly cast in supporting roles. In a display of great foresight, he had purchased about 740 acres of what was then cheap land in the San Fernando Valley in 1934; after retiring from the film business in 1958, Lederer made his fortune in real estate.

Carl Esmond, born Karl Willy Simon in Vienna, made his stage debut at age twenty-one at the Burgtheater. He adopted his mother's maiden name, which sounded less Jewish, and went by Willy Eichberger at first, a stage name he changed again after the English press turned "Eichberger" into "Iceberg." He became a star of the silver screen in 1933, when he played in *Liebelei*, an adaptation of the Arthur Schnitzler play, directed by Max Ophüls. In January 1938 he went to Hollywood—not as a persecuted emigrant but at the invitation of Louis B. Mayer. Esmond turned down the first offer he received—a role in *Three Comrades*, based on a Erich Maria Remarque novel—because *Das Schwarze Korps* (The Black Corps), an SS publication in Germany, crowed that he could never return to the country if he accepted. The annexation of Austria soon meant there was no going back, anyway; his father died in the Theresienstadt "camp-ghetto" in 1942. With costars Errol Flynn and David Niven, Esmond played a German flying ace based on the "Red Baron" Manfred von Richthofen in the antiwar drama *The Dawn Patrol*. Though he shared the screen with giants such as Gary Cooper, Spencer Tracy, and Katharine Hepburn, it pained Esmond to play Nazi characters, the roles he was almost exclusively offered. He finally managed to establish himself as a character actor after the war, though he then mostly appeared in made-for-TV movies, miniseries, and commercials. When he died in Brentwood in 2004, at age 102, the German daily newspaper *Die Welt* remembered Esmond as "the last refugee in Hollywood."[18]

Despite her limited aptitude as an actor, the beautiful Hedy Lamarr would achieve even greater fame. Style icon, sex symbol, and a model not only for countless women but for Walt Disney's animated Snow White as well as the original comic-strip Catwoman, Lamarr was born Hedwig Kiesler in Vienna in 1914. As a nineteen-year-old, she caused an unspeakable scandal at home when she appeared in a nude sex scene and acted out an orgasm in the film *Ekstase* (*Ecstasy*). The pope himself publicly condemned the work. The same year she married Fritz Mandl, fourteen years her senior and one of Europe's biggest arms manufacturers, who did business with Adolf Hitler and Benito Mussolini. Mandl forced her to convert to Catholicism, forbade her from acting, and ultimately locked her up in his hunting lodge like a prisoner. She escaped in disguise in 1937, selling her jewelry for the money she needed to get to Paris, then London. There she met Louis B. Mayer, who signed the raven-haired vamp (along with thirteen other European beauties) for MGM, dubbed her Hedy Lamarr, and branded her the most beautiful woman in the world. At the height of her fame, she and the composer George Antheil devised a way to equip radio-guided torpedoes with a secret communications system, which they patented in 1942. The method they employed, known as frequency hopping, is a key component of WiFi and Bluetooth communications today.

Berlin-born Conrad Veidt, a leading figure in expressionist film who appeared in such films as *The Cabinet of Dr. Caligari*, shot his first Hollywood film in 1927, then left Germany with his wife in 1933, never to return. In England he played the title role in the 1934 film *Jud Süß* (*Jew Süss*), adapted from Lion Feuchtwanger's novel, then portrayed the capricious Grand Vizier Jaffar in the 1940 color film *The Thief of Bagdad*. Veidt is best known today for depicting Maj. Heinrich Strasser, the stone-cold antagonist in *Casablanca*. The film functioned as a sort of reunion for exiled film actors in 1942, with roles ranging from Carl, the head waiter at Rick's Café Américain, played by Szöke Szakall (credited as S. K. Sakall), and the pickpocket, performed by Curt Bois, to a far larger number of uncredited appearances: Hans Heinrich von Twardowski and Richard Ryen (a.k.a. Révy, a renowned stage director in Germany until 1936) are members of Strasser's entourage; Lotte Palfi hawks jewelry; Helmut Guttmann (now Dantine) plays roulette while Trude Berliner tries her luck at baccarat; Wolfgang Zilzer, who soon changed his name to Paul Andor, is in trouble because his documents have expired; and Ludwig Stössel and Ilka Grüning steal the show as a touchingly out-of-touch older couple trying their best at English: "Sweetness heart," he says, "what watch?" "Ten watch." "Such much?"

In *Casablanca* Paul Henreid plays the resistance fighter Victor Laszlo, whom viewers register primarily as the destabilizing force in the love affair between Rick Blaine, played by Humphrey Bogart, and Ingrid Bergman's character Ilsa Lund. (Henreid's father had changed the family name from Hirsch to Henreid after leaving the Jewish religious community.) He became a legend of the silver screen playing the continental lover, a romantic image cemented by an iconic scene in the melodrama *Now, Voyager*: Henreid lights two cigarettes at once, then places one between Bette Davis's lips. He lived in Pacific Palisades for twenty years until his death in 1992. In his front yard at 18068 Blue Sail Drive, just above the Getty Villa, he hoisted the Austrian flag along with the Stars and Stripes every morning. Henreid outlived his friend Conrad Veidt by nearly half a century. Though Veidt did not spend his final years in Pacific Palisades, he did spend his final hours there: he died of a heart attack while on the links at Riviera Country Club in 1943.

PACIFIC PALISADES did not become a true magnet for film exiles until the 1940s. Four are worth discussing in closer detail. None were happy, though they all had respectable careers to look back on. Ludwig Hardt, born in the northwestern German town of Neustadtgödens in 1886, was a versatile elocutionist best known for his recitations of German literature. He captivated audiences in Berlin and around the world, with such authors as Franz Kafka, Thomas Mann, and Erich Kästner numbering among his fans. Because of his Jewish background, Hardt was limited to working within the Kulturbund Deutscher Juden, or Cultural Federation of German Jews, from 1933 on; he first emigrated to Austria, then to Czechoslovakia, and finally to the United States, where he; his second wife, Gertrude; and their ten-year-old daughter, Hanna, arrived in New York aboard the SS *Île de France* on August 18, 1938.[19] In Pacific Palisades Hardt purchased a modest home at 418 Mount Holyoke Avenue. Los Angeles was not exactly a hotspot for German recitation, and, besides, many of Hardt's contemporaries thought his recitation style was outmoded. Brecht, for instance, described his recitations as "applesauce-filled words" and tried in vain to "get him interested in a new approach to recitation."[20] Forced to supplement the occasional gig, including a recitation of Heinrich Heine's poetry, Hardt tried his luck with supporting roles in Hollywood films. He appeared in *Arizona*, a 1940 western starring William Holden, as well as the 1941 psychological thriller *Rage in Heaven*, with Robert Montgomery, Ingrid Bergman, and Oscar Homolka.

In 1946 Thomas Mann wrote about Hardt to Homolka's mother-in-law, the wealthy publicist Agnes E. Meyer:

> His is a melancholy and hopeless cause, and nothing to be done about it. I have known the fellow, who is short and ugly, for many years. Though gifted in acting and rhetoric, he was not suited to the stage and turned to recitation out of a sincere love of literature, language, and composition. . . . In Germany one could make a living as an elocutionist. Here you can't, as the genre is utterly unknown. . . . Here in Pacific Palisades he lived with his wife in a nice little house that cost him almost nothing, and he got by fine because his wife had some money. And because he just couldn't help it and needed the illusion of success, he often hosted a circle of German emigrants for evening lectures at his home. Then, out of an untamable drive to act, he tried to go higher. With commendable but utterly useless fervor, he studied English, thinking he could switch languages; he rehearsed an English program and performed in public. I had warned him not to, but ended up helping him. That evening was probably the bleakest thing I've sat through. Scholem Asch, who had also come out of kindness, almost cried. Unfortunately, one of the agent Colston Leigh's staffers was there, who convinced [Hardt] that it had been a success and he should go east and make money with it. Shake our heads as we might, the fool sold his little house and moved to New York, where he bought a much more expensive one and spent as much to heat it as he did on all his living costs here. His hopes and dreams all failed, of course. He got what he deserves—which is what makes it so sad and pitiable. The best thing would be for him to go to Berlin or Vienna and starve with the others, but at least find some appreciation for his skills.[21]

SINCE 1939 Rose Stradner had lived at 694 Amalfi Drive. Born in 1913 in Vienna, Stradner enjoyed considerable success on stage, playing the teen innocent and grand dame at the Theater in der Josefstadt before landing lead roles in German film opposite such actors as Hans Albers, Werner Krauss, and Heinrich George. In 1937 she was recruited by MGM and took the same ship to the United States as Hedy Lamarr, only two months sooner. She spent four months practicing the pronunciation of *th*, then starred alongside James Stewart and Edward G. Robinson in *The Last Gangster*. After wrapping her next film, in 1939 she remarried: Joseph L. Mankiewicz was the son of Jewish immigrants from Berlin, a screenwriter, film producer, and director who rose to fame in 1946—his major movies include *Cleopatra*, starring Elizabeth Taylor and Richard Burton. Stradner had two sons and temporarily withdrew from the business. Her third Hollywood appearance, *The Keys of the Kingdom* with Gregory Peck in 1944, fell short of a comeback and would remain her final film. Following years of psychiatric care and threats of suicide, Stradner, who suffered from depression and alcoholism, overdosed on sleeping pills at age forty-five.

MOST FAMOUS OF ALL—though her name is scarcely known today—was Luise Rainer. She was the first female actor to win two Oscars back-to-back for best actress, a feat that would take another three decades and the likes of Katharine Hepburn to reprise. When Rainer moved to Pacific Palisades in 1941, however, her career in film was already over. "She had something working for her, she had them interested, she could've really rolled," another character says of protagonist Holly Golightly in *Breakfast at Tiffany's*, Truman Capote's 1958 novella. "But when you walk out on a thing like that, you don't walk back. Ask Luise Rainer. And Rainer was a star."[22]

Rainer had been performing for some time and toured Europe with Max Reinhardt when Bob Ritchie, a talent scout for MGM, pegged the twenty-four-year-old as the next Greta Garbo and offered her a five-year contract. In 1935, accompanied by her Scottish terrier named Johnny, Rainer boarded the SS *Île de France* in Le Havre and sailed to New York. She spent the first few months in a furnished beach house in Santa Monica, lonely and soon certain she had made a huge mistake. She took English lessons from a fellow (American) actor and waited for the right role to come her way. Then, because Myrna Loy had quit after two weeks of filming and Rainer happened to bump into screenwriter Anita Loos on the beach, she was cast (at Loos's insistence) in the role of Leopoldine in *Escapade*. Rainer was known as an Austrian actor from then on, despite having been born in Düsseldorf in 1910, the daughter of a German Jewish businessman. After her second, similarly lachrymose role, she was called

"The Viennese Teardrop"—a name the MGM marketing team was happy to promote in an effort to conceal Rainer's German heritage.

In *The Great Ziegfeld*, Rainer plays Ziegfeld's extravagant first wife, Anna Held. When Anna discovers her husband has left her for a new love, she calls him and stoically wishes him all the best, then dissolves into silent tears. This famous telephone scene would win her an Oscar, and Rainer maintained that she wrote it herself, inspired by Jean Cocteau's play The Human Voice. In 1937 she wowed critics and audiences alike with a very different, much bigger yet nearly silent role: that of the devoted Chinese farmer's wife, O-Lan, in the film adaptation of Pearl S. Buck's *The Good Earth*, the most expensive MGM project since *Ben-Hur*.

Rainer, who had escaped racism in Germany, ultimately had racism in the United States to thank for the latter role. The Chinese American actor Anna May Wong was in line to be cast as O-Lan, only to be passed over. After appearing in films such as Douglas Fairbanks's *The Thief of Bagdad* in the 1920s, Wong had emerged as the first Hollywood star with Asian roots, although producers typically cast her in the role of "China doll," the stereotypical racist portrayal of Asian women as exotic, servile, and sexually submissive, or that of the "dragon lady," a kind of treacherous femme fatale of the Far East. In the late 1920s she went to Germany and secured her standing as a film icon, and she was rumored to have had lesbian affairs with Leni Riefenstahl and Marlene Dietrich. In 1932, after Wong had returned to Hollywood, she starred opposite Dietrich in *Shanghai Express*, though by then the Hays Code prohibited her from kissing white actors on screen. Ethnic "mixing" was frowned on, meaning white actors (such as Luise Rainer) in yellow face were cast as Asian characters. What remained for actors like Wong were supporting roles, depression, and alcohol.

Rainer was not happy, either. In an interview with a fan magazine in 1937, she lamented,

> Hollywood is dead. . . . Everything about it is dead, even the beautiful hills. . . . I look at those hills. I know they are beautiful, and I ask myself what is it I don't like, and the answer is . . . they are dead. The

> air surrounding them is heavy, not like mountain air. There is no exhilaration, no sparkle. The people here are like that, too, all impersonal, all cold, with no feeling. . . . I came here. And I worked very hard. But I regret they have no feeling for personal art. It is heartbreaking to develop a part and have it go into the hands of strangers when you can do nothing about it. This is not acting! This Hollywood picture business is like a factory or a big machine. My part that I work on so hard is sent through the cutting-room, like a loaf of bread.[23]

Her consecutive Oscars were the worst thing that could have happened to her, Rainer later said. She hated the glamorous lifestyle she felt forced to lead, though the weekly $250 she had made filming *The Good Earth* ranked her MGM's worst-paid star. She no longer saw herself as an artist but as "one of the horses of the Louis B. Mayer stable." When she told the studio director that her well had run dry and there was nothing left inside for her to draw on, Mayer asked incredulously what she needed a well for if she had a director. Rainer suggested more substantive roles, but Mayer kept casting her in frivolous comedies and melodramas. In 1938 she returned to Mayer's office and resigned. "We made you, and we are going to kill you," Mayer is said to have bellowed in response. Rainer stood her ground: "Mr. Mayer, you did not make me. God made me. I am now in my 20s. You are an old man . . . . By the time I am 40 you will be dead."[24] Her prediction was not entirely accurate. Rainer was 47 when the film mogul died, though she would outlive him by 57 years. She was nearly 105 when she died, making her the longest-living Oscar winner of all time.

In 1938 Rainer temporarily moved to New York to join her husband, the playwright Clifford Odets, whom she had married the year before. The marriage was troubled from the start, not necessarily because of Odets's jealousy—in a rage he mutilated a photo of Albert Einstein with a pair of scissors after the physicist had flirted with Rainer—but because he struggled with her Hollywood success; she, meanwhile, envied the artistic work he did with New York's ambitious Group Theatre collective. They divorced in May 1940, and Rainer returned to the West Coast. The following year, she moved into the ranch-style house at 740 Amalfi Drive, where Thomas Mann and his family had lived.

In 1943 Rainer encouraged Bertolt Brecht to adapt a fourteenth-century Chinese drama, *The Chalk Circle*. Brecht had fled Germany in 1933, first to Denmark, then Sweden, then Finland, before immigrating to the United States in 1941, thanks to the affidavit Rainer always claimed to have provided. On July 21 Marta Feuchtwanger and the actor Alexander Granach met Brecht; his second wife, Helene Weigel; their children, Stefan and Barbara; and Brecht's mistress, Ruth Berlau, at the docks in San Pedro. It was Feuchtwanger, along with Fritz Lang's girlfriend Lily Latté, who had found them a place at 1954 Argyle Avenue in Hollywood. Initially Lang and William Dieterle helped the four-person family cover costs, though the monthly $120 they provided made for lean living.

Before long the Brecht family moved to Santa Monica. First they rented a "horrible bourgeois villa with a tidy little yard" at 817 Twenty-Fifth Street, and Brecht felt cramped: "My room measures 11 feet by 12 feet, the air is suffocating, the doors pink." Besides, he groused, the house was surrounded by "whorish bourgeois villas with their depressing prettiness."[25] In August 1942 the family moved to 1063 Twenty-Sixth Street: "The house is among the oldest, around 30 years old, a californian wooden house, whitewashed, with 4 bedrooms upstairs. i have a long (almost 23 feet) study that we whitewashed first thing and furnished with 4 tables. there are old trees (pepper and fig) in the yard. rent $60 per month, $12 more than 25th street."[26]

Still, Brecht was not much happier there. He complained that he "could not breathe in this climate"; that the air was "utterly odorless, the same morning and night"; and that there were "no seasons."[27] The landscape was attractive, "but it all exists as though behind glass, and without meaning to, i search each line of hills or every lemon tree for a little price tag. one looks for these price tags on people, too." He got upset about "colonial capitalism" and the "advanced mercantilism of art" and lamented the spiritual isolation: compared to Hollywood, he declared, the Swedish village of Svendborg was a bustling global hub.[28] "Every morning, to earn my bread / I go to the market where lies are traded / In hope / I take my place amongst the sellers," reads a famous poem of Brecht's.[29]

Considering the fact that at the time university professors earned an annual $5,000 before taxes, and the immigrant population in the United States averaged around $19 a week, Brecht had hit the jackpot. In 1942 he was paid $10,000 for his work on *Hangmen Also Die!* Fritz Lang's anti-Nazi film about the assassination of *Reichsprotektor* Reinhard Heydrich in Nazi-occupied Prague. Nevertheless, Brecht complained bitterly about Lang and accused him of churning out "squalid sentimentality and untruths . . . for the box office" and producing "vile tripe."[30] He was further angered when, in an authorship dispute with John Wexley, who had also worked on the screenplay, the Writers Guild sided with the American, who was credited in the film as the sole screenwriter. As an American, Wexley needed the nod, the guild reasoned, since Brecht would return to Germany eventually.

Brecht finished the rough draft of *The Caucasian Chalk Circle* in June 1944 and sent it to Rainer, although by that point he said the actor was "pretty repellent [to me], it will not bother me if she rejects the piece," which was her intention, anyway: "He was like a spider, something I didn't want to touch."[31] Brecht modified the lead role, which he had created with Rainer in mind, into a duller, less cloying, and less Broadway-friendly character named Grusche. Opposite Grusche was Adzak, a role intended for the Viennese actor Oskar (now Oscar) Homolka, who was as lumbering as he was lively.

Homolka, an actor renowned for his menacing, libidinous roles, was the first to portray Brecht's character Baal in 1926. He left Germany by choice in 1935 and arrived in the United States in 1936. By the mid-1940s he was living in Bel Air and would later move to 914 Corsica Drive in Pacific Palisades. His fourth wife, Florence, was the eldest daughter of *Washington Post* publisher Eugene Miller and the publicist Agnes E. Meyer, Thomas Mann's greatest patron. Florence was the photographer behind famous portraits of Charlie Chaplin, the Feuchtwangers, the Mann family, and others. The Homolkas were central figures in the émigré community; Florence was often found cavorting with Thomas Mann, while Oscar and Brecht were close friends. And although Brecht lived in Santa Monica, the original version of *The Caucasian Chalk Circle* came together largely in Pacific Palisades—Homolka was joined in the task of translating the play by the Englishmen Aldous Huxley, who had risen to international fame with his 1932 dystopian novel *Brave New World*, and Christopher Isherwood, whose memories of Berlin would be memorialized on stage and screen in *Cabaret*, as well as Hans Viertel, Salka's eldest son. Thomas Mann's son-in-law Wystan Hugh Auden was responsible for the US adaptation.

TO THIS DAY Martin Kosleck is remembered as "the man who was Goebbels." He was rather slight, just over 130 pounds, with expressive, defined facial features and intense gray eyes. Though Kosleck, who was gay, battled depression, suicidal tendencies, and alcoholism for years, he was one of the few emigrants to establish himself in Hollywood. He became popular as "the most hateful, inhuman celluloid Nazi in Hollywood film" and as the star in horror films.[32] In the early 1940s, film company press agents seized on the legends surrounding Kosleck's emigration: it was said that, as an opponent of the National Socialists, he had incurred Goebbels's hatred early on and that he was wanted by the police and sentenced to death in absentia but had managed to escape persecution just in time by fleeing Germany. In reality Kosleck—the son of a forester, born in 1904 in the Pomeranian town of Barkotzen, and later an actor with whom Klaus Mann would "fall endlessly in love"—came in 1931 to Hollywood, where his friend Hans Heinrich von Twardowski was acting in German-version films.[33] Unable to find work as a performer, Kosleck turned to visual art. He painted portraits of stars such as Joan Crawford, Bette Davis, and Greta Garbo and created a series of surrealistic paintings of famous film directors at work. He appeared on camera just once during those early years, in the role of "Dance Director" in William Dieterle's musical comedy *Fashions of 1934*. He had one inconsequential line: "The fitter is waiting, Mr. Nash."

In 1939 the filmmaker Anatole Litvak invited Kosleck to screen testing for *Confessions of a Nazi Spy*. Other emigrants involved in the project included Hans Heinrich von Twardowski, Wolfgang Zilzer, Rudolph Anders, Lotte Palfi, Louis Adlon, and Lionel Royce. Known as Leo Reuss during his career in Europe, in 1936 the Austrian Jewish actor concealed his true identity by growing out and bleaching his hair and beard and presenting as a naturally talented rustic named Kaspar Brandhofer. His performances on the Viennese stage were celebrated until an old colleague recognized and outed him. Reuss signed a contract with MGM in the summer of 1937 and would go on to play the "bad German" in more than forty films.

Kosleck did not land the leading role in *Confessions of a Nazi Spy*. Instead, it went to Franz Lederer, an emigrant and former classmate of his at Max Reinhardt's acting school, while Kosleck was cast as the Reich minister for public enlightenment and propaganda, Joseph Goebbels. Though his appearance was brief and his name passed over in the opening credits, this was Kosleck's breakthrough, followed by thirty more films by war's end. He played Basil Rathbone's lover in *The Mad Doctor*, appeared in Alfred Hitchcock's *Foreign Correspondent*, and enjoyed tremendous success for his performance as Colonel Heller in *Underground*, an anti-Nazi film that seems to feature half the émigré community. He portrayed German spies and agents, concentration camp overseers, and the propaganda minister in another four films. To protect his mother and other relatives still in Germany—his nephew and two half brothers had been conscripted into the Wehrmacht—Kosleck claimed his name was a pseudonym, and he had actually been born Nicolai Yoshkin. (The first name was borrowed from an uncle, the surname inspired by a past stage role.)

Bolstered by his success, though ever wary of artistic stagnation, Kosleck tried to push back against typecasting. He was invited to audition for more interesting roles, but these often went to competitors, Peter Lorre chief among them. He had been promised the role of Colonel Heinze in *Casablanca* when producer Steve Trilling swapped him out for Richard Ryen (born Révy), whose rates were lower. Kosleck managed to pivot genres: in 1944 he played the lead in the Universal horror film *The Frozen Ghost*, and two months later he portrayed Ragheb in *The Mummy's Curse*. Many similar jobs would follow.

Kosleck, though not an A-lister, was famous enough that studio dictate compelled him, like many of his gay contemporaries, to cultivate a heterosexual image. The most popular means of reinforcing this image were press releases. Warner publicity, for instance, announced that twelve schoolgirls from Santa Ana had stormed the studio and demanded bigger roles for Kosleck, who they insisted was the only Hollywood actor to be both sinister and sexy. Kosleck's personal press agent Ewald André Dupont, who worked for the Columbia

Publishing Corporation ("Names for the News—News for the Names"), published snippets such as "the pretty blonde accompanying Martin Kosleck to the city's bistros is none other than Gwili Andre."[34]

Kosleck suffered from severe depression for years. He was hospitalized several times and underwent electroshock therapy. After the collapse of his relationship with Twardowski and a string of increasingly disastrous affairs, in 1947 he married another lonely emigrant, "so as not to be alone."[35] His wife, Eleonora von Mendelssohn, once unhappily in love with Max Reinhardt and Arturo Toscanini, was a longtime morphine addict and Broadway performer with varying degrees of success. Despite his marital status, from 1949 Kosleck lived alone in a room at the Santa Ynez Inn at 17310 Sunset Boulevard in Pacific Palisades; the building, located at what was once the heart of Inceville, is now home to Westside Waldorf School. For many years the hotel housed Pacific Palisades' only restaurant, its lounge a popular hangout for stars such as Cary Grant and Joan Crawford.

Having returned to Manhattan at his wife's insistence, in 1951 Kosleck fell in love with Christopher Drake, a colleague twenty-five years his junior. The feeling was not mutual, however, and a spurned Kosleck climbed onto a windowsill and threatened to take his own life if Drake refused to listen to him. At 3:05 a.m. Kosleck jumped from the fourth floor and was hospitalized with critical injuries. He told the investigating officer from the East Seventy-Fifth Street Station that it was an accident, that he had been trying to repair the window. While Kosleck was in the hospital, his wife, Eleonora, committed suicide. He died forty-three years later at a nursing facility in Santa Monica.

"YOU LOSE YOUR HOME AND THERE'S NO FINDING A NEW ONE"

THE FIRST TRUE EXILE to settle permanently in Pacific Palisades in 1936 was lauded as one of the greatest composers of the modern age. In 1962, two years before his death, he would describe himself with resignation as the "most forgotten composer of the twentieth century."[1] Ernst Toch was born the son of a Jewish leather merchant in Vienna, his upbringing artistically barren. He enrolled in medical school but studied piano and composition on the side under Robert Fuchs, who had once taught Gustav Mahler and Erich Wolfgang Korngold. While studying medicine, Toch was awarded the Mozart Prize in 1909 for a string quartet and his Chamber Symphony in F Major. This great honor entitled him to study at Hoch Conservatory in Frankfurt, an offer Toch accepted. In 1921 he received his doctorate from the University of Heidelberg (his dissertation was titled "Contributions to the Stylistics of Melody"), and in 1928 he moved to Berlin, where he wrote his operas *The Princess and the Pea* and *Egon and Emilie*, among other works.

Toch was attending a conference in Florence on January 30, 1933. He recognized the signs of the time sooner than many others and did not return to Germany but instead went to Paris. He sent a telegraph to his wife, Lilly, who immediately followed with their daughter, Franziska; then the family continued on to London. While there, as though foreshadowing what was to come in Pacific Palisades, Toch—whose New Objectivity compositions the Nazis would deem "degenerate"—wrote the music for *Little Friend*, a film by Berthold Viertel with a screenplay by Christopher Isherwood. "The very prospect of an emigration visa, with the subsequent possibility of becoming an American citizen, sparks great longing," he wrote to friends.[2]

On September 25, 1934, he and Lilly arrived in New York on the SS *Laconia*.

With letters of recommendation from the conductors Arturo Toscanini and Bruno Walter, Toch found work teaching composition at the New School for Social Research. There he met George Gershwin, who put him in touch with people in Hollywood. Although Toch's first project with Warner Brothers fell through, it was enough to pique interest at rival studio Paramount. While Toch and his wife were on a private visit to their native Vienna in the summer of 1935, the composer received an offer by telegram to score the Gary Cooper melodrama *Peter Ibbetson*, a job that paid a handsome $750 a week. He returned to the United States immediately, only to learn that work on the project had to wait seven weeks; he was, however, paid on the spot. During that time he stayed with Vicki Baum and Richard Lert at 1461 Amalfi Drive in Pacific Palisades. The film—which tells the story of a man who reconnects with his childhood sweetheart, only she is sentenced to life in prison after accidentally causing her husband's death—was an artistic success that, despite its Jewish composer, opened in German theaters on May 15, 1936. His Hollywood debut earned Toch his first of three Oscar nominations.

Toch returned to New York for one last teaching gig. He, Lilly, and Franziska—who had followed her parents to the United States from Great Britain in October 1935—relocated to the West Coast in the summer of 1936, settling down in Pacific Palisades. The local paper the *Palisadian* welcomed the famous newcomer with open arms and urged him to compose a symphonic poem that captured Pacific Palisades' irresistible charm, as the rather overwrought article reads: a piece that weaves the area's heartbeat into a musical composition, that emerges from the natural beauty of the landscape, that resounds with the hopes and pleasures, desires and dreams of its founders and pioneers—it was an invitation to which Toch never responded.[3] The Palisadians, who were not yet as accustomed to celebrities as they are today, were proud of their new neighbor. One even knocked on Toch's door to express his admiration for the man who had composed the *Geographical Fugue* for spoken chorus ("Trinidad! / And the big Mississippi / and the town Honolulu / and the lake Titicaca"), a classic piece of the modern age that is now better known than the composer himself: the enthusiastic young fan was John Cage, who at the time lived at 545 Swarthmore Avenue. The Tochs first rented a Spanish colonial house on

De Pauw Street that tumbled into Potrero Canyon several years later. In 1937 they moved to 601 Toyopa Drive, the same year Toch became a professor of composition and music theory at the University of Southern California, where Arnold Schoenberg was also an instructor.

Although Pacific Palisades was a tranquil place at the time, Toch desired greater seclusion. He rented a plot of land on Coral Beach, north of Malibu, for one hundred dollars a year. There he built Villa Majestic, the name incongruous with the small, L-shaped structure he fashioned out of the shipping containers in which the family's belongings had made their way to the United States. The dwelling was furnished with little more than a thirty-dollar piano, sofa, and kitchenette, and, although it had power, there was no telephone. One of the first people allowed to visit the composer at his self-imposed hermitage, on April 11, 1938, was Elizabeth Sprague Coolidge, the country's greatest patron of chamber music. In 1937 she had commissioned Toch's Quintet for Piano and Strings, Op. 64. The composers Paul Hindemith and Ernst Křenek came to see him in Malibu, as did Emanuel Feuermann, whom many considered the greatest cellist of all time and who spent the last two summers before his death in 1942 at 444 Chautauqua Boulevard in Pacific Palisades. Gasoline rationing after the United States entered the war in 1941 put an end to Toch's time at Villa Majestic, which was thirteen miles from his home on Toyopa Drive; as it was, power was cut along the coast at night, for fear of Japanese attacks. Toward the end of the war, the spartan structure was destroyed in a storm, and the debris washed out to sea.

Lilly Toch shielded her husband from disturbance, as he preferred a quiet, cloistered life. She worked to manage his life perfectly, inconspicuously, and to secure the conditions he required for work. Despite this avowed commitment, she loved hosting parties at their house in Pacific Palisades, where guests included Emil Ludwig, Bruno Frank, Salka Viertel, Alma Mahler-Werfel, and Thomas Mann—who loved delving into musical topics with Toch—as well as musicians such as Hanns Eisler, Paul Dessau, Eric Zeisl, and Erich Wolfgang Korngold. Toch, who supported Lilly in her social pursuits (he maintained a detailed record of what food they had served which guest), grew increasingly uncomfortable with these large gatherings, which as cohost he had a hard time avoiding. He became more sensitive to noise and was especially upset by the cacophony of voices talking over one another. Years later he parodied this cocktail-party chatter in his piece *Valse*: "My, how super-dooper / Hold your tongue, you strapper / Let's behave, not like babies, but grown-ups / She is right / She is right!"[4] At bigger dinner parties, he could often be found sitting in a room off the parlor, speaking with a small clutch of friends.

The Toch household included Lilly's mother and Ernst's sister, cousin, and his cousin's daughter. They decided to build a bigger house at 811 Franklin Street in Santa Monica, financed by a loan from the Federal Housing Authority, which covered 82 percent of the cost. Lilly was especially opposed to hiring their friend Richard Neutra as the architect; she found that Neutra, who had come to the United States from Vienna in 1923, was overly orthodox, dogmatic, even tyrannical about his ideas. Instead, the job went to Liane Zimbler, who had emigrated to the States from Austria by way of the Netherlands and Great Britain; in February 1938 she had become the first woman in Austria to become a licensed civil architect. The Toch residence was her first major project in exile. After arriving in Los Angeles, Zimbler first worked at a packaging paper plant, then in 1940 joined Anita Toor's interior design firm, which she would take over after Toor's death. Zimbler's design for the Tochs' house was outwardly conventional, the structure consisting of various cubes with a flat hipped roof. Most of the rooms merged into one another, some separated by sliding doors, others only by curtains; fluid floor plans, often achieved by means of flexible walls, were a hallmark of Zimbler's. The largest room downstairs was Toch's study, which was soundproofed against the surrounding din. The composer had a magnificent view of the Santa Monica and San Gabriel mountain ranges and the eucalyptus groves edging Brentwood Country Club, but he habitually drew the curtains to limit distractions.

Optimal as these conditions may have been, they were not enough to avert a creative block in the 1940s. Toch, who was naturalized in 1940, may well have been exhausted by the unremitting fight for affidavits and visas for his relatives, including sixty-four cousins. Despite his efforts, more than thirty family members did not make it out of Europe; Lilly's sister died in Theresienstadt. Toch's enthusiasm for film work waned, and he sank into depression. In 1937 he had anonymously composed a few sequences for the Shirley Temple film *Heidi*; in 1939 he arranged the "Hallelujah" theme for William Dieterle's *The Hunchback of Notre Dame*, which was reused in 1943 in the screen adaptation of Franz Werfel's novel *The Song of Bernadette* as well as the biblical epic *The Robe* in 1953. He was under contract with Columbia Pictures from 1941 on. His very first project, the score for Charles Vidor's spine-chilling *Ladies in Retirement*, received an Oscar nomination, as did his music for the 1945 film *Address Unknown*. Toch, who had a knack for chase scenes and suspenseful climaxes, wrote just sixteen film scores, yet even the four he produced for Columbia would be recycled in nearly forty other films. Over time he developed a real aversion to the film industry. He thought he was prostituting his talent and turned increasingly to forms of absolute music, yet his productivity flagged.

After suffering a life-threatening heart attack in 1948, Toch resigned from his teaching position at the University of Southern California and dedicated himself solely to composition. Within no time he completed seven symphonies. In the hopes of drawing on his earlier accomplishments in Europe, he began to split his time between the two continents. As was the case for many targets of Nazi persecution, however, his name was all but forgotten in Europe. Those who did remember him felt that Toch—whose standing in academic circles once rivaled Schoenberg's—had undone that reputation through his film work. Despite the Pulitzer Prize and Grammy he had won, the "echolessness of the monstrous American space" (as his friend Křenek once put it) had left scars.[5] The outcome of Toch's life could be summed up pretty concisely: "You lose your home and there's no finding a new one when you emigrate. It happens to everyone."[6]

IN 1936, the same year as Toch, Gertrud Zenzes arrived in Pacific Palisades. Zenzes, who was Jewish, was the poet Gottfried Benn's ex-lover and close intellectual companion until his death. Born in 1894 in Hirschberg, in the Giant Mountains, Zenzes had a PhD in economics and emigrated to the United States in 1926. In 1931 she opened the first German-language bookstore on the

West Coast, which existed for five years. The famed coloratura soprano Miliza Korjus, who had relocated to Pacific Palisades in March 1936, invited Zenzes to stay in a guest cottage at her estate at 13525 D'Este Drive; Zenzes worked during that time as Gert von Gontard's private secretary.

On his father's side, Gontard was part of a Huguenot family elevated to the nobility under Frederick the Great, while on his mother's side, he was a member of the immensely wealthy US brewing dynasty Anheuser-Busch. In 1929, at just twenty-three, Gontard had founded the *Neue Revue* in Berlin, a magazine whose staff included George Grosz and Erich Kästner. In 1933 he went into exile in the United States, first in New York, then Los Angeles. Gontard lived at 22360 Malibu Road in Pacific Palisades and taught at the Max Reinhardt Workshop for Stage, Screen and Radio in 1938.

His on-again, off-again partner, the German actor Hilde Krüger (born in Cologne in 1912), can justifiably be described as the most dubious figure in the German-speaking scene in Los Angeles. Not only was the blonde bombshell a protégé of Goebbels', but rumors of an intimate relationship with Hitler swirled about the industry; her personal relationship with him was well documented. Krüger arrived in Los Angeles shortly after the war began and took a different lover, who was willing to ignore her dalliance with Gontard: the oil magnate J. Paul Getty, one of the richest men in the world, a Nazi sympathizer whom the FBI investigated between 1940 and 1943. In 1945 Getty bought a nineteenth-century ranch house in Canyon de Sentimiento in Pacific Palisades and opened a museum for his collection of antiquities and paintings in an eastern annex in 1953. In 1974, two years before his death, he moved the collection to a new building located nearby, at 17985 Pacific Coast Highway, and modeled on the Villa of the Papyri in Herculaneum. Today the Getty Villa in Pacific Palisades and the Getty Center in Brentwood are the J. Paul Getty Museum's two branches.

Boasting a letter of recommendation from Getty and allegedly on behalf of the Abwehr, the German military intelligence service, Krüger moved to Mexico in 1941. She quickly found her footing in society and became the mistress of the minister of the interior and later President Miguél Alemán Valdés, who is said to have provided the necessary visas (at her insistence) to allow Germany to plant around three hundred spies in the country—although none of this has been proven. In 1942 Hilda Krüger, as she was now known, was detained as a spy, though Alemán intervened and she was soon released. She married Nacho de la Torre, a rich playboy and grandson of former president Porfirio Díaz, and was remarried in 1956 to Julio Lobo y Olavarría, the "Sugar King of Havana."

Zenzes had met Krüger in 1940 in Pacific Palisades through Gontard, whom she soon followed to New York, where he founded and ran a German-language theater for exiles, Players from Abroad. In 1948 Zenzes became Krüger's personal assistant, secretary, and closest confidante, though she maintained a critical distance: "For all intents and purposes she's a tramp, a gypsy, and cannot live without an aim to steal, without tricks, intrigues, transactions, and packed suitcases in some hotel room. She is truly a Loreley with a Cologne dialect, a golden comb and Guerlain perfume and maidservant's sense of romance, cold and tattered, and she delights in the little ships that shatter against her rocks," Zenzes wrote to Gottfried Benn in 1953.[7]

Like Zenzes, Francesco Mendelssohn (born in Berlin in 1901) settled only temporarily in Pacific Palisades in 1936. Whereas Toch suffered from his dwindling importance but kept up a fairly successful track record, "Cesco," as pals called him, hit rock bottom in exile. Back in Berlin Cesco had once strolled down Kurfürstendamm like a bird of paradise in a canary-yellow silk dressing gown and frequented clandestine gay bars with friends such as the pianist Vladimir Horowitz and the silent film star Ramón Navarro. Cesco was eccentric, Konrad Kellen recalled, "but really, truly eccentric, and not just pretending. He was actually pretty crazy. He was a strange bird, almost spooky in how far removed he was from everyday life."[8]

Cesco, the son of a banker, was heir to a great fortune and carried a great name, as a direct descendant of the Jewish philosopher Moses Mendelssohn. He was a talented cellist and relatively successful stage director, who had premiered two pieces by Ödön von Horváth in Berlin and staged the first Broadway performance of Brecht's *Threepenny Opera* in 1933, yet the unstable man's decline in exile was extreme. He felt "melancholissimo" and "death-obsessed" in America and, driven by loneliness and boredom, even toyed with returning to Nazi Germany.[9] "He's homesick," his sister Eleonora wrote to her friends Salka and Berthold Viertel,

> and it's impossible to explain to him that the thing he misses no longer exists. . . . Cesco is in real and immediate danger of being sent to a concentration camp, if only for the ransom he would fetch. He knows it, too, but thinks that if he didn't pay, they would get bored, or it would impress them. He loses all sense of danger and anyway: his contrarian spirit. He wants to see it *himself*, know it *himself*, experience it *himself*. Employ him in some way. I'll send you the money from Amsterdam. He is *never* to find out about it, though, nor anyone else. But give him work. I beg you.[10]

Cesco, who had first emigrated to New York in 1935, within a few months relocated to 515 Radcliffe Avenue in Pacific Palisades. The house was built in 1932 and boasted magnificent views of Temescal Canyon and the ocean. He made his way from Pacific Palisades to Mexicali, then reentered the United States in Calexico with a permanent visa on May 27, 1936. Cesco applied for citizenship; worked as Max Reinhardt's assistant in New York; briefly rented a house in the Hollywood Hills; directed another performance of *The Threepenny Opera* in Paris; returned to New York; joined the San Antonio Symphony Orchestra, which soon dismissed him over issues related to his heavy drinking; and spent more and more time in hospitals and psychiatric clinics. He even spent time in police custody as the result of physical violence.

California suited his depression so well, Cesco mused in 1944, but by then ruin had set in. "How eerie: the news about Francesco Mendelssohn's madness. 'He is locked in'—: The way it was *bound* to happen. . . . The—fluid—boundary between snobbish eccentricity and clinical insanity suddenly breached with the courage of desperation," Klaus Mann had observed years earlier, on January 9, 1940.[11] Berthold Viertel also described a "mad Francesco": "Shaves himself bald (branding himself a prisoner). Willful seediness of clothing, the mark of a pariah. . . . No one wants him around; he feels erased, thus the final resort: drawing attention, causing a stir. Hangs cowbells round his neck, finally forcing his arrest." Lying on Max Reinhardt's couch, Cesco told him he could not stand it in America any longer and asked him to hit him "in the kisser."[12] Following his sister's suicide in 1951, the "glamorous boy" of Berlin, who admitted he had been "reduced [to a] wreck," underwent a lobotomy.[13]

The fêted bohemian of the past spent the final years until his death in 1972 as a "totally uninteresting, phlegmatic creature" in the care of an Austrian woman in New York.[14] "I have never had such an unsettling reunion as that hour spent with a person I last saw thirty years ago, but whom I had previously experienced so often and so closely," the German diplomat Dieter Sattler reflected, who had been in Cesco's friend group in Berlin:

> It was him, and it wasn't. The same person, yet a different one too. The uncanny impression of a kind of magical conjuring that pastes a person back together and sends him onto the stage, though he has actually been dead or crazy for a long time. He could remember earlier years relatively well, but as though through a pane of glass—everything sedated, without excitement, without danger, and without luster. All the magic of this unspeakably talented, imperiled and imperiling person had been distilled out of him. All the audacious, cheeky, shameless comments, but all the keen, lightning-quick, brilliant ones too—they were gone. The sweet seriousness of an old family, an old race, a long tradition of the deepest artistic knowledge and experience, which was what was most thrilling about Francesco—gone. Instead, a polite, mannered older gentleman with a friendly smile and carefully chosen—well, certain words and phrases that he—or the woman—had prepared—prefabricated—practiced, and that he put steady effort into neither doubting nor allowing to be toppled. . . . He did not remember much from recent years—or he could not, did not want to, or was not allowed to speak of them. Of course I did not ask. It all remained behind a pane. Was it still there, was that bubbling, abysmal and exultant life still in him—no one knows.—At the end, just as I was leaving, suddenly his voice broke through: Please come again! The most unset-

tling ruined life I have ever seen. As I made my way home through the city—I was in a daze—it began to rain.[15]

The playwright Ernst Toller's life ended in tragedy much more quickly. Toller, who wrote *Die Wandlung* (*Transfiguration*) and *Masse Mensch* (*Man and the Masses*), arguably the two most important pieces of expressionist theater, lived briefly in Pacific Palisades in 1937. Although sources state that Toller lived in Santa Monica, which he also provided as his return address, the house—built in 1928 and barely changed since—is located at 413 West Channel Road, within the bounds of Pacific Palisades.

Born in 1893 in the province of Posen, Toller was arrested in June 1919 for his involvement with the Bavarian Soviet Republic. He was charged with high treason and sentenced to five years in prison. The German state expatriated him in 1933 on the basis of his politics and Jewish heritage. Following stints of exile in Zurich, Paris, and London, he and his wife, Christiane Grautoff, twenty-three years his junior, reached New York on October 12, 1936. In February 1937 he signed a yearlong contract as a screenwriter at MGM. In keeping with the image of a well-paid, successful author, he first resided at the sumptuous Miramar Hotel perched atop the Santa Monica bluff—a favorite haunt for stars such as Greta Garbo and Jean Harlow—then moved to the Sovereign Apartments at 205 Washington Avenue in Santa Monica. Toller earned $1,000 per week drafting scripts for a Lola Montez feature and a film about the construction of the Suez Canal, but no one discussed his work with him, the pictures were never filmed, and his contract was not extended.

Grautoff wrote about that time: "Every morning ET went into his air-conditioned cell, where the beige Venetian blinds were always down, not only to keep out the glaring sunlight, but to ensure no one saw that he was not at his desk writing films, but rather lying on the divan reading magazines."[16] Toller moved to the comfortable house in Pacific Palisades in December 1937, after a six-week trip around Mexico. On February 18, 1938, he returned to New York, where on May 22, 1939, he hanged himself at the Mayflower Hotel. For years he had suffered from bouts of depression and always traveled with a length of rope.

THE AMERICAN WRITER David S. Malcolmson settled in Pacific Palisades in 1928, first at 533 Mount Holyoke Avenue, then at 544 Rustic Road, before hiring Richard Neutra to build him a guesthouse at 491 Mesa Road in 1936. In early 1939 he worked closely with Ruth Landshoff-Yorck, who had emigrated to the United States in March 1937. Born Ruth Levy in 1904, her uncle was the famed Berlin publisher Samuel Fischer and one of her cousins the important émigré publisher Fritz Landshoff. During the Weimar Republic, Landshoff-Yorck had been one of the first-ever "it girls," an androgynous fashion icon who wrote effervescent essays for the arts pages and published several novels. Now in exile she struggled to make ends meet. "One is industrious, swift, indefatigable; meanwhile, at a painfully slow pace, the apocalypse takes shape," Klaus Mann wrote her on February 4, 1939.[17]

Now an avowed anti-fascist, Landshoff-Yorck coauthored *The Man Who Killed Hitler* with Malcolmson in Pacific Palisades. The novel tells the fictional tale of Dr. Karl Moeller, a psychiatrist in Vienna whose Jewish wife, Grete, is kicked to death by Nazis after the Anschluss in 1938 while trying to shield fellow Jews from attacks on the street. In the heat of passion and still in shock, Moeller murders an SS-*Mann* named Severin Braun, who has been institutionalized for schizophrenia and believes himself to be Hitler. To avoid prosecution Moeller smashes his victim's head and trades their clothing and identities. Pretending to be Braun, he explains that the doctor had antagonized him with anti-fascist slogans; the ruse works, and Moeller makes his way to Berlin with the intention of assassinating Hitler, only the opportunity eludes him. Heinrich Himmler then summons him to the Reich Chancellery, where the führer informs him in private that he has selected him as his double. Without a knife at hand, Moeller seizes a bust of Hindenburg and bludgeons the man to death. Then the real Hitler enters the room, revealing that the doppelgänger simply murdered another doppelgänger. Moeller's execution is assured.

The novel was published anonymously by George Palmer Putnam, the legendary pilot Amelia Earhart's widower, a necessary precaution in Landshoff-Yorck's case, as her parents still lived in Berlin. On May 12, 1939, Putnam was overpowered by two masked men, abducted, and left bound and gagged at a construction site. He eventually managed to call for help. The following morning Putnam told the press that the men had been speaking German; one of them, he said, had asked who provided the details for the book.[18] The German consul general, Manfred Freiherr von Killinger, declined to comment, while Hermann Schwinn, "Gauleiter" of the German American Federation in Los Angeles, registered doubt that Germans had been involved in the kidnapping. In fact, certain details suggest that this was a public relations stunt, as Putnam soon caused a splash by revealing Landshoff-Yorck's identity. Landshoff-Yorck helped shape postwar American culture more than most any other German-speaking exile: she became a venerated mentor in experimental, off-off-Broadway theater in New York. This brought things full circle for her, as she had been an actor herself in younger years and worked with Max Reinhardt.

REINHARDT SETTLED in Pacific Palisades in 1940. "It's wonderful here on the Pacific, a thousand times nicer than living in New York, but I grew up on the fourth balcony of the Burgtheater," Reinhardt, who shared the same fame as Thomas Mann and Lion Feuchtwanger, complained.[19] According to a popular bon mot, many of those stranded there had been world-famous back home in Germany, but Reinhardt—ostracized in the Third Reich—truly was revered halfway around the globe. Stars never tired of mentioning the training they had received at his prestigious acting school, including Marlene Dietrich, who never actually enrolled. Reinhardt was born Maximilian Goldmann in Baden bei Wien in 1873, though his parents hailed from the Hungarian town of Stampfen, near Pressburg. As an adult in Berlin, he was the ruler of an entire theater empire. He founded the Salzburg Festival in 1920 and in 1924 took over the Theater in der Josefstadt in Vienna. His guest performances earned him international fame, and even in the United States he had been celebrated as a "magician" of the theater since 1911. During his first trip to Los Angeles in 1926, he met with studio people and began envisioning arts festivals in California, plans he would revive in the 1930s.

Reinhardt's final production on German soil premiered on March 1, 1933. One week later he turned his back on the Third Reich, defamed by the *Völkischer Beobachter* newspaper as a "marcelled lion of the stage" once admired by "'German' citizens of Jewish faith" who had now fallen to little more than a "domesticated prop cat."[20] Goebbels allegedly offered him "honorary Aryanism" and thus the option to return, but Reinhardt ("actually Goldmann the Jew," as the Nazis were wont to say) declined.[21] After nearly three decades as Germany's most important figure in theater, he now worked exclusively outside the country. As he wrote to a friend, "I condemn what the Nazis did, especially in the field of theater, not only as barbaric cruelty, a crude and cowardly act of violence, but as an instance of outrageous stupidity. They expelled people, the only people in the world who were truly in love with the essence of Germanness. This love yielded great fruit in the arts. Karstification is now setting in, a wasteland that Austria is doing what it can to revive."[22]

Many of Reinhardt's ambitious plans in the United States failed, usually for lack of funding, but in 1934 he produced *A Midsummer Night's Dream* at the Hollywood Bowl. His rather presumptuous suggestions for casting were not borne out: he wanted Charlie Chaplin as Nick Bottom, Greta Garbo as Titania, and Fred Astaire as Puck, with Clark Gable, Gary Cooper, Joan Crawford, and Myrna Loy playing the two pairs of lovers. As usual, Reinhardt's staff prepared the production, the man himself absent until thirteen days before the premiere. It was a risky move on his part, between the unknown actors, his shaky grasp of English, and the rabid interest among Hollywood producers. The show was a runaway success, thanks in no small part to fourteen-year-old Mickey Rooney as Puck.

Reinhardt, who had come to the United States on a tourist visa, saw his future in the country. He made his way to Mexicali with Helene Thimig, his mistress of seventeen years who would become his second wife after the divorce battle with Else Heims, which had started in 1924, finally ended. "The place was terribly dirty and crowded with poor, filth-gazing people," Thimig later recalled. "After a long search, our lawyer found us a hotel room. It was the only time during our twenty-five years together that we slept in a double room. Although it's going too far to say 'slept.' The room was crawling with bedbugs, and we were terrified we'd be eaten alive. We sat fully clothed on two wobbly chairs and waited for morning."[23] Reinhardt and Thimig returned to US soil in Calexico on April 2, 1935, and applied for citizenship in Los Angeles on August 21. Salka Viertel and William Dieterle's wife, Charlotte, acted as character witnesses; in the years to come Charlotte did more to support refugees than almost anyone else.

As Wilhelm Dieterle, William had been a star of the German stage and screen in the 1920s and made his debut as a film director in 1926. Since 1930 he had gained a reputation in Hollywood as an expert in European literature and as a "women's director." His wife was an actor and was known professionally by her maiden name, Hagenbruch. Like the Viertels' home in Pacific Palisades, the Dieterle residence on North Knoll Drive was a haven for emigrants. "First things first: they prepared the starved soul to sow new seed," the composer Friedrich Hollaender recalled. "The hungry gathered there, many newly arrived, and lay on the carpet, paging through his beautiful art books, engravings and discoveries from Mexican, Aztek, and Etruscan times. But then—this soon became more important—they helped with the steps toward legal immigration. What came next was not entirely without risk, namely traveling to Mexico and, if all went according to plan, entering the country legally."[24] The Dieterles retained several lawyers who dealt with such cases and managed the paperwork; issued countless affidavits that made entry into the States possible; provided newcomers with loans, including Max Reinhardt; and collected money for friends such as Bertolt Brecht, who arrived in 1941.

William Dieterle also funded a show that went down in exile history: Leopold Jessner's production of Friedrich Schiller's *William Tell*, which premiered at El Capitan Theatre in Hollywood on May 25, 1939. The ensemble featured Ernst Deutsch, Alexander Granach, Christiane Grautoff (whose husband Ernst Toller had committed suicide three days earlier), Ernst Lenart, Lionel Royce (a.k.a. Leo Reuss), and others, many of whom barely spoke English and had memorized their lines phonetically. It was a financial disaster: Dieterle lost $20,000.

Reinhardt's 1934 staging of *A Midsummer Night's Dream* had been such a success that Warner Brothers agreed to a lavish film version, a prestige picture with a generous budget of $1.3 million and another $500,000 to promote it. Reinhardt was paid a princely sum of $100,000, whereas Dieterle, an experienced Hollywood man, earned just $19,000 as codirector. The pioneering film went down in history, received multiple Academy Award nominations, and won for best cinematography and best film editing. It also launched the careers of Olivia de Havilland, whom Reinhardt had discovered and who dazzled in her debut role as Hermia, and Erich Wolfgang Korngold, summoned from Vienna at Reinhardt's request, who would become a leading Hollywood film composer. Nevertheless, *A Midsummer Night's Dream* was not the money-maker its backers had hoped.

Disappointed by this outcome, Reinhardt—who in 1936 was nominated for the Nobel Peace Prize for his services to international understanding by a group that included the king of Sweden and Albert Einstein—turned his attention back to the stage. On January 7, 1937, he premiered the most expensive Broadway production to date: the "colossal, Jewish-national extravaganza" *The Eternal Road*, a kind of biblical revue that depicted the exodus of the Jewish people and their persecution across the ages.[25] Reinhardt brought Franz Werfel and Kurt Weill on board, though they were not exactly a great fit: although Weill was the son of a cantor, his close collaboration with Bertolt Brecht had earned him the reputation of a cultural Bolshevist; Werfel had embraced Catholicism under the influence of his antisemitic wife, Alma, the rather matronly widow of the composer Gustav Mahler. Once admired for her beauty, Alma was an ex-lover of the painter Oskar Kokoschka and ex-wife of the architect Walter Gropius.

The Eternal Road took half an eternity to open, its production postponed ten times by funding and technical snags, but it was a tremendous success for Reinhardt when it finally did. Lion Feuchtwanger described the spectacle as a "Jewish-American Oberammergau," but he was one of few critics who found the play trivial and vulgar, boring, too long, and a huge waste of money.[26] The production had, in fact, cost $463,000. A total of $60,000 had gone to the 757 spotlights needed to achieve the desired effects. Stagehands, technicians, and administrative staff, numbering 159, were on the payroll; 208 people worked on stage; and the wardrobe held 1,772 costumes. The show recorded nightly losses, even with a sold-out house, and its run ended after 153 performances. It had a record deficit of $500,000, and, although Reinhardt's artistic standing remained intact, it ruined his reputation as a businessman.

The Salzburg Festival, directed by Reinhardt, enjoyed one final display of international artistry and attendance in the summer of 1937. The "taste of the ephemeral was on the tongue," Carl Zuckmayer wrote. "What makes these festival summers so wonderful is that each could be the last."[27] The following year, after German troops invaded and Austrian chancellor Kurt von Schuschnigg resigned on March 11, 1938, the National Socialists forced the festival in line with their cultural and political goals, in a process of compulsory coordination known as *Gleichschaltung*. They expelled Reinhardt and taunted him with the lines, "Run your *Everyman* if you please / Across the mighty sea. / Now we're safe from its grasp / From Hamburg down to Brenner Pass."[28]

By this point Reinhardt had left Europe for good. At age sixty-five and accompanied by his cook, Friederike Josefa Vogl, Reinhardt arrived in New York aboard the SS *Normandie* on October 14, 1937—Helene Thimig, now his wife, would follow on November 8. Things in the United States had changed for him though. No longer a guest, he no longer had guest performances to do, and invitations dried up. The tragic decline that now set in was undoubtedly tied to his new status as an emigrant. All his film projects flopped, including a version of *Hamlet*, starring Greta Garbo in the title role. Warner Brothers terminated his contract, waiving the advances. "Like my ancestors I walked on dry feet through the sea and into the desert and spent seven lean years in Hollywood. There the Warners and other nonbelievers thought me too ponderous for the dance around the Golden Calf," Reinhardt summed up his experience in 1943.[29]

In the summer of 1938, he rented a building on Sunset Boulevard from CBS Studios and opened the Max Reinhardt Workshop for Stage, Screen and Radio. In 1941 the rather pompously renamed Max Reinhardt Theatre moved to the site of an amateur dramatics school for service members on Wilshire Boulevard. The endeavor, which Reinhardt hoped would become the standard-bearer his schools in Vienna and Berlin had been, was creatively unfulfilling from its founding until its closure in October 1942; students rejected what Reinhardt taught as "artificial" and "sophisticated."[30] It was a financial disaster too and, ultimately, a depressing defeat. "On top of it all, I handed over my name and almost (as for Hollywood, definitely) lost it," Reinhardt admitted with resignation.[31] As his projects failed, interest in working with the old luminary waned; accustomed to his employees in the past addressing him as "Professor," he had difficulty getting used to the fact that even his students now casually called him "Max."

By the time Reinhardt was naturalized, on November 29, 1940, he had spent all $600,000 he had earned at Warner Brothers. Thimig, who had a more practical head on her shoulders, described his failed attempts to improve his relationship with money as "distressing and sometimes touchingly funny." The couple was forced to sell their ostentatious villa in Outpost Estates, north of Hollywood Heights. Yet again Reinhardt, who valued beautiful homes above all else, lost his lordly abode—as he had lost his apartment in Berlin, located in the court gardener's house at Bellevue Palace, to Prussian State Theater director Gustaf Gründgens in 1936; and as he had lost Leopoldskron Palace outside Salzburg, purchased in 1918, the "production that made Reinhardt most proud."[32] The latter was seized by the Nazis in 1938 and turned over to Princess Stephanie von Hohenlohe, a Nazi spy and friend of Hitler's, a *Volljüdin* and half sister of Gina Kaus, the exiled writer living in California and Vicki Baum's best friend.[33]

Reinhardt and Thimig moved into what they considered a modest Mediterranean villa at 15000 Corona del Mar, on the cliffs overlooking the beach in Pacific Palisades. The plot was three-quarters of an acre, and more important to them than the breathtaking view of the ocean toward Catalina Island, the shady eucalyptus trees, night-blooming jasmine, hibiscus bushes, and bougainvillea was the arable land: "Behind the profusion of flowers out front, the garden now has an Austrian interior: vegetables. Beans, savoy cabbage, red cabbage, onions, red peppers, carrots, lots of white radishes, corn, cucumbers, lettuces, spices, potatoes."[34] This saved them money on groceries. "If we had a cow or goat and a few chickens, we would be totally self-sufficient," Thimig wrote to her husband.[35]

They knew just one of their neighbors, the actor Charles Laughton. He and Elsa Lanchester, who had made a name for herself in the horror film *Bride of Frankenstein*, lived at 14954 Corona del Mar. "We heard they were an extraordinarily interesting and intelligent couple"—Laughton, who was gay, and Lanchester were married, their relationship characterized by tolerance and respect—"and though we lived so close, we never spoke a single word," Thimig wrote.[36] Thomas Mann, on the other hand, was a frequent guest at Reinhardt's "house, a true display of stagecraft, compared to which ours is of sober practicality," as was Bertolt Brecht, who noted on May 15, 1942, "one of those days of lunch at max reinhardt's with feuchtwanger. he lives in a big villa on the sea, filled with his berlin furniture and artworks. the old magician, short and sure-footed, discolored like a blotted pen-and-ink drawing, with his slow, effective movements, the deep voice, tongue still rolling appreciatively inside his cheek, and thimig, a tired, worn out angel of death."[37] It was in Pacific Palisades, where the network of emigrants was small and tightly knit, that Reinhardt finally met Brecht, although he had employed him as a dramaturge at his theater in Berlin in 1924.

The actor Fritz Kortner, who lived in neighboring Brentwood, sniped that Reinhardt, accustomed as he was to profligacy, approached his new residence "as if he were forced to live in a collier's shack."[38] Only a handful of callers knew that the couple had given up many valuable pieces of furniture and art and relied on credit accounts and their friends' generosity to get by. Of course, poverty is relative; before Thimig returned to Austria in the summer of 1946, almost three years after Reinhardt's death, she auctioned off their eighteenth-century French furniture, English crystal, Meissen porcelain, silverware, and a mere fifty-five Persian carpets.

While in 1937 Reinhardt had dreamed of "building a Californian Salzburg in Hollywood," he now had to accept that his ambitions for theater in Los Angeles were dead on arrival. He wrote to a friend, "In a city dominated by the surface (the surface of the screen, which has undoubtedly been enlivened artistically by Chaplin, Disney, and a few others), one cannot justifiably expect the three-dimensional art of theater to develop. Living here is more pleasant, freer, and tranquil than anywhere else in the world at the moment."[39] He hoped for a comeback in New York but grew resigned to the fact that his name no longer drew funding, that he was no longer "the man of the hour," as Thomas Mann put it.[40]

Thimig taught acting in Pacific Palisades and occasionally took on bit roles of her own, despite initial concerns that appearing in anti-Nazi films could endanger her parents and brothers in Vienna. She was in sixteen Hollywood productions, including playing Hitler's half sister Angela Raubal in *The Hitler Gang*. For the most part, however, she had to make due with the twenty dollars of unemployment insurance she received every Wednesday. As money got tighter, she tried to "prepare the house for a temporary sublet, i.e. to put all personal belongings in one room, the library possibly in storage," Thimig wrote to her husband in August 1942, "then I'll just go to some other room whenever I still have to be here."[41] The search for a subletter failed. Salka Viertel suggested it to Greta Garbo, who did not want to live on a cliffside: "She's afraid of falling. She decided that sight unseen."[42] Garbo's fear was by no means irrational: in 1944 a landslide destroyed a significant part of Charles Laughton's property.

Reinhardt celebrated his seventieth birthday in September 1943 in New York. He was "the only one who could today be crowned king of the realm of that human dream called theater," Franz Werfel's histrionic birthday message read. The letter, signed by everyone from Heinrich and Thomas Mann to Berthold and Salka Viertel, went on to call Reinhardt the "powerful sovereign of imagination" and a "darling of the gods."[43] A few days later, while taking a walk on Fire Island, Reinhardt had a stroke, followed by a second in October. He could no longer speak or move his right arm and had to be fed. "His current state is worse than death," Reinhardt's son Gottfried wrote to Salka Viertel and asked bitterly, "Will no one live to see the end of Hitler?"[44] The next day an unsuspecting Thimig arrived in New York from Pacific Palisades, having received an alarming telegram sent anonymously by the actor Elisabeth Bergner. Reinhardt's mistress, Eleonora von Mendelssohn, had to clear out before her rival arrived but allegedly left the windows open to ease Reinhardt's suffering. He developed pneumonia and died in the early morning hours of October 31, 1943, "euthanized by Ela," the theater critic Leo Lerman wrote.[45] Fritz Kortner reflected, "Now, on the eve of Hitler's demise, I would have hoped a different homecoming for him."[46]

PAYING HOMAGE TO GOETHE IN HOLLYWOOD

"WHILE IN EXILE in America, Thomas Mann played a role he had never sought: he was the emperor of German emigrants, a patron of the writers' tribe, in particular," the philosopher and writer Ludwig Marcuse, who had settled in Beverly Hills in 1939, reflected, looking back on the most famous—and, in the postwar years, most controversial—German emigrant. "Everything was expected of him, everything was thanks to him, everything was his responsibility. He was the focus of all devotion and all rebellion," Marcuse said of Mann, whom people referred to ironically was "His Emigrance."[1] Mann's contemporaries in "German California" could not help but envy the unshakably self-satisfied author for his book sales, pay, popularity at the lectern, and relatively luxurious life "with roast pigeons and champagne," as Mann himself noted in his diary.[2] Exile in the United States was a struggle for most, and those whose stock-in-trade had been the German language often foundered. Many succumbed to depression and alcoholism.

Thomas Mann was born the son of a merchant in Lübeck in 1875 and awarded the Nobel Prize for Literature in 1929 for his 1901 debut novel *Buddenbrooks*. He and his wife, Katia, née Pringsheim, who was eight years younger and came from a wealthy Jewish family in Munich, were on vacation in Arosa, Switzerland, following a lecture tour in 1933 when they heard about the Reichstag fire in Berlin on the evening of February 27. Their eldest children, Erika and Klaus, made it clear to them by telephone that a return to Munich was out of the question. Thomas Mann, who at the time was fairly naive about politics, complained that "while you're out, your country is running away somewhere." Initially, the Manns lived in exile in Switzerland, as they thought to wait out the political situation in the Reich, which was still considered opaque, and set about "creating a temporary personal base and place to live." Mann once again proved himself to be a highly sensitive, demanding, and easily offended aesthete. "I feel unwell, and the visit, which left a hideous and oppressive impression of declassed existence, worsens the state of my nerves, which at home yielded to tears," he noted after viewing a villa in Riehen, a posh Basel suburb.[3] Erika ultimately found an acceptable residence for her parents in Küsnacht, on Lake Zurich.

In 1934 Mann visited the United States for the first time, where he was best known for writing *The Magic Mountain*. The following year he and Albert Einstein were conferred honorary doctorates from Harvard, and Mann was invited to the White House by President Franklin D. Roosevelt, whom he idolized. He returned to the States in 1936 and in the spring of 1938. "Where I am, there is Germany. I carry my German culture in me," Mann told reporters awaiting his February 21, 1938, arrival in New York on the *Queen Mary*.[4] Accompanied by Katia and Erika, Thomas Mann traveled across the country—with a brief stay in Toronto, as the immigration paperwork had to be filed from abroad—on a fifteen-stop lecture tour, which paid three times the annual salary of a US university professor. His thick accent prompted one sarcastic attendee to comment that Mann should have just spoken in German, so at least a few in the crowd could have understood him. During his four-week stay at the Beverly Hills Hotel in Los Angeles, he visited Max Reinhardt in Outpost Estates and admired the view of the city lights. In Pacific Palisades he met with Aldous Huxley, attended a soirée hosted by Vicki Baum, and lunched with Salka Viertel.

Mann was of course invited when Bruno and Liesl Frank threw a hundred-guest party in their backyard, which was overgrown with huge eucalyptus trees. Bruno, the son of a Stuttgart-based banker, and Liesl, the illegitimate daughter of Fritzi Massary and Count Karl-Kuno von Coudenhove, had been the Manns' neighbors in Munich before emigrating to Lugano, Switzerland, shortly after the Reichstag fire. Then, like so many exiled writers, they went to the south of France; the Franks later left Sanary-sur-Mer and alternated between Aigen, near Salzburg, and London. In 1937 Bruno, whose works had been translated into English in the 1920s, moved to the California coast with his wife and in 1938 signed a lucrative contract as a screenwriter with Universal Pictures, with a weekly salary of $850.

Like Bruno Frank, Thomas Mann was interested in Hollywood. He hoped to see his tetralogy *Joseph and His Brothers* optioned, the first three books of which had been published in 1933, 1934, and 1936. Just a day after he arrived, the Franks took Mann to Paramount Studios, where among others he spoke with the Viennese director Fritz Lang. Even Lang, the giant behind such seminal silent films as *Destiny*, *Die Nibelungen*, and *Metropolis* as well as the talkie *M*, had faced an uphill battle in Hollywood after escaping Germany. (Per Nazi classifications, Lang was a "half-Jew," whereas his girlfriend and later wife, Lily Latté, was Jewish.) Lang had managed to make only three Hollywood films to date: *Fury*, starring Spencer Tracy, in which Lang, like in *M*, depicts the mental state of a man pursued by the mob; *You Only Live Twice*, with Henry Fonda and Sylvia Sidney, a critical portrayal of mass hysteria born of stupidity and narrow-mindedness; and the comparatively frivolous musical romantic comedy *You and Me*, a bust with critics and at the box office.

A week later Warner Brothers boss Jack Warner invited Mann as a guest of honor to a fundraising dinner for German refugees. The event was attended by such stars as James Cagney and Miriam Hopkins and authors Dorothy Parker and Lillian Hellman, along with the Dieterles and the Franks. In the following weeks, Mann visited Disney Studios, where he was shown a Mickey Mouse film; attended shoots at the MGM lot in Culver City; toured Universal Studios, which was under Carl Laemmle's management; and went to Fox Studio, where he watched the making of a film with Peter Lorre and Shirley Temple. He had lunches with Adrian, the foremost costume designer in Hollywood, and Carl Laemmle and supped with the Lubitsches and Dieterles. On another trip to Hollywood in April 1939, Mann met with filmmakers and returned to MGM Studios and Warner Brothers. Before screening what Mann called the "very useful and impressive" anti-Nazi film *Confessions of a Nazi Spy*, he met for lunch with "members of the production. Remarque and Dietrich, inferior."[5]

Marlene Dietrich appeared on camera in the United States directly following her success in Josef von Sternberg's *The Blue Angel*, based on Heinrich Mann's novel, in 1930. She was one of a handful of European artists to become a major star, though her career had its ups and downs. Having unequivocally rejected all offers to return to Germany and clearly taken sides against the Nazis, Dietrich was now an exile. She earned the Presidential Medal of Freedom for entertaining US troops during the war, but in postwar Germany she became known as a traitor and was spat at during a concert in Düsseldorf in 1960. She wrote, "These people clearly mourn the end of Hitler's regime. Incited by newspaper articles and flyers, some fanatics went so far as to threaten to plant bombs in the theaters where I was performing. . . . I never returned to Germany after that. I'd had more than enough of being spat at, enough of the 'demonstrators,' enough of that love-hate relationship."[6]

The Osnabrück native Erich Maria Remarque had risen to international fame for his 1929 novel *All Quiet on the Western Front*, which describes the horrors of World War I and sold 3.5 million copies within the first year and a half. He left Germany for Switzerland in 1932 and moved to the United States in 1938, probably at Dietrich's urging. Remarque had a long-standing, by no means uncomplicated romantic relationship with the older actor. It was followed by an intense but brief affair with Luise Rainer and another that fizzled amicably with Greta Garbo. After a stay at the elegant Beverly Wilshire Hotel, in May 1940 he rented a house at 1050 Hilts Avenue in Westwood. At Dietrich's suggestion, he enlisted Martin Kosleck and Galka Scheyer to furnish his new home, and he sent for his valuable art collection from Switzerland, which included pieces by Van Gogh, Cézanne, Renoir, Picasso, and Toulouse-Lautrec. When a fellow party guest of Salka Viertel's once asked if he didn't miss Germany, Remarque is said to have replied, "Why would I? *I'm* not a Jew."[7]

In 1946 Remarque would learn the fate of his younger sister, Elfriede Scholz, who had been a seamstress in Dresden: she had been arrested in August 1943, denounced by a client after criticizing the regime in passing. Her trial took place on October 29 before the People's Court in Berlin. The judge, Roland Freisler, would oversee the trials against the July Plot assassination attempt the following year. "Your brother unfortunately slipped through our fingers, but not you," Freisler is reported to have said.[8] Scholz's lawyer also referenced the famous author in a clemency appeal, arguing that "her being the sister of the notorious Remark, whose beliefs she often heard in her youth, could play a role. . . . As she has not had any contact with her brother in 13 years, however, any direct influence is no longer the case."[9] This letter was as unsuccessful as subsequent appeals. Scholz was executed by guillotine on December 16, 1943, in Berlin-Plötzensee. Her sister Erna Brames had to pay a 300.00 reichsmark fee for the death penalty, plus 122.18 reichsmarks for the execution itself and 73.50 reichsmarks for costs incurred during Scholz's imprisonment—plus 12 pfennigs postage.

It was after the war that Marlene Dietrich, too, learned the fate of her older sister, Elisabeth, who had stayed in Germany. In May 1945 Dietrich rushed to the Bergen-Belsen concentration camp, where she expected to find her sister. It turned out that Elisabeth and her husband, Georg H. Will, had run a cinema at the Belsen barracks, where the murderers went for entertainment. Dietrich disowned her sister for the rest of her life. Whatever Mann's reasons for disliking Dietrich and Remarque—the most famous representatives of a "better" Germany alongside Albert Einstein and Mann himself—they all avoided further encounters in their joint exile.

Mann and his wife, Katia, who had first moved from Küsnacht, Switzerland, to Princeton, New Jersey, in September 1938, spent the summer of 1940 at 441 North Rockingham Avenue in Brentwood, "an elegant house in a beautiful hilly area," not far from Arnold Schoenberg's estate.[10] The Manns had met the composer at a soirée of Vicki Baum's in 1938. The conductor Bruno Walter and his wife, Elsa, greeted the newcomers with flowers; Bruno and Liesl Frank brought Gugelhupf cake. That summer Mann wrote to his patron Agnes E. Meyer, "We have taken possession of an amazingly well-situated, spacious house with a yard and swimming pool. The surroundings are truly Tuscan, the hills of Fiesole cannot compete, and I now have what I have wanted for so long, namely beautiful weather every day. We have gotten together several times with our friends here, the Walters and Franks."[11] From then on he noted "bathed in the pool at lunchtime" in his diary as routinely as he did his walks with Niko, the black poodle, along the shore in Santa Monica, where he also went for regular pedicures—but not haircuts. "Went to get a haircut, but the place disgusted me," he wrote rather sullenly after his first outing in Santa Monica. Two days later he found a hairdresser to his liking: "Went to Westwood at noon for a haircut, only again they asked, 'Are you English?' Call me Swiss."[12]

Mann traveled primarily to Westwood to see films such as *The Jungle Book*, captivated by the young actor Sabu's "expressive face and beautiful body." Mann, who cut an aloof figure, placed tremendous value on propriety and outward appearances and sublimated his homosexual tendencies all his life. He commented in his diaries about *Pride of the Yankees*, a "very American baseball film with the charmless [Gary] Cooper"; the "lovely" Disney film *Bambi*; the "abjectly stupid" anti-Nazi film *Hitler's Children*; and the "extremely awkward" Franz Werfel adaptation *The Song of Bernadette*.[13]

WORKING WITH AN AGENT and the Hungarian architect Paul László, who had emigrated from Stuttgart to Beverly Hills in 1936, Mann began looking for property on which he could have his own house built. He was especially taken with the Riviera in Pacific Palisades, and on September 12, 1940, he signed the contract for "lot 41": Mann paid $6,500 for a site on San Remo Drive, a street lined in eucalyptus, California live oak, and cedar trees. "Some Hollywood film man had purchased it but lost interest, then let it go cheap," Katia Mann wrote. "The location was beautiful, with a magnificent view of the sea and of Catalina Island, and with palm, orange, and lemon trees on a large plot."[14]

The Manns left the house in Brentwood on October 6, 1940, to spend another six months in Princeton. On April 8, 1941, they moved into a rented ranch-style house at 740 Amalfi Drive. About five weeks later, Thomas Mann ordered construction on his nearby property to begin, though he would question this decision as the price climbed. He considered collaborating with Paul László or Richard Neutra, probably the biggest name in modern architecture, but ultimately hired Julius Ralph Davidson for the project. Davidson, another titan of California modernism, was born in Wrocław and had lived in the United States since 1923; he had created the sets for a number of Cecil B. DeMille's films and redesigned the fabled Cocoanut Grove Restaurant in Hollywood. Other emigrants involved in the job were the building contractor Ernst Schlesinger as well as interior designer Paul Huldschinsky. A square study on the ground floor was connected to the main part of the house by a narrow corridor that led directly into a spacious living room, while the bedrooms were upstairs.

On February 5, 1942, the Manns moved into their $30,000 Bauhaus-style villa at 1550 San Remo Drive, for which they had taken out a mortgage. "You should see the landscape around our house, with a view of the ocean," Mann wrote to Hermann Hesse. "Cheery impressions are no trivial matter in such times, and the sky here is cheerful almost year-round and sends out an incomparable light that beautifies all it touches."[15] In her memoirs Katia Mann wrote,

> It was a charming house. My husband always said it was the best study he ever had, and he felt completely at home there. . . . The beach was only ten to twelve minutes away by car. Every day I drove my husband to the promenade overlooking the ocean, and while he took a walk, I went swimming. I drove him there and picked him up again. I never accompanied him on his walks, except perhaps a little way now and then. . . . But every couple of days a car would stop and someone would ask, "May we give you a ride?" Then he would say, "No, thank you, I'd rather walk," and usually all the dogs would follow him. Americans don't walk much; in any case, they didn't at that time.[16]

Paradoxically, Thomas Mann distanced himself from Hollywood after settling in Pacific Palisades, though the industry had been of such interest to him once. In a letter to his son Klaus, he referred to people in film—some of whom were his neighbors, such as *Casablanca* screenwriter Howard W. Koch, who lived at 1341 San Remo Drive, and Gregory Peck, at number 1700—as "movie rabble."[17] Mann made few serious attempts now to pitch his novels to studios or even to establish himself as a screenwriter. In 1942 he supplied the story "Thou Shalt Have No Other Gods before Me," based on the First Commandment, for an episodic film intended to denounce the Nazis' violations of the Ten Commandments, though the film was never made. The same year he wrote an exposé for a film about a farmer who organizes resistance against German and Italian occupiers in Thessaly. This idea bore as little fruit as a 1946 screen adaptation of *The Magic Mountain*, meant to star Greta Garbo as Clavdia Chauchat and Montgomery Clift as Hans Castorp. "A film that took place solely among the infirm," the screenwriter and director George Tabori later reflected, having met Mann at Salka Viertel's house in Pacific Palisades and been involved in the planning, was "unthinkable in the Hollywood of that time."[18]

THE KING OF PACIFIC PALISADES HELPS DISPOSE OF THE DEAD MICE

THE FEUCHTWANGERS were in the market for a house with ocean views and a big yard. The English real estate agent, whom Marta Feuchtwanger had enlisted to help with the search, took her to Paseo Miramar. In 1926 Arthur A. Weber, a former judge turned lawyer; the building contractor George W. Ley; and a few others had purchased Miramar Estates, a steep hillside covered in brush. The 1.3-square-mile property was terraced according to designs by the famed landscape architect Mark Daniels, its subdivided plots then listed by the Frank Meline Company at prices between $10,000 and $150,000. The Miramar Estates Sales Corporation hoped for a $200 million return on its $8 million investment. The first house built there was Ley's, a Spanish colonial-style home that cost $40,000; the film director Robert Z. Leonard, who specialized in lavishly produced star vehicles, had his house built for $100,000. There were now nine houses there, almost all of them for sale, because schools, stores, and medical care were difficult to reach, a daily commute to work downtown impossible in light of gasoline rationing. "Pacific Palisades doesn't exist; it's just trees and hills," Bertolt Brecht once commented. "When someone is sick there is no doctor; when you need a pharmacy, there's nothing to buy. You cannot live so far away from civilization."[1]

Marta and Lion Feuchtwanger first set their sights on 846 Paseo Miramar, a five-thousand-square-foot house built on the hilltop in 1929. Shortly after they signed the contract, however, seller Glenn A. Doughy, a prominent building contractor, backed out because he wanted to keep using it himself. The agent showed Marta an even bigger villa just down the hill, at 520 Paseo Miramar. The art patron Peggy Guggenheim and Katia Mann had also shown interest in the property but changed their minds, as they found it too rundown. Marta, however, took a shine to it. She and her husband acquired the neo-Hispanic villa for the comparatively low price of $9,000, $4,000 of which they paid upfront, thanks to the sale of Lion's novel *The Lautensack Brothers* to *Collier's Magazine*.

The Miramar Estates Sales Corporation had built the house in 1927–28. The "Los Angeles Times Demonstration Home" was modeled on a small castle that Arthur Weber and his family had seen near Seville and intended as an "ideal dwelling."[2] Mark Daniels, who designed homes as well as landscapes, was the architect. The villa was called "Miramar"—the "Villa Aurora" sign was not added until the early 1960s, though Marta rarely used the name—and was meant to persuade solvent Angelenos to buy in the new residential area on the northwestern edge of Pacific Palisades. In September 1927, while work was underway (the *Los Angeles Times* reported regularly on its progress), the Casa Miramar Café was opened on the construction site for potential buyers to enjoy refreshments. On October 13, around a thousand people were invited to a barbecue there. Rodney Benson, of Barker Brothers, oversaw the home interiors, while designer Thorwald Probst based its carved and painted wooden doors and ceilings on Mudéjar art found in the Cathedral of Santa María de Mediavilla in Teruel, Spain. The model home was equipped with the latest gadgets, from an electric refrigerator and dishwasher to a futuristic appliance that could beat eggs and polish silver to a pest-proof safe for fur coats; the door to the three-car garage opened automatically.

From April 29 to June 10, 1928, there were daily guided tours of the finished house between 11:00 a.m. and 6:30 p.m. These featured talks by Mark Daniels, Thorwald Probst, Jack Rennick (who had made all the furniture, including some replicas of museum pieces), renowned carpet importer and dealer Najeeb S. Hanief, and Bertha Townsend Coler, who lectured on the harmonious play of colors in the home's curtains and sofa cushions. Marion Rouzie provided afternoon entertainment, performing works by Antonín Dvořák, Jules Massenet, Franz Schubert, and others on the house organ built by the Artcrafts Organ Company of Santa Monica. On opening day ten thousand visitors viewed the house, but Alphonzo E. Bell's plans to built a cement factory in Santa Ynez

Canyon killed all interest in Miramar Estates properties. Moreover, feeling the effects of the stock market crash, from 1931 to 1939 Weber and his wife, their son, and his mother and her three siblings lived as tenants at 520 Paseo Miramar, which now belonged to a bank. Weber died of a heart attack in a courtroom on September 7, 1943, and, after he and his family left the house, it fell into disrepair, despite the caretaker's presence.

The Feuchtwangers spent the first few nights at their new home outside in sleeping bags in the overgrown yard. The affluent attorney Eric Scudder, a "great admirer" of Lion Feuchtwanger and known as the "King of Pacific Palisades," sent over a worker, and, with this man's help, Marta shoveled the layers of dirt, detritus, and dead mice and lizards littering the floors into bags, hauled them onto the terrace, and dumped everything into the garden as fertilizer. "[In] the basement, the spider webs were so thick, you needed an axe to go through."[3] Though nearly all the windows were broken, the structure was sound, as were the plumbing and wiring.

Isabel von Ostheim, who lived half a mile up the hill, at 815 Paseo Miramar, offered to help as well: "I wanted to tell you that in a way we are related." Her husband was Count Hermann von Ostheim, born in 1886 as heir to the throne of the Grand Duchy of Saxony-Weimar-Eisenach, then excluded from the succession to the throne in 1909 because of his dissolute lifestyle; he came from the family of Duke Karl Alexander of Württemberg, who had employed Joseph Süß Oppenheimer as court Jew. Feuchtwanger's 1925 novel *Jud Süß* (*Jew Süss*) was based on Oppenheimer's life. Marta joked in response that "[maybe] I could be related with King David, but not with a count in Germany."[4]

With antiques she had bought for a song, Marta and Lion gradually furnished the upstairs bedrooms and studies; the parlor, with its fireplace and home organ; an adjoining room to the west originally intended as a billiard room; and the breakfast and dining rooms, which were next to the tiled kitchen:

> With the movie people there are certain fads, certain styles, and this was the time where they all of a sudden wanted all French furniture, Louis XVI mostly, you know, those little chairs which are golden. I hate this style. . . . So I went to secondhand stores, and all the movie

> people, the great directors and producers, they all threw their furniture out. They were glad that people took it out for nothing, and they didn't even sell it sometimes; they just were glad that somebody picked it up. And I found the most beautiful antique things there. And they had their golden little chairs. And I found—for instance, I found out that in West Los Angeles, on Santa Monica Boulevard, there are all kinds of junk stores. I drove very slowly through, and I saw sometimes . . . the most beautiful things. People were so glad they got rid of it.[5]

Lion combed the used bookshops of Los Angeles to rebuild his library for the third time in his life. (His first, numbering around ten thousand volumes, had been left behind in Berlin in 1933; his second, in Sanary-sur-Mer, left behind in 1941.) The collection soon included such treasures as the *Nuremberg Chronicle* of 1454, the definitive edition of Goethe's *Faust II*, and first editions of Shakespeare, Corneille, and Balzac. Meanwhile, the plot now cleared of weeds, Marta planted vegetables, bougainvillea, roses, and mimosas as well as eucalyptus, palm, and cedar trees: "I plant trees because paper is made of trees."[6] Over time the estate grew as Feuchtwangers purchased adjacent plots. The veritable park they created on the south side, complete with tropical fish ponds, soon became a local attraction for raccoons, gophers, skunks, deer, and the occasional cougar.

THE FEUCHTWANGERS had been married for more than thirty years at this point, though there had been bumps in the road, as theirs was an open marriage. Lion especially had numerous affairs. "I married my comparative form," Marta was fond of saying, in reference to the *-er* ending of Lion's surname: she and her husband, who was born in 1884 in Munich, could trace their ancestry to the town of Feuchtwangen, and one of Marta's great-grandfathers was a Herr Feuchtwang.[7] Marta Löffler was born in Munich in 1891, her parents wealthy merchants. She met her "comparative form" in 1910. Lion came from an upper-class, Orthodox Jewish family of factory owners and had completed his doctorate with a dissertation on Heinrich Heine; by the time he met Marta, the same year his debut novel, *The Clay God*, was published, his reputation as a rather dubious bohemian preceded him. Two years later the young lovers' fathers met: "My son is a scoundrel, and if your daughter marries him, she's not much better," Siegmund Feuchtwanger declared.[8] Reservations aside, Marta, a tall, exotic-looking beauty, married Lion, an ordinary, rather gnome-like fellow, less than four months before their daughter Elisabeth was born, though the baby died two months later.

What followed was the happiest time in the couple's life together: a two-year trip to Côte d'Azur, Italy, and North Africa. Back in Munich after serving in the military, Lion's writing career took off, and he earned good money producing articles and theater pieces. The couple led a glamorous social life. In 1925 he published the historical novel *Jud Süß*, the tale of Württemberg court Jew Joseph Süß Oppenheimer, which Lion had completed back in 1922. It sold one hundred thousand copies in its first year. The first English translation appeared in 1926, under the title *Power*, and sold well in the United States; translations into more than fifteen languages followed. In Nazi Germany the film director Veit Harlan used the same title—*Jud Süß*—for one of the most antisemitic propaganda films ever made.

In 1925 Bertolt Brecht, a friend and collaborator of Lion's, urged the Feuchtwangers to move to Berlin. It was there that Lion wrote *Success*, his greatest novel. In the winter of 1932–33, a book tour brought him to the United States for the first time. He explored the country from New York to Los Angeles, where Charlie Chaplin pitched a film adaptation of *Jud Süß*; Lion vehemently rejected the proposal and offered an alternative. In his diary he wrote, "Chaplin is taken with my idea of a Hitler film," and in 1940 Chaplin's masterpiece *The Great Dictator* opened in theaters.[9] The German embassy had planned an official reception for Feuchtwanger in New York on January 30, 1933. At ten o'clock that morning, a German legation counselor turned up at Feuchtwanger's hotel and informed him that Reich president Paul von Hindenburg had appointed Adolf Hitler as Reich chancellor.

Feuchtwanger would never return to Berlin. He finished his US tour, declared "Hitler means war," and in early March boarded the SS *Aquitania* to Cherbourg, then took a train by way of Paris to Tyrol, where his wife was on a ski vacation.[10] The Nazis had since looted the Feuchtwangers' Berlin home, seized their assets, and revoked Lion's doctorate. Joseph Goebbels branded the successful author the "worst enemy of the German *Volk*."[11] In April the Feuchtwangers moved to Sanary-sur-Mer in the south of France, a precursor to Pacific Palisades as a hub for German-speaking émigrés. They lived there for the next few years, their stay interrupted only by Marta's annual ski vacation and Lion's trips to London, Paris, and, in the winter of 1936–37, Moscow, where the writer—who had socialist leanings—also met Stalin.

Feuchtwanger first toyed with the idea of emigrating to the United States in 1938, the thought being to settle down in Santa Fe, New Mexico. On September 14, 1939, less than two weeks after the German invasion of Poland, the French government ordered all male nationals of enemy states detained, even those who had entered the country as political refugees. Three days later Feuchtwanger was interned at Les Milles but was released from the camp in late September following international outcry. He had a tourist visa for the United States, yet he could not bring himself to leave France.

Then the German Wehrmacht invaded France, and on June 22, 1940, the Franco-German Armistice was signed. The country was divided into a German-occupied northern zone and "free zone" in the south, with the seat of government in Vichy. "Enemy aliens," this time including women, again became targets for arrest, and since Article 19 of the armistice agreement stipulated that France had to extradite all persons requested by the German Reich, the Feuchtwangers and other refugees were in serious danger. Lion was imprisoned again at Les Milles and later transferred to San Nicolà, a camp outside Nîmes. Marta was interned at a camp near Hyères before being sent to Gurs. Thousands would be deported to Auschwitz from Gurs in the coming years, but Marta managed to escape with the help of the US consulate in Marseille. Vice Consul Hiram Bingham Jr. and his colleague Miles Standish persuaded Lion to get into their car while he was walking along a river near the camp, an outing permitted because escape seemed so unlikely. He passed through all the checkpoints to Marseille disguised as a woman, wearing a lady's coat and scarf arranged round his head.

There the American political scientist and journalist Varian Fry arranged the flight of prominent refugees on behalf of the European Rescue Committee.

One of the first groups—Franz Werfel, who had a heart condition; his wife, Alma; Golo Mann; his sixty-nine-year-old uncle, Heinrich Mann; and Heinrich's wife, Nelly—crossed the Pyrenees on foot in sweltering summer heat. The Feuchtwangers followed within days. Lion's visa was issued under "James Wetcheek," the literal translation of his last name a rather thin cover, and the Spanish border guards were bribed with cigarettes. Marta and Lion traveled by train from Port Bou to Barcelona and on to Lisbon, where Lion boarded the US liner SS *Excalibur* and arrived in New York on October 5. The next day the *New York Times* published an article in which the author, whose novel *Exil* (*Paris Gazette*) came out later that year, revealed details about the secret escape routes from Europe, which many fellow exiles resented. Five weeks later Marta followed him aboard the SS *Exeter*.

The Feuchtwangers spent the first few months in New York, then moved to Los Angeles in February 1941. They stayed at 2088 Mandeville Canyon Road in Brentwood, the home of the painter, illustrator, and caricaturist Eva Herrmann, one of Lion's many lovers since 1935 and the "muse of exile," as her biographer Manfred Flügge put it. She was born in Munich in 1901, the daughter of a wealthy American painter and a German woman from Romania, both of whom were Jewish. From 1922 to 1924, Herrmann had been together with the expressionist poet and later author of the East German national anthem, Johannes R. Becher. She had moved into her own studio in New York in 1925 and become close friends with Erika and Klaus Mann in 1927. Herrmann traveled to the Côte d'Azur in 1931, where she made friends with Aldous Huxley and his wife, Maria, who had lived there since the year before; she rented a Provençal stone cottage on the outskirts of Sanary-sur-Mer, which had become an important meeting place for intellectuals in the early thirties. As a US citizen, she had no trouble relocating to the United States in October 1939. The Huxleys had been living for several months in an ostentatious home leased from Dr. George H. Kress at 701 Amalfi Drive in Pacific Palisades, so Herrmann made her way to Los Angeles and purchased the Mandeville Canyon Road property. In 1940 she let Ludwig Marcuse and his wife, Sascha, use it for a spell, then in 1941 she rented it out to the Feuchtwangers; in 1960 Vladimir Nabokov wrote the screenplay for Stanley Kubrick's film *Lolita* there.

Since Thomas Mann's arrival in California, "Gemme"—as he usually referred to Herrmann in his diary—was part of the family's inner circle. She helped with practical matters and in 1942 became godmother to Thomas Mann's favorite grandson, Frido. In 1943 she moved to Pacific Palisades, first to Max Reinhardt's onetime residence at 15000 Corona del Mar, with a brief interlude at 533 Spoleto Drive. In 1947 she had a bungalow built on the grounds of Uplifters Ranch, at what is now 790 Latimer Road. By then she had begun exploring parapsychological phenomena with the Irish medium Eileen J. Garrett, whom Herrmann had met through the writer Mercedes de Acosta and the Huxleys, who were also taken with spiritualism and hosted Garrett at their home. (De Acosta, whose dalliances with rival goddesses of the silver screen Greta Garbo and Marlene Dietrich set tongues wagging, was born in 1892 to a Cuban father and a Spanish mother descended from the Dukes of Alba and had lived at 740 Amalfi Drive before the Manns.) Herrmann later recorded messages from the deceased, as relayed by the medium, and in 1976, two years before her death in Santa Barbara, published them in a work titled *Von drüben* (From over there)—complete with a postmortem afterword by Thomas Mann.

The Feuchtwangers left Herrmann's house on Mandeville Road for Nogales, Mexico, and reentered the United States with permanent visas on February 10, 1941. Salka Viertel arranged for them to rent the house at 1650 Amalfi Drive in Pacific Palisades, though they had to move when the owner, film producer Dudley Murphy, returned six months later. They returned to Mandeville Canyon, this time to a Spanish-style villa at 1744 Mandeville Canyon Road, with a huge garden, "almost a plantation of avocados and persimmons. There were so many fruits that we could have sold them and make lots of money."[12] In the fall of 1942, the Feuchtwangers moved back to Pacific Palisades, first to 13827 Sunset Boulevard, then to a house built in 1936 at 689 Amalfi Drive, and finally to Paseo Miramar.

The Feuchtwangers' day began with exercise. Marta was a dedicated athlete. She skied until age seventy and well into old age took daily walks down Paseo Miramar and swam in the ocean, whatever the weather. After breakfast Lion reviewed the previous day's work until his secretary Hilde Waldo, a Jewish woman who had fled Berlin for America, arrived around ten. She sat at one of the four bargain tables Lion had set up in the middle of his upstairs study and typed as he dictated to her from a standing desk overlooking the Pacific—he still wrote his books in German.

The Feuchtwangers' residence soon became a favorite gathering place among exiles. Pacific Palisades felt like "a kind of gigantic Sanary" to Lion.[13] Recalling the evenings spent at 520 Paseo Miramar, Ludwig Marcuse wrote, "Frau Martha [*sic*]—tall, tanned day and night, summer and winter, in Provence and on the Pacific Ocean, rising from the floodwaters every morning, not unlike the elegant wife of an Indian chief—was the most gracious hostess."[14] It was here that Charles Laughton recited Shakespeare's poems, here that Lion discussed the *Life of Galileo* with his friend Brecht. Thomas and Katia Mann were among the guests, though the connection to Heinrich Mann was much deeper. Bruno Frank was Lion's closest friend in exile, though they were drifting apart, as Frank objected to Lion's relationship with Brecht. Hanns Eisler; the cellist Gregor Piatigorsky and his wife, Jacqueline; and the actor Edward G. Robinson routinely stopped by. The Feuchtwangers also became close with Charlie Chaplin and his wife, Oona.

Every few months no more than forty-four guests (the number of chairs the Feuchtwangers owned) would gather for a reading from Lion's latest work; as his shrill voice filled the room, Marta served sherry and port, Italian or Russian salad or tuna on black bread, and homemade apple strudel with whipped cream for dessert. The readings began at eight o'clock sharp to accommodate Thomas Mann's wish to be home by eleven and were followed by a discussion—Mann was always allowed and expected to speak first. He never voiced what he supposedly confided to his fellow attendee George Tabori:

> Young man, did you notice the perfection of the furnishings, the 18,000 leather-bound books, all of which he has not only read, but understood and retained, the variety of desks, one to write at lying down, another to write at seated, a third for standing, and the splendid writing implements, the various typewriters, the battery of fountain pens, pencils, erasers, the superb quality of paper, the ingenious little nook for his secretary, always close at hand, the view of the Pacific Ocean,

> the perfume of exotic flora, that giant, discreet, ever helpful wife, who reminds me of an Indian chief, and what does all this perfection produce? Pure shit.[15]

Mann himself occasionally read from his works at the Feuchtwangers' house. Lion returned the favor on San Remo Drive, though he rarely left home. As Marcuse noted, "He socialized, but not too often. Invited people over; not overeagerly. But really preferred being undisturbed."[16]

"AND THAT SUBSTANCE IS OUR WORK"

THOSE WHO DID NOT COME to Los Angeles in the hopes of finding work in Hollywood—or with a studio contract already in hand—generally chose the area because the cost of living was much lower than in New York and because, like Thomas Mann, they preferred the West Coast weather. Franz Werfel, who first moved to a house in Outpost Estates situated above the Hollywood Bowl, then bought a bungalow in Beverly Hills, raved about the "unique" climate and the unaccustomed comforts of American homes: "You press a button and it gets warm in ten seconds."[1]

Pacific Palisades' sublime surroundings were another major draw: "The elevation is relatively high, so the fog from the sea does not reach it, and there is a beautiful view of the mountains," Max Horkheimer wrote to Theodor Adorno.[2] For writers and philosophers, unlike film people, proximity to the studios was not a deciding factor, so many settled in the west of Los Angeles, an area whose beauty—according to Adorno—was

> so incomparable that even such a hardboiled European as myself can only surrender to it. The proportion of mountains to sea initially reminds one strongly of the French Riviera, for example San Remo or Mentone, except that it is not so divided and "privé," but rather much more long-lined and open. The shape of the mountains themselves, however, is more reminiscent of Tuscany. . . . But best of all are the incredibly intense, in no way reproducible colours; a drive along the ocean around sunset is one of the most extraordinary impressions that my—by no means highly responsive—eyes have ever had. All the red, blue and violet activity found there would appear laughable on any illustration, but it is overwhelming if one sees the real thing.[3]

Horkheimer suffered from heart and circulatory conditions, including rheumatism, and in 1941 he made the move from New York to Pacific Palisades for his health. His wife preferred the weather there too. Incidentally, his relationship with Rose Riekher, his father's private secretary, had once caused a rift between Max and his father, Moses (or Moritz), a wealthy manufacturer of synthetic cotton. Already furious that his son chose to attend university rather than take over the family business, Moritz opposed his involvement with Riekher, who was Christian and eight years older than Max. It was only after a ten-year courtship that the two had dared to marry in 1926.

Moritz Horkheimer was a conservative Jew and German patriot of the National Liberal persuasion; in 1917 King Ludwig III of Bavaria awarded him the title of *Kommerzienrat* (councillor of commerce) for his charitable work. Max, however, born in Zuffenhausen in 1895, was influenced most by his mother, whom he described as an "especially loving woman," because "one cannot learn love by way of messages, but by the shine in a mother's eye, by her love and the way she speaks."[4]

Horkheimer was taken out of secondary school early to train at his father's textile factory, and by 1914 he was a junior manager. He was drafted into the army in 1917, then discharged for health reasons and sent to Munich to convalesce; there he experienced the end of the war, November Revolution, and Bavarian Soviet Republic. Horkheimer completed his Abitur examinations to secure his secondary school diploma and in 1919 enrolled at the University of Frankfurt to study philosophy, psychology, and political economy. In 1921 he moved to Freiburg for two semesters, where he studied under Edmund Husserl. He presented his dissertation "Zur Antinomie der teleologischen Urteilskraft" (On the antimony of teleological judgment) in Frankfurt in 1923 and completed his postdoctoral qualification two years later with a work titled *Über Kants* Kritik der Urteilskraft *als Bindeglied zwischen theoretischer und praktischer Philosophie* (Kant's *Critique of Judgment* as a link between theoretical and practical philosophy). His hopes of filling the vacancy at the University of Frankfurt left by his erstwhile professor, the neo-Kantian philosopher Hans Cornelius, were dashed when Max Scheler was appointed; a few months later, after Scheler's death, the existential theologian Paul Tillich was named to the position. In 1930, however, Horkheimer was appointed professor of social philosophy, a position created for him that ran in tandem with the directorship of the Institute for Social Research, which was associated with the university.

The man (and money) behind the institute was Felix Weil. His father, Hermann, who came from the village of Steinsfurt in southwestern Germany, had emigrated to Argentina in 1888 and become one of the country's top three wheat exporters, then returned to Germany in 1907 as a multimillionaire. During World War I, Hermann Weil served as an adviser on trade war issues to General Erich Ludendorff and Emperor Wilhelm II himself.[5] Hermann's son Felix, born in Buenos Aires in 1898, was moved by the patriotic spirit of the time and volunteeredin 1917 for military service in the Imperial German Army, which granted the Argentinian citizen an exemption that allowed him to join.

When the Workers' and Soldiers' Council took control of Frankfurt in November 1918, Felix Weil joined the revolutionary body, was briefly appointed head of its provisional police force known as the "workers' defense," and turned his attention to Social Democratic writings. He was refused a doctorate at the University of Tübingen in 1920 because of his socialist activities and expelled from the state of Württemberg—an alleged housing shortage meant the number of international students had to be capped. The same year Weil submitted his dissertation on the concept of socialization to the University of Frankfurt. In 1922 he organized a "Marxist Week" in Ilmenau, Thuringia, then decided to make things more official with a privately funded institute; he prudently concealed the Marxist element from his father, an enlightened liberal, as well as from the university. But university finances were so precarious in 1923, a year marked by crisis and inflation, that it would have been difficult for administrators to refuse. The Frankfurt Institute for Social Research opened in 1924, with a research focus on political economy through the lens of historical materialism. Weil continued to finance it with his father's help, then drew from his considerable inheritance after Hermann died. Weil supported the painter George Grosz, theater productions by Erwin Piscator, and the German adaptation of Sergei Eisenstein's silent film *Battleship Potemkin*; he was also a main shareholder of Malik, a publishing house run by brothers Wieland Herzfelde and John Heartfield, which had ties to the Communist Party of Germany and specialized in socially critical and avant-garde literature.

Another central figure at the Frankfurt Institute since its founding was Friedrich Pollock. He and Horkheimer had signed a "friendship contract" with each other in 1911, when they were still boys. Pollock had helped Horkheimer break free from his domineering father and remained a devoted friend until his death in 1970. Leo Löwenthal joined the institute in 1926, followed in 1930 by the psychoanalyst Erich Fromm and in 1932 by Herbert Marcuse. On January 30, 1933, the Nazi paramilitary Sturmabteilung seized Horkheimer's house in the tony Frankfurt suburb of Kronberg. Sensing what might happen, Horkheimer and his wife had checked into a hotel several days earlier and in short order emigrated to Geneva. After the Nazis became the second strongest party in the Reichstag elections of September 1930, Horkheimer had a branch of the Frankfurt Institute established in Geneva, and in 1931 the foundation's assets were transferred to the Netherlands for safekeeping. The Nazis shuttered the Frankfurt Institute for Social Research on March 13, 1933, due to "subversive activities" and confiscated the sixty-thousand-volume library. Max Horkheimer, Theodor Adorno, Friedrich Pollock, and others had already been stripped of their teaching licenses per the "Aryan paragraph" in Nazi legislation that barred Jews and other non-Aryan people from many professions and aspects of public life. In 1934 the institute moved to Columbia University in New York, where the Austrian sociologist Paul Lazarsfeld was already running the Bureau of Applied Social Research.

The Institute for Social Research, with Horkheimer and Pollock at the helm, administered around $200,000—thanks in large part to Weil—to over two hundred German Jewish scientists and issued countless affidavits to enable researchers of Jewish descent to immigrate to the United States. Whereas the institute had once embraced Marxist language, Horkheimer now prohibited its use. "Capitalist social order" thus became "modern industrial society," and "class struggle" was replaced by "conflict."[6]

When Horkheimer and his wife, who went by Maidon, arrived in Pacific Palisades in 1941, they waited out the first four weeks in another house until their villa in the Riviera was ready: "All that '20 minutes to Hollywood' and '30 minutes to Los Angeles' is pure bluster. It's about twice that, and only if you include tickets for speeding," Horkheimer groused in a letter to his friend Pollock, who had stayed in New York for the time being.[7] In June the Horkheimers moved into their spacious bungalow at 13542 D'Este Drive, a nearly half-acre plot, today the site of a home built in 1996. The housewarming party on July 12, 1941, turned into a "buffet dinner that lasted well into the night and a rather torturous orgy of historical, political, and philosophical discussion," the newcomers' neighbor Thomas Mann wrote in his diary. "The Jews have a sense of Hitler's greatness that I can't stand."[8]

In Pacific Palisades Horkheimer continued to meet regularly with other institute members: Friedrich Pollock, who always had a bedroom reserved for him at the Horkheimers'; Theodor Adorno, who lived in nearby Brentwood; and Herbert Marcuse, who lived in the "professors' part" of Santa Monica and whose house had a sign that read "Institute of Social Research, Office Los Angeles," "as if made for our purposes," Horkheimer wrote to Leo Löwenthal.[9] To distinguish between Herbert Marcuse and the philosopher and essayist Ludwig Marcuse and his wife, Erna (also known as Sascha), who had emigrated to Los Angeles in 1939, Horkheimer referred to the latter two as "the poor Marcuses," and with good reason: in 1941 he wrote to Pollock, "Sascha Marcuse needs another typewriter. Hers is broken. She heard from David, who supposedly heard it from our Marcuse, that we get lower prices. . . . If there is a way to give the poor Marcuses one we no longer need, or to get one otherwise, it would of course be very nice."[10] Sascha Marcuse was just one of the many women in exile who kept their hapless husbands afloat while the men clung to their old, now unprofitable jobs. She trained as a medical massage therapist and practiced for many years.

Ludwig Marcuse was not alone—the philosopher Ernst Bloch lived in a state of precarity as well. Adorno reported to his friend Horkheimer, "On top of it all, Bloch has been fired from his job as a dishwasher because he couldn't keep up with the pace, and now earns his living bundling old paper in a dirty hole. His wife worked as a waitress, but lost her job due to illness and can't find anything in the arms industry, either, because she is an enemy alien."[11] At least the "beardy philosopher," as Thomas Mann dubbed Felix Weil, lived without financial woes.[12] Weil had returned to Argentina, then moved to New York in 1935 and authored a major study on Argentina's politics and economics, *The Argentine Riddle*, at the Institute for Social Research. In 1945 he and his fifth wife, Helen, settled in Pacific Palisades. Weil invited friends to his new home, a villa built in 1938 at 533 Spoleto Drive, where Eva Herrmann had lived for a spell: Max Horkheimer and Theodor Adorno, the Feuchtwangers and Dieterles, Charlie Chaplin, and Thomas Mann, who enjoyed "discussions on Wagner that mixed enthusiasm and malice" with Hanns Eisler but criticized the "sweet punch" as "unnecessary and unpalatable as anything."[13]

Horkheimer also fraternized with Eisler and the Feuchtwangers. Marta, who found the philosopher as handsome as he was humorous, appreciated the tolerance he expressed in nearly all his discussions. The film director "William Dieterle with his enchanting wife and her mother [were] truly delightful friends" of the Horkheimers.[14] Neighborly relations with Thomas Mann, who had once "tangled" with Horkheimer in Germany and declared that "he could not talk to Marxists," also grew more cordial, and they visited each other regularly.[15] Whenever the Nobel laureate was away, the Horkheimers looked after things next door, watered the flowers, and welcomed him home with "cream, milk, cake, flowers."[16] In 1944 the Horkheimers, who had been naturalized in 1940, served as witnesses at the naturalization ceremony for Thomas and Katia Mann, which they celebrated in true American style with pancakes and maple syrup.

"Our lives are very regular," Horkheimer wrote to a friend in 1942:

> I get up around 9 in the morning and breakfast is ready. On the days we have a girl, we eat in the dining room, on the others in the kitchen. I routinely insist that I don't want anything more than a glass of water, at most, then find myself talked into having tea, eggs, sausages, jam, toast, and all sorts of other things. Then I either race to my study or the garage to go see Teddie [Adorno], who lives exactly 2½ miles away. Maidon calls after me to be back no later than 12:30, and I accommodate her request by returning a few minutes past 1:30. The same happens in the afternoon, only with adjusted times; I maintain a buffer

> of about 65 minutes. Maidon spends part of the day on housework, the other part on gardening, but I prefer the latter because housework generally has a bad effect on ladies' moods. The idea of cleaning, sweeping, and purging is known to be linked to warlike, pleasure-hating, downright antisemitic instincts. . . . When I nudge Maidon to slow down and garden more, she of course reminds me that I have to eat, too. Unfortunately it's true. Admitting this cannot, however, prevent my enjoyment of every chicken in the pot being tarnished by the thought that it has to be washed.[17]

It took seven minutes to drive to Adorno's house at 316 South Kenter Avenue in Brentwood. Theodor Wiesengrund was born in Frankfurt in 1903. His father was a German Jewish wine wholesaler, and his mother—whose maiden name he came to adopt—was a singer of Corsican descent. Adorno studied philosophy, psychology, music, and sociology and in 1924 earned his doctorate with a dissertation titled "Die Transzendenz des Dinglichen und Noematischen in Husserls Phänomenologie" (The transcendence of the material and the noematic in Husserl's phenomenology). Adorno also studied composition with Alban Berg in Vienna, took piano lessons from Salka Viertel's brother Eduard Steuermann, and served as an editor of the avant-garde music magazine *Der Anbruch* (The advent). Following his habilitation on Kierkegaard, titled *Die Konstruktion des Ästhetischen bei Kierkegaard* (*Kierkegaard: Construction of the Aesthetic*), Adorno became a private lecturer at the University of Frankfurt in 1931 and a contributor to the *Zeitschrift für Sozialforschung* (Journal of social research), published on behalf of the Institute for Social Research. In February 1938 Horkheimer invited him to the United States, where he joined the Institute for Social Research and directed the musical component of the Radio Research Project, an initiative at Princeton funded by the Rockefeller Foundation to examine the role of radio.

Like his friend Horkheimer, Adorno moved west in 1941. Impressed by Adorno's 1943 essay on Arnold Schoenberg, Thomas Mann turned to him for advice on music theory for his novel *Doctor Faustus*. The twelve-tone technique invented by the novel's protagonist, Adrian Leverkühn, is based on Adorno's

Schoenberg essay. In his "novel of a novel," *Zur Entstehung des Doktor Faustus* (On the origins of Doctor Faustus), Mann praised Adorno's involvement, although he deleted some parts before publication at the insistence of his daughter Erika, who could not stand the philosopher. Nevertheless, Mann inscribed a first-edition copy for Adorno with the words "To my secret advisor." Mann did not, however, tell Adorno that he had also conferred with Schoenberg. Mann had sought Adorno's help behind the composer's back, because Adorno and Schoenberg did what they could to avoid each other, although they were practically neighbors in Brentwood. After *Doctor Faustus* was published, Schoenberg felt the author had not sufficiently credited him as the creator of the twelve-tone technique; he terminated their friendship and publicly accused Mann of intellectual-property theft. In 1951, shortly before he died, Schoenberg finally suggested in a letter to Mann that they "bury the hatchet."[18]

While many of his contemporaries were resigned to the global political situation, Horkheimer—who was driven by rebellion against injustice, violence, and suffering as by a longing for truth, happiness, and the dissolution of authoritarian conditions—demanded full dedication of his employees. As he wrote to Weil, "The possibility, indeed the likelihood of death tomorrow does not relieve us of responsibility today. The fact that one will 'just be in a concentration camp in three years' does not justify any behavior, unless that behavior is taking even greater care of the substance of life. And that substance is our work."[19] In 1939 Horkheimer had decided to conduct a scientific study on Nazism and antisemitism, and in 1943 the American Jewish Committee finally agreed to finance it. Several members of the Institute for Social Research contributed to the project. Researchers analyzed antisemitic articles and speeches, created a scale for evaluating antisemitic opinion, and examined the psychology of antisemitism. To help coordinate, Horkheimer returned to New York for several months in 1944 and 1945. In Pacific Palisades he continued collaborating with Adorno on the seminal text of critical theory, *Dialectic of Enlightenment*, which they dedicated to Friedrich Pollock. The work—a collection of notes that bear the subtitle "Philosophical Fragments" in the original German—was published in 1944, the first run consisting of just five hundred hectographed copies.

SALKA VIERTEL SERVES SAUSAGE SOUP, AND ALFRED DÖBLIN SEARCHES FOR GOD

ON NOVEMBER 5, 1938, at the Hollywood agent Paul Kohner's urging (and in his office), the European Film Fund was established. Its founders were Charlotte Dieterle, Ernst Lubitsch, Liesl Frank, and the screenwriters Heinz Herald, a longtime dramaturge at Max Reinhardt's Deutsches Theater in Berlin; and Felix Raphael Joachimson, known in the business as Felix Jackson, who wrote flighty films for Columbia. As the best-known European in Hollywood, Lubitsch was appointed president. Frank volunteered as acting secretary, managing affidavits, collecting money, and finding apartments for new arrivals. Her husband, the writer Bruno Frank, was none too happy about his wife's involvement and wanted her close by at all times.

The situation in Europe had worsened since Austria went "back home to the Reich." In response the nonprofit European Film Fund aimed to field the countless requests—for affidavits, jobs, money, and other aid—from filmmakers in Europe who were being forced to emigrate (or who already had) and coordinate between them and more established émigrés in Los Angeles. Instead of supporting other filmmakers individually, those emigrants who could were encouraged to make donations to the fund, which disbursed a mix of loans and grants. Many donated a percentage of their earnings—for those Kohner's agency represented, the money was automatically deducted—while others, such as the big-time directors Michael Curtiz and William Wyler, routinely sent in larger sums. Accordingly, records preserved in Kohner's papers reveal the range of donations made between May 1, 1941, and April 30, 1942: the journalist Josef Mischel, who was hungry for screenplay commissions, sent in $2.00. The actor Erwin Kalser, who had occasionally played cultivated older gentlemen in Hollywood since 1939, gave $7.67. Albert Bassermann donated $20; Vicki Baum, $50; Charlotte Dieterle, $300; Ernst Lubitsch, $1,200; and Henry Koster, $1,300.

On October 24, 1939, at a meeting in Fritzi Massary's house in Beverly Hills, the European Film Fund devised a plan to rescue some of the most famous German-language authors. Kohner pitched the plan to the major film studios as a solid investment and in 1940 helped secure one-year contracts with a weekly salary of one hundred dollars, five times the average income of refugees from Nazi Germany. The studios hired the writers, few of whom had any film experience, to help them obtain visas to immigrate. Leonhard Frank, Heinrich Mann, Alfred Neumann, and Friedrich Torberg worked for Warner Brothers, while Alfred Döblin, Walter Mehring, Alfred Polgar, Wilhelm Speyer, and Jan Lustig—the only one whose contract was extended—went to MGM. These men of letters, whose pronounced elitism compelled them to despise the pictures, often struggled to accept the charity that had saved their lives. "There they sat at these production companies; not speaking English, unfamiliar with film-making, brimming with contempt for the industry," Ludwig Marcuse wrote.[1] It turned out these writers were in the same boat as so many European actors in Hollywood: "If I film one or even two days a week, I'm making a decent annual income. Acting in the pictures isn't work," Richard Révy wrote to a friend. "Unless you're Chaplin, it's day labor peppered with boredom."[2]

Curt Goetz, the leading Germany comedy writer of his day, rejected a five-year, $500-a-week contract with MGM and purchased a chicken farm in Van Nuys instead. He said he would rather peer "under the tailfeathers" of two thousand chickens than look one Hollywood producer in the face.[3] Arnold Schoenberg was also unwilling to meet the demands of film production. In her memoir Salka Viertel recalled a telling exchange between the composer and the great American film producer Irving Thalberg:

> I still see him before me, leaning forward in his chair, both hands clasped over the handle of the umbrella, his burning, genius's eyes on Thalberg, who, standing behind his desk, was explaining why he wanted a great composer for the scoring of the *Good Earth*. When he

> came to: "Last Sunday when I heard the lovely music you have written. . . ." Schoenberg interrupted sharply: "I don't write 'lovely' music."
>
> . . . [In] a surprisingly literary though faulty English, [Schoenberg] conveyed what he thought in general of music in films: that it was simply terrible. The whole handling of sound was incredibly bad, meaningless, numbing all expression; the leveling monotony of the dialogue was unbearable. He had read the *Good Earth* and he would not undertake the assignment unless he was given complete control over the sound, including the spoken words.
>
> "What do you mean by complete control?" asked Thalberg, incredulously.
>
> "I mean that I would have to work with the actors," answered Schoenberg. "They would have to speak in the same pitch and key as I compose it in. It would be similar to 'Pierrot Lunaire' but, of course, less difficult." He turned to me and asked if I remembered some verses of the Pierrot and would I speak them. I remembered very well: "*Der Mond, den man mit Augen trinkt. . . .*" ("*Augen*" high and long.) I reproduced it quite faithfully, watching Thalberg's face. He must have been visualizing Luise Rainer and Paul Muni singing their lines in a similar key. But he did not move a muscle of his face. "Well, Mr. Schoenberg," he said, "the director and I have different ideas and they may contradict yours. You see, the director wants to handle the actors himself."
>
> "He could do that after they have studied their lines with me," offered Schoenberg magnanimously.[4]

Amazingly, Thalberg was undeterred. Negotiations fell apart only when Schoenberg doubled "the price of prostitution" the next day to an unheard-of $50,000.[5] The composer, who earned a modest $4,800 a year as a visiting professor at the University of California, Los Angeles, could have lived comfortably off the project for years. "If you sell your soul to the devil, you'd better charge a very high price," Schoenberg said. He turned down all the film scoring offers he received, calling the underpaid work "artistic suicide."[6] When he was forced to retire in 1944, he was making $5,100 annually, and his finances were shakier than ever. He collected a small pension, calculated according to years of employment, which initially came out to $26.60 per month. This increased to $40.38 per month in March 1945, earnings from which he had to support himself, his wife, and three children.

Leonhard Frank, a successful novelist since before World War I, described his unfulfilling work as a Hollywood screenwriter in his autobiographical novel *Links, wo das Herz ist* (*Heart on the Left*), the protagonist Michael Vierkant a stand-in for Frank:

> At Warner Brothers' Studio, Michael was provided an office, a secretary who spoke English and German, and enough writing supplies for a dozen screenplays. For weeks nothing happened. . . . Michael had to report for work at nine on the dot every morning. The studio receptionist marked his arrival. He left at five after a day's idling and received a hundred-dollar check for his boredom every Saturday evening. The American screenwriter in the next office, who earned $3,500 a week, cleared up the puzzle as to why no one sent work Michael's way. He said, with a companionable grin, "They figure there's no way a writer who works for a hundred bucks a week could write anything decent." . . . Successful German film people in Hollywood, who for years had earned huge sums and lived the lives of millionaires in sumptuous mansions, flocked to Michael and drove him to their magnificent palaces in the latest Cadillac models. But as soon as they realized he wasn't destined for stardom in the Hollywood firmament, they forgot his name.[7]

Frank was nearing sixty when his contract with Warner Brothers expired, and he was forced to rely on donations. Early on he would drive to the Pacific coast and "stare into the distance, overcome by yearning for Europe, with the feeling that it lay beyond every horizon."[8] A few weeks passed before he realized he was looking in the wrong direction—toward Asia.

Alfred Döblin, best known for his 1929 novel, *Berlin Alexanderplatz*, had two targets on his back in Nazi Germany: he was both a Jew and a Social Democrat. In 1933 he fled to Switzerland, then on to France and Portugal. He made it to the United States in 1940, thanks to a contract with MGM. The weekly hundred-dollar pay was plenty for Döblin; his wife, Erna; and their youngest son, Stephan, as rent was just sixty dollars for their unit at 1842 North Cherokee Avenue, a Hollywood apartment complex the actor Alexander Granach and the director Leopold Jessner called home for a while as well. After one year exactly, on October 7, 1941, Döblin's contract expired. Brecht wrote in his journal, "he's left with nothing, yet that old berlin sense of humor remains. what kind of business could he open? to become a doctor he'd have to study for a year and to become a healer he'd need to know english (i can't put a man under hypnosis then ask him to help me find the word i'm looking for)."[9] For six months after his termination, Döblin collected eighteen dollars' a week unemployment, but, after those benefits expired, the family relied on help from wealthier acquaintances. From November 1942 on, they lived in very humble circumstances at 1347 North Citrus Avenue for thirty-five dollars a month.

When Warner Brothers ended Heinrich Mann's screenwriting contract after a year, money soon became so tight that he had to pawn the cheap furniture he had bought on credit, for which $13.50 was due the fifth of the month. Brecht journaled on December 3, 1941, "he receives welfare, picks up his 18$ 50 unemployment benefit every week, as his contract with the movie company ran out, like döblin's. he's over 70. meanwhile his brother thomas is building himself a big villa."[10] Given his visibility within the emigrant community, Thomas Mann had little choice but to support his indigent older brother, first directly and later through the European Film Fund.

There was nothing unusual about these men's fates, as most exiled writers remained unknown to the American public. Those who did well were the real exceptions, best-selling authors such as Vicki Baum, Emil Ludwig, or Franz Werfel, whose wildly kitschy *The Song of Bernadette*, a novel that tells the story of the nineteenth-century French saint, sold three hundred thousand copies in its first three weeks. Twentieth-Century Fox acquired the rights to the book for a handsome $125,000. The film, starring Jennifer Jones, premiered in late 1943, received twelve Oscar nominations, and won four of the coveted statuettes.

ROMANISCHES CAFÉ had been a hub of intellectual and artistic life in Weimar Berlin. The coffeehouse was a forum for new ideas, a meeting place for producers and agents, a job fair for fresh talent, and a workplace for writers. Many geniuses considered it their own private study. Patrons—some might say residents—lingered for hours over a single cup of coffee, certain they would bump into someone they knew. Everyday life looked much the same for the literary class in Vienna, Prague, and other big cities. These people now felt adrift in Los Angeles—a series of suburbs in search of a city, they scoffed—where a car and telephone were all they had to protect themselves from utter seclusion.

This isolation worsened for exiles when the United States entered the war in 1942. A curfew between 8:00 p.m. and 6:00 a.m. was imposed on all "enemy aliens," who had to stay within five miles of home during the day, "which makes personal interaction in this sprawling city all but impossible," Lion Feuchtwanger explained to a friend.[11] Erich Maria Remarque, who lived in a lavish bungalow at the Beverly Wilshire Hotel, complained, "The curfew makes everything more surreal somehow; it's a kind of glassy waiting; I'm not reading, moving, working any more, sleeping—it's all quite absent, without rebellion or excitement, simply accepting the facts,—that we don't live in Germany because of our democratic thinking;—& are now half-confined in a democracy because we come from Germany."[12] Thomas Mann and Albert Einstein tried in vain to intercede. The regulation was not in effect on the East Coast, where there was understandably less fear of a Japanese invasion. Curiously, however, it did not apply to Austrians nor to Germans who had gained citizenship in other countries before the United States joined the war, such as Thomas Mann, a Czechoslovak citizen since 1936.

WEALTHY ÉMIGRÉS such as William Dieterle or Erich Wolfgang Korngold would occasionally treat guests to lunch at Musso and Frank's Grill, a fabled oak-paneled eatery in Hollywood, while Thomas Mann and Alma Mahler-Werfel were known to enjoy champagne and caviar at Romanoff's, but inevitably a culture of private gatherings developed.[13] Not only were these get-togethers an indispensable outlet for exchange, given the loss of coffeehouse culture; they were a form of social existence, the absence of which immediately translated into loneliness. One was less of a stranger when in the company of other friendly strangers, Ludwig Marcuse mused. As Fritz Kortner described in his memoir, however, socializing in Hollywood was dictated by "caste. For the most part, people associated with those who earned about the same."[14] Christiane Grautoff reported a similar phenomenon: "All the screenwriters, illustrators, and transcribers who earned five hundred a week stuck together and never let themselves be seen with those who were paid a thousand. Of course, those who fell into the three-to-five thousand dollar category had a broader range of cohorts to choose from. From five grand upwards, one was free to just pick up the phone and ring L. B. Mayer directly."[15]

This did not, however, apply to Sunday afternoons at Salka Viertel's in Pacific Palisades, which set these gatherings apart and prompted Berthold Viertel to describe them as a "refuge of humanity."[16] Salka's guest list was motley by comparison to those at the Santa Monica or Bel Air homes of Hollywood tycoons or even those at the Feuchtwanger or Mann residences in Pacific Palisades. She was no less welcoming to emigrants who lived off hundred-dollar paychecks, unemployment benefits, or donations from friends than she was to Hollywood stars and publishing magnates. Nowhere else did the successful and the unsuccessful, the nobodies and the nobility, members of different income brackets, nationalities, professions, and otherwise segregated spheres mingle as naturally as on Mabery Road, where there was neither a dress code nor opportunity for vanity and self-promotion. Some people stuck to Hollywood parties "because their agent thought it better, as they were bound to meet someone wildly important there," then did everything they could "to catch the eye of the person they hoped would give them their next role," but Sundays at Salka's were *gemütlich* (cozy, familiar, easy), as Helene Thimig would say.[17]

Thomas Mann traded in his champagne and caviar for "sausage soup" and beer, conversed with Adorno, laughed at Chaplin's impersonations of Churchill and Gandhi, and relished the comic's "careful listening" as Mann told him about *Doctor Faustus*.[18] Chaplin brought Hanns Eisler on board as a musical ghostwriter, and the eccentric Mercedes de Acosta fell in love with Garbo, who was busy planning a film adaptation of *Hamlet* with Max Reinhardt. Salka displayed "a kind of generosity . . . as a hostess and in conversation," Fritz Kortner's daughter Marianne, who often visited Mabery Road as a child, recounted: "She was different than most women of her generation. She was independent. She was not shy, didn't hold back, and participated actively in discussions but was never overbearing. She had an amazing way of talking to people and drawing the best out of them. She also knew how to listen. Many of her parties were planned such that certain Americans and certain emigrants would meet, and that was very deliberate on her part. She helped countless people in every way. One felt protected by her, and truly, I believe everyone felt that."[19]

Early on nearly all Salka's guests worked in film. In the 1930s and 1940s, stars of the stage and screen were joined by luminaries of other fields. The roster included George Cukor, Ernst Deutsch, Ernst Lubitsch, Fritzi Massary, Tallulah Bankhead, Jean Renoir, Marlene Dietrich, the producer Gottfried Reinhardt—Max Reinhardt's son and Salka's lover from 1933 to 1943, who was twenty-two years her junior and helped host the salons when Berthold was away—Eleonora and Francesco von Mendelssohn, Humphrey Bogart and Lauren Bacall, Charles Laughton, John Huston, Montgomery Clift, and Judy Garland, as well as the psychologist Alfred Adler, Arnold and Gertrud Schoenberg, the conductor Leopold Stokowksi, Albert Einstein, and the writers Aldous Huxley, Lion Feuchtwanger, Bertolt Brecht, Bruno and Liesl Frank, Franz Werfel and Alma Mahler-Werfel, Erich Maria Remarque, Clifford Odets, André Malraux, and Norman Mailer. Brecht's assistant and lover, Ruth Berlau, and Christopher Isherwood lived in the Viertels' in-law apartment above the garage at different times.

Exiles and Americans interacted in many ways, of course, and the influence of emigration on American culture cannot be understated. Victor Gruen, for instance, was born Victor David Grünbaum in Vienna in 1903, emigrated to the United States in 1938, settled in Hollywood in 1940, and is credited with inventing the shopping mall, that emblem of suburban America. One of Arnold Schoenberg's many students was Oscar Levant, who at the height of his popularity was the highest-paid concert pianist in the United States, beating out Horowitz and Rubinstein; it was through Levant that Schoenberg met his future tennis partner George Gershwin as well as John Cage, who became one of the twentieth century's most influential composers. The painter and gallery owner Galka Scheyer introduced Cage to the pioneering filmmaker Oskar Fischinger, who was born in Gelnhausen in 1900 and emigrated to the United States in 1936. Fischinger's abstract works are considered the forerunners of the modern video clip, and Cage was swayed by the auteur's notion that it was possible to free the soul inherent in all objects by drawing sound from them. Tennessee Williams drew inspiration from Thomas Mann, whose writing he first encountered in 1935, in such works as *Mysteries of the Joy Rio* and *Hard Candy*. It is doubtful, however, that Christopher Isherwood took him to meet Mann on San Remo Drive in 1943, as the playwright claimed.

"IN THE WORLD OF ÉMIGRÉS everyone has [an] open house, and so in California we saw more German writers than we had in Munich," Katia Mann wrote in her memoir.[20] When she hosted, she was known to serve "dumpling soup, roast beef, [and] ambrosia."[21] Friendships and collaborations like the one between Lion Feuchtwanger and Bertolt Brecht deepened—they invited each other over, spoke regularly on the phone, celebrated Christmas together (first in 1941 with Elisabeth Bergner, Alexander Granach, and Fritz Lang, then in 1942 with Eisler and Homolka)—yet they maintained the formal *Sie* form of address; Brecht's letters always opened with "Dear Doctor." Old neighborly relationships were revived, like those between the Manns and the conductor Bruno Walter or Bruno and Liesl Frank, but new acquaintances were made as well: Mann and Schoenberg first met in 1938, at a soirée hosted by Vicki Baum in Pacific Palisades, then didn't see each other again until 1940, at the Viertels' house. In 1942 Hanns Eisler introduced Brecht and Schoenberg. The circle was small, the network tightly woven. At one point Brecht, Horkheimer, Adorno, Eisler, and Kortner all employed the same housekeeper. The author and film editor Albrecht Joseph worked as a secretary for the European Film Fund as well as for Emil Ludwig, Franz Werfel, Thomas Mann, and Bruno Frank. He had an affair with Bruno Walter's daughter Lotte; married and divorced Lella Simon, who later married the composer Franz Waxman; and then married his second wife, Alma Mahler-Werfel's daughter Anna.

Émigrés met for tea, small dinner parties that grew larger over the course of the evening, and big garden parties. People played tennis and cooled off in the pool, despite concerns about loved ones in Europe who were desperate for visas or had already been deported. They experienced real qualms about living in a paradise like Pacific Palisades at a time when millions were being murdered, but "not enjoying the water or blocking out the sun wouldn't have been much help to Hitler's victims," Albrecht Joseph commented.[22] Charades, which everyone just called "The Game," was a favorite pastime. Even Thomas Mann would shout out guesses. Whether he refused to take a turn, as some claim, or excelled at pantomime, as others insist, we will never know. Birthday parties were a particular highlight, guest lists curated with extra care. As Berthold Viertel reflected, "One of the loveliest aspects of our life as exiles in Hollywood is the warmth with which birthdays are celebrated. They are not only milestones of time in our decidedly timeless existence here; they are occasions—almost the only occasions—on which the colony is reminded of its togetherness."[23]

On May 2, 1941, forty-five people gathered at Salka Viertel's house for a belated birthday celebration for Heinrich Mann, who had turned seventy in March. They gathered around Ping-Pong tables set for the event and feasted as they once had in the old country: there was turtle soup, trout Meunière, beef tenderloin and veal medallions with Burgundy sauce, served with French fries and asparagus in mayonnaise. The evening may have been the final moment of happiness for Heinrich Mann, whose years in exile were characterized by loneliness and poverty. The Mann brothers' speeches lasted so long, the meat ended up terribly overcooked, "but the guests were elated and hungry and did not mind," Salka Viertel recalled.

The Mann brothers' relationship had once been defined by embittered rivalry. Heinrich, born in 1871, emerged as a leading satirist of the Wilhelmian era, with his novels *Professor Unrat* and *The Patrioteer*. He enjoyed greater fame until his younger brother overtook him. From the first Thomas—who sublimated his homosexuality—had expressed disgust at Heinrich's sexual indulgence and dissolute ways. The two had also fallen out over their divergent political views. They avoided each other for years but now rejoined in exile;

Heinrich, whose fame had faded, was touchingly attached to his brother, who was very aware of his power.

In recounting Heinrich Mann's birthday party, Salka Viertel wrote,

> Bruno Frank's and Lion Feuchtwanger's speeches were brief and in a lighter vein. The dessert, my chocolate cake, a "specialty of the house," was served and disappeared rapidly. Toward the end of the dinner Martha [*sic*] Feuchtwanger spontaneously offered a toast, "To Nelly, who saved Heinrich Mann's life, practically carrying him in her arms on their rough trek through the Pyrenees. She supported him with her loving strength and gave courage to us all."
>
> Nelly hid her face in her hands when we surrounded her to clink glasses and then, screaming with laughter, pointed to her red dress, which had burst open revealing her bosom in a lace bra.[24]

Nelly Mann, a "dreadful trollop," was a thorn in Thomas Mann's side. His journals mention "ghastly behavior by Heinrich's *Weib*" or that "the *Weib*'s conduct was appalling."[25] Katia, too, was upset by her sister-in-law "running riot in a drunken state."[26] Nelly was scarcely an outlier in the family—Erika was a drinker, her brother Klaus was addicted to drugs, and even Thomas was hooked on pills—but there was very little patience when it came to Nelly's indiscretions, especially after she was arrested for drunk driving on February 26, 1942. After a night spent at the police station, she was released on $250 bail—money that Thomas and Katia had to front. To repay them Nelly pawned all her furniture, even the curtains. Ten days later she received a suspended sentence of sixty days' jail time; within two weeks she was given a probationary driver's license, and four weeks after that her full driving privileges were restored. Not only did her husband rely on her to get around, but Nelly needed to be able to drive to the many different jobs she held. She worked washing clothes and delivering milk; she even worked as an overnight guard at a hospital. "My wife works to put food on the table," Heinrich Mann told a friend.[27]

On November 10, 1943, Nelly hit an oncoming Pontiac and was due to appear in court on January 7. Had it been established that she was driving under the influence, her suspended sentence would have been added to the new one. Three days before the hearing, Nelly was admitted to the hospital after overdosing on sleeping pills. It was not her first suicide attempt, nor would it be her last. On December 17, 1944, Heinrich discovered his wife unconscious in their bedroom. Word got around that the ambulance tried hospital after hospital, "because the scruffy old man accompanying the dying woman didn't look too trustworthy—or should we say, creditworthy."[28] When one clinic finally admitted her, Nelly died of respiratory paralysis. Thomas Mann was compelled to pay for the funeral of "Heinrich's unfortunate wife, who did him much harm."[29]

HELENE WEIGEL threw Döblin's belated sixty-fifth birthday party. Lion Feuchtwanger, Leopold Jessner, and Thomas Mann were among the 180 illustrious guests who gathered on August 14, 1943, at El Pablo Rey Playhouse, a theater and event space in Santa Monica, to honor the increasingly isolated and impoverished writer. Heinrich Mann gave the welcoming address; Eduard Steuermann performed pieces by Hanns Eisler, Arnold Schoenberg, and Ernst Toch; Friedrich Hollaender's ex-wife, Blandine Ebinger, crooned old Berlin chansons; and Alexander Granach, Fritz Kortner, and Peter Lorre read from Döblin's books. Ludwig Hardt unintentionally amused the audience with his recitation of Heinrich von Kleist's "Gebet des Zoroaster" (The prayer of Zarathustra): when he got to the part about overlooking the follies and errors of humankind, Hardt mistakenly replaced the word *Gattung*, meaning "species" or "kind," with the word *Gattin*, or "wife"—most in attendance knew that Döblin had just spent the weekend with Hardt's wife at their house in Pacific Palisades.

Brecht, who was among the partygoers, noted that "at the end döblin delivered a speech against moral relativism and in favor of concrete religious measures, which hurt the irreligious feelings of most of the revelers. the more rational listeners were gripped by awkwardness." Döblin had left the Jewish faith in 1912 and been baptized a Catholic in 1941 but had concealed his conversion until then, perhaps so as not to upset his friends, out of solidarity with the persecuted in Nazi Germany, or because he relied on financial support from Jewish organizations in the United States. Brecht felt betrayed that his friend and role model was turning his back on atheism and thus on their shared worldview and approach to life. Döblin further alienated his guests by acknowledging his guilt in Hitler's rise, "because i didn't seek god."[30] It was an absolute scandal, and several people left without saying goodbye.

EXILE IN PACIFIC PALISADES was not all friendship and respect, anyway. Those less fortunate, for instance, were disgusted by Erich Maria Remarque's flashy lifestyle. The disparities that existed within the community were magnified in the microcosm of Pacific Palisades, home to four of the most affluent émigré households: Mann, Feuchtwanger, Ludwig, and Baum. Bruno Frank was piqued by Lion Feuchtwanger's warm relationship with Brecht, whom he found repellent. As for Brecht, he fraternized with Heinrich Mann but despised his younger brother, Thomas, whom he called "the reptile" and considered a politically opportunistic spokesperson for the bourgeoisie. Brecht dismissed *Joseph and His Brothers* as "the encyclopedia of petty bourgeois know-it-alls."[31] He also took digs against Adorno, though they regularly saw each other, and railed against the "double-clown horkheimer and pollock."[32] He had as little to do with Bruno Frank, Erich Maria Remarque, and Marlene Dietrich as he did with the pious Franz Werfel, whom he called "saint frunz of hollywood"— in this regard alone, Brecht agreed with Thomas Mann, who also mocked Werfel's Catholic faith. Hanns Eisler described Schoenberg's music to Brecht as "establishing naive miscalculation in music."[33] Katia Mann did not think Schoenberg a "very winning man," and she "took an immediate dislike to his wife, Gertrud," though she admits Gertrud "didn't have a very easy time of it with her tyrannical husband." She also felt that Alma Mahler-Werfel "always drank far too many sweet liqueurs and was rather malicious by nature."[34] Emil Ludwig spoke "very poisonously" of Thomas Mann, which Ludwig Hardt immediately reported back to him.[35]

"FOOLISH PERSON," was all Thomas Mann had to say in his diary after bumping into Emil Ludwig.[36] Despite having spent time with Ludwig back in Switzerland in the 1930s, here in Pacific Palisades Mann gave him a wide berth. Ludwig was born in Breslau in 1881. His father, Hermann Ludwig Cohn, was a liberal-minded, assimilated Jew who worked as an ophthalmologist. His uncle, Fritz von Friedlaender-Fuld, had made his fortune trading in coal and lignite, but by 1905 Ludwig—who had also earned a doctorate in law—turned his back on a respectable career at his uncle's company in favor of a more bohemian existence as a poet. In 1906 he and his wife, Elga, moved to Moscia on Lake Maggiore in southern Switzerland, not far from Monte Verità, which at the turn of the century was a destination for nude sun worshippers, occult charlatans, and upper-crust anarchists. These prototypes of future hippies and tree huggers lived off raw fruit and vegetables, wore flowing robes or "air dresses" (i.e., nothing at all), weeded the gardens stark naked, and danced and tumbled in the buff.

Ludwig's poetry did not receive much attention or remuneration, but in the 1920s his fortunes turned with his own shift to literary biographies of famed artists and statesmen, written with a keen sense of storytelling. His largely anecdotal and eulogistic portraits of Goethe, Rembrandt, Napoleon, Wilhelm II, Otto von Bismarck, Abraham Lincoln, Michelangelo, and Heinrich Schliemann were translated into two dozen languages and sold countless copies worldwide. Ludwig, who drew a clear line between his work and historical fiction, was more of a psychographer than historian or a biographer (which was how he introduced himself). Ludwig, who looked to Goethe as a role model for his righteous dilettantism, explained his approach:

> I was never moved to find new sources, but rather to draw on common knowledge to reshape these figures so vividly that the man on the street can see them before his very eyes. What could be better than to inspire people, especially the youth, with tales of great men and to show them that even they were just humans who faced all the same hurdles and difficulties, confusion and suffering, yet they reached the pinnacle! It is only those who, unlike Olympic demigods, reveal their human character—that is, the struggle of genius with itself—who inspire young people to emulate them.[37]

Ludwig's renown as a journalist grew after an interview with Stalin in December 1931, in which he courageously reproached him for his ruthless response toward detractors. A year later he employed a clever interview technique to make Mussolini describe himself as a fascist Caesar. "Emil Ludwig doesn't have it easy," Kurt Tucholsky stated in 1932. "What he should do is send his critics a circular: 'Please pardon me for being so successful.'"[38] The Nazis burned Ludwig's books in 1933: "No to falsifying our history and belittling its great figures. Yes to reverence for our past!"[39] Ludwig's 1936 novel *The Davos Murder* tells the story of the Jewish student David Frankfurter, who that year had shot Wilhelm Gustloff, the Swiss branch leader of the Nazi Party. After reading it Joseph Goebbels fumed in his diary, "It's enough to make you antisemitic, if you weren't already. This Jewish pestilence must be obliterated."[40]

After the Anschluss in 1938 and the start of the war in 1939, Ludwig—who even in the 1920s had represented an "other," European-style Germany—no longer felt safe in Switzerland in the face of a possible German invasion. He emigrated to California, first to Montecito near Santa Barbara, then to Beverly Hills, and finally to Pacific Palisades in 1942. He lived in Aldous Huxley's rambling former residence at 701 Amalfi Drive (the house was torn down and replaced in 1965), and in 1944 Ludwig moved into a two-story house built ten years earlier, at 303 Grenola Street. He was a sociable fellow and would invite musicians such as Ernst Toch or Eric Zeisl over to play four-handed Viennese waltzes on the piano; he saw Bruno Frank some, though the two fell out in 1941; and he was friendly with Lion Feuchtwanger, but he does not seem to have integrated himself fully into any of the various circles. And although he was extremely generous and helped out many an impecunious fellow exile, there was not much warmth directed toward him. In his memoir Albrecht Joseph put it this way: "Emil Ludwig was a very sensitive, well-educated, gifted person, amiable and amusing, but all these excellent qualities were encased in a cloak of claptrap that ultimately made him insufferable."[41] Brecht was no less sparing: "a very inhibited, somewhat drunken, subaltern person, but with a 'spark,' utterly spiritless, unoriginal, but at the mercy of the original, foolish, but appreciative of wisdom."[42]

"TERRIBLY DISTURBED BY THE DWINDLING SENSE OF JUSTICE IN THIS COUNTRY"

BEYOND THE PETTY ANIMOSITIES and rampant gossip—Thomas Mann and Fritzi Massary, for instance, whispering about Maestro "[Arturo] Toscanini's venereal activity at age 82"—there were serious conflicts too.[1] The questions of German collective guilt and what should happen to Germany after the war split the exile community. There were acrimonious debates about "hard" or "soft" peace. On August 1, 1943, a group met at the Viertels' home in Pacific Palisades to issue a statement on the founding of the National Committee for Free Germany in the Soviet Union, a matter evidently reserved for men. While Heinrich and Thomas Mann, Lion Feuchtwanger, Ludwig Marcuse, Bruno Frank, the philosopher and physicist Hans Reichenbach—who had been teaching at the University of California since 1938—Bertolt Brecht, and Berthold Viertel deliberated on the second floor, Salka Viertel, Liesl Frank, Sascha Marcuse, Marta Feuchtwanger, Elisabeth Reichenbach, and Helene Weigel visited downstairs. The players upstairs drafted and signed a declaration that emphasized the need to "draw a sharp distinction between the Hitler regime and its associated classes on the one hand and the German people on the other" and that expressed their confidence that a democratic Germany could be built after the war. Brecht was infuriated by the fact that Thomas Mann, in a display of doleful "katzenjammer," withdrew his signature by telephone the following day, saying he did not want the Germans to be able to deny their culpability too easily.[2]

It had taken Mann three years before joining the fight against Nazi Germany in 1936. He had since made a public display of his support of Franklin D. Roosevelt and US policies, and he contributed to the war effort in whatever way he could. For four years Mann—who had been declared "vermin" (*Volksschädling*) and stripped of German citizenship—addressed his former fellow citizens in Germany in the monthly radio program *Deutsche Hörer!* and recorded more than fifty speeches, mostly at the NBC studio on Hollywood Boulevard, "to arouse resistance within Germany."[3] As early as September 1941, he spoke of crimes against "Poles and Jews"; in November he mentioned "mass gassing operations" for the first time; and in June 1942 he confronted his listeners with the "brutal mass murder at Mauthausen."[4]

The global response was tepid, and on April 10, 1943, a disillusioned Mann wrote in his diary, "The slaughter of the Jews has been met with general approval, or at least indifference."[5] Unlike many exiles, he saw Germany through the eyes of the victims of German aggression. He felt the Royal Air Force was justified in bombing his hometown of Lübeck on the night of March 29, 1942, after the German Luftwaffe had destroyed Coventry, and he "had no objection to the doctrine that everything must be paid for."[6] On July 18, 1944, Mann wrote, "The news about the bombardment of Munich with 6,000 dead and 100,000 homeless, destruction of the Brown House, Palace of Justice, etc.—Cannot suppress feelings of satisfaction."[7]

Mann was criticized alternately for advocating for soft peace and for espousing Vansittartism, the latter swipe clearly intended to tarnish his reputation. Sir Robert Gilbert Vansittart was an English diplomat who was elevated to "Lord" in 1941. A Francophile and Germanophobe, Vansittart blamed World War II not only on the Nazis but on the Germans before Hitler came to power. He was accused of "anti-German racism" and allegedly considered Germans incurably aggressive and warlike by nature. As the jacket to Vansittart's 1941 book, *Black Record: Germans Past and Present* reads, "[The German] has always been the barbarian, the war-lover, the enemy—furtive or avowed—of humanitarianism, liberalism and Christian civilisation."[8] In a speech delivered to the Library of Congress on May 29, 1945, Thomas Mann maintained that "there are not two Germanies, a good one and an evil one, but only a single one, which turned its best by devilry into bad."[9] After all that had happened, he wrote to Agnes E. Meyer, there could be no limit to the depths of "the fall and the penance."[10] Brecht did not hold back in excoriating Mann, whom he disliked anyway, in his satirical poem: When "the Nobel Prize winner Thomas Mann granted the Americans and English the right to chastise the German people for ten long years for the crimes of the Hitler regime."[11]

In response to Germany's defeat on May 7, 1945, Mann noted, "It is not exactly elation I feel. . . . So far, there has been no disavowal of Nazism, no word that the 'seizure of power' was a terrible misfortune, its authorization and facilitation a crime of the highest order. The denial and condemnation of the deeds of National Socialism inside and out, the declaration of wanting to return to truth, to justice, to humanity—where are they? The ridiculous rifts among the émigrés, the envious hatred of my stance and of me contribute to tamping down the joy.—Physical survival provides a certain satisfaction."[12]

Not two months later, however, he was rattled by "the disposal of Germany. The preposterous expansion of Poland to the Oder. The mass dislocation into the constricted country, in an orderly and decent way. The reduction to an agricultural status (while partitioning main agricultural areas) with some harmless industry for domestic use. Presumably planning to reduce the population to 40 million or so. No surprises there, but still shocking as a definitive plan." Mann also spoke out against the possible division of Germany. On December 17, 1945, he signed a statement—albeit "not entirely lightheartedly"—calling on the United States to tread lightly in its policies toward Germany, which was threatened by hunger and economic calamity.[13] He himself stressed that he had no intention of ever leaving the United States again.

Emil Ludwig, who was in poor health and, unlike Mann, really did subscribe to Vansittartism, had by this point returned to Germany and made his way to Weimar, where he discovered the lost coffins of Goethe and Schiller. He ultimately returned to his old home in Moscia and set about writing his memoirs. Ludwig, once spoiled by success and now nearly destitute, tried in vain to find a German publisher before his death in 1948. That year Erich Maria Remarque moved back to Switzerland, after having left Los Angeles for New York in 1942 and become a US citizen in 1947. He settled in Porto Ronco, not far from Moscia, and lived there until his death in 1970 with Paulette Goddard, Charlie Chaplin's ex-wife, whom Remarque married in 1958.

Filmmakers such as Billy Wilder and Otto Preminger were not unique in calling the United States home, having established their lives and careers stateside. For Ludwig Marcuse, who became a US citizen in 1944, a new chapter opened when he was appointed professor of German literature and philosophy at the University of Southern California in 1945: "Until 1945, I was still living in Germany, even if my address read Beverly Hills, California." It was only then that Marcuse—who had moved mainly in emigrant circles, written in German, and spoken almost exclusively German—began an intensive study of English. In 1949 he visited Germany for the first time in sixteen years, although he rejected the widespread critical attitude toward emigration there: "The stupidest line you heard in Germany after 1945 was that we [exiles] had been perched in box seats, enjoying the distant spectacle through opera glasses. What we did see with great clarity was the very people who later said such things—they were living off a plundered Europe."[14] Marcuse and his wife moved back to Germany after his retirement in 1959 and settled in the Upper Bavarian spa town of Bad Wiessee.

Leonhard Frank, whose novel *Carl and Anna* was unexpectedly optioned by MGM in 1945, took the money and left "the eternally sunny, out-of-touch hell of Hollywood" for New York, where he devoted himself to writing.[15] When he returned to Germany in 1950, the onetime bestseller had to face the fact that he was largely forgotten there. Alma Mahler-Werfel, who was naturalized in 1946, a year after her husband, Franz Werfel, died, relocated to New York in 1951 as well. When she developed diabetes, this inveterate antisemite declared that she could not possibly have such a Jewish disease and continued to drink her daily bottle of sweet Bénédictine against her doctor's orders. Between her poor hearing and complicated personality, she grew increasingly isolated.

THE RED SCARE swept the United States in light of the looming Cold War between Western powers and the Soviet Union that followed the end of World War II and the death of President Franklin D. Roosevelt. Calls to attack the resurrected red specter reached a fever pitch. An emotionally charged, if not outright hysterical, hunt for subversive communist elements in the country began. Joseph McCarthy, a farmer's son from Wisconsin, became one of the most powerful US senators in history by exploiting the fears of the postwar period. He suspected Soviet agents everywhere, even in the White House. The Federal Bureau of Investigation, which was under the aegis of the dictatorial, arch-conservative administrator J. Edgar Hoover, completed successful purges of government offices, then moved on to target American artists and intellectuals—the exiles among them.

The feds had begun compiling a dossier on Lion Feuchtwanger in November 1940, not least because of his visit with Stalin in 1937. The FBI surveilled and interrogated him, intercepted his letters and telegrams, monitored his bank accounts, and enlisted residents on Paseo Miramar to report the license plate numbers of cars parked outside his house. Marta and Helene Weigel are rumored to have spent hours on the phone exchanging recipes from a Polish cookbook to annoy the FBI, which had tapped both their phone lines; the bureau was also checking the Brechts' mail, recording all visitors, and rummaging through their garbage.

Nearly all the exiles were spied on, including Thomas Mann, though all the dirt his neighbor could produce was that he was arrogant and received visitors at all hours. Erika Mann was a target too, though she had offered to help the FBI track down fascist spies. Klaus Mann's "sexual perversion" was enough to attract the bureau's attention.[16] In 1948 he was living with his partner, Harold—whose last name was never used in either diaries or letters—in a nearby apartment at 395 Amalfi Drive, where Klaus would first attempt suicide on July 11.

On October 30, 1947, Brecht was summoned to appear before the House Un-American Activities Committee (HUAC), a committee of the US House of Representatives tasked with investigating the alleged infiltration of US society by communists. Brecht testified that he had never belonged to a communist party and the next day boarded a plane for Paris, never to set foot in the despised nation again. Helene Weigel, who had tirelessly arranged parcel deliveries to friends in Germany and Austria since the end of the war, was also happy to return home. Shortly after Brecht's departure, she and their daughter, Barbara, got on a ship to Europe. Her brother Stefan, who had been granted citizenship through his military service, was the only member of the family to remain in the United States.

Hanns Eisler was questioned by HUAC from September 24 to 26, 1947. When asked if he had ever been a member of the Communist Party, the composer responded that he had applied, "but I neglected the whole affair":

> THE CHAIRMAN: Then your answer is you were never a member of the Communist Party?
>
> MR. EISLER: Yes—this is hard to be correct. I want to be correct. You can put it that way—that a man who made an application to join was.
>
> THE CHAIRMAN: Were you a member?
>
> MR. EISLER: Not in the real sense.[17]

In a similar vein for the next three days, the legislators questioned witnesses and probed any and all of Eisler's artistic endeavors they deemed suspicious.

Hanns Eisler was born in Leipzig in 1898. He was the youngest son of Rudolf Eisler, a Viennese university lecturer and descendant of the great Rabbi Loew of Prague—who, according to legend, had created the Golem. In Vienna in 1919, the younger Eisler became a pupil of Arnold Schoenberg, who taught him free of charge for four years. Eisler came to criticize Schoenberg's music as "art for art's sake" and tasked himself with creating a unique proletarian musical style that would set itself apart from the elitist and, as he saw it, bourgeois avant-garde. He relocated to Berlin in 1925 and established himself as probably the most important composer of the agitprop movement. He composed innovative choral works, political battle songs, and eventually film music. He first collaborated with Brecht in 1928, and in 1930, after the playwright's estrangement from Kurt Weill, Eisler became his closest creative partner.

In 1933 Eisler emigrated to London by way of Czechoslovakia and France, and in 1935 he accepted a position teaching music history and composition at the New School for Social Research in New York City. After time in Spain and with Brecht in Denmark, he and his second wife, Lou—the Hungarian aristocrat Louise Anna Gosztonyi von Abalechota—returned to the United States on January 21, 1938, and Eisler resumed his employment at the New School. His attempt to secure a permanent visa was a real odyssey: Eisler, who had been expatriated and was therefore stateless, applied for an immigrant visa at the

US consulate in Havana in March 1938. The process dragged on, however, as US authorities had informed the consulate that Eisler's views were "anti-fascist and pro-communist" and that he was "not eligible for an immigrant visa."[18]

Still, the Eislers' tourist visas were extended. The influential journalist Dorothy Thompson rallied support from prominent figures, Eleanor Roosevelt among them, but it was no use. The Eislers were set to be deported on March 2, 1939, after their tourist visas finally expired, but, in an about-face, authorities granted two requests to extend the deadline for leaving the country. Celebrities again lobbied for the composer, and finally Mexican president Lázaro Cárdenas del Río—after receiving telegrams from Albert Einstein, Thomas Mann, Ernest Hemingway, and others—granted the couple entry into his country and arranged a guest professorship for Eisler at the National Conservatory of Music in Mexico City. Hanns and Lou received new tourist visas on September 7, 1939, and returned to the States. They overstayed the two-month limit and went on living illegally in New York.

When an arrest warrant was issued for passport violations on July 17, 1940, the Eislers fled to Mexico. At the US consulate in Mexicali, they finally managed to obtain nonquota visas—like those issued to foreign academics engaged by US universities—presumably because the official handling their application was unaware of their previous difficulties and neglected to review their file. Still they were barred entry in Calexico. Eisler was interrogated and detained. He filed an official complaint with the Board of Immigration Appeals in Washington, and on October 16 his appeal was granted. Hanns and Lou stepped onto US soil on October 22 and headed straight for New York. Eight days later the arrest warrants were retracted.

In April 1942 Hanns traveled to Los Angeles without his wife in search of work. In mid-August Lou followed, and the two moved into an apartment in Brentwood. With Brecht's help Hanns was commissioned to score Fritz Lang's anti-Nazi drama *Hangmen Also Die!*, which would earn the composer his first Oscar nomination in 1944. The money from that project enabled the Eislers to rent a sprawling, 6,200-square-foot villa built in 1928 at 1650 Amalfi Drive in Pacific Palisades, where the Feuchtwangers had lived for a spell. The next year they moved south to 689 Amalfi Drive, a comfortable, 4,000-square-foot house that the Feuchtwangers had *also* occupied at one point. They eventually settled in neighboring Malibu.

Hanns Eisler had been on the FBI watch list since 1943. In 1947, now a tenured professor at the University of Southern California, he was dragged into the witch hunt against his brother Gerhart Eisler. Gerhart had been defamed by their sister, the former head of the Communist Party of Germany, Ruth Fischer, who had become a radical opponent of Stalin. (Charlie Chaplin once quipped that Eisler family dynamics resembled those found in Shakespearean histories.) Gerhart was arrested on February 4, 1947, for a passport violation; held on Ellis Island; then imprisoned in New York and released on $20,000 bail. He was indicted for having worked as an agent of a foreign power plotting a communist coup in the United States. The indictment was followed by conviction, release, rearrest, and renewed questioning. In 1949, facing five years in prison, Gerhart escaped as a stowaway on a Polish ship to Great Britain. He continued by way of Prague to the German Democratic Republic (GDR), where he would later become a member of the Party Central Committee.

The year of Gerhart's arrest, 1947, countless media reports covered both him and his younger brother, despite Hanns's never having been politically active in the United States. Lou described it to a friend in London, "Our life has become very unpleasant. For months, Hanns has not been able to turn on the radio without hearing idiotic stories about either Gerhart or himself. Hanns has become a monster in this country, an outcast, a subversive character. As you know, the country is already flooded with hatred against the Reds."[19]

Thomas Mann commented on the situation in his diary on October 3, 1947: "Shocked by the news that H. Eisler was to be arrested and deported to Germany by order of the Department of Justice, on the recommendation of the Un-American Committee. Terribly disturbed by the dwindling sense of justice in this country, the supremacy of fascist violence. Nervous dreams of protest, accusation, and self-sacrifice, undoubtedly a foolish thing to do that no one would thank me for."[20] A group of public figures formed the National Committee for Justice for Hanns Eisler but were unsuccessful in their efforts.

Despite public protests and appeals made by Thomas Mann, Charlie Chaplin, and Albert Einstein, the Justice Department ordered Eisler's deportation and future entry ban.

On February 28, 1948, Leonard Bernstein and Aaron Copland hosted a farewell concert at the Town Hall in New York, and on March 26 Hanns and Lou Eisler left the United States and flew to Vienna. Their furniture and other household effects had been seized for back taxes. In late October 1948, Eisler wrote the music for Johannes R. Becher's "Auferstanden aus Ruinen" (Risen from ruins). It would become the national anthem of the GDR, which was founded on October 7, 1949. Eisler lived in East Germany until his death in 1962. West German media had a field day when, in July 1953, Eisler, who was still an Austrian citizen, was found drunk in West Berlin and escorted to the border by police, and when, in 1958, Peter Kreuder accused Eisler of plagiarism, claiming that the GDR anthem was based on his hit tune "Goodbye Johnny," sung by Hans Albers.

Heinrich Mann also wanted to settle down in the young country, which awarded him the National Prize of the German Democratic Republic in 1949 and invited him to head the newly founded Academy of Arts in 1950. Everything was ready for his move from Santa Monica to East Germany when he died of a stroke.

As soon as the war ended, Alfred Döblin was among the first exiles to return home to help build a democratic Germany. He served as a French cultural officer for the military government in Baden-Baden. From 1953 to 1956, he lived in France, where he was treated for Parkinson's disease. By the time of his death in 1957 in Emmendingen, many of his top titles from the past had been forgotten.

Max Horkheimer decided to return to Germany in 1950 as well, though he was intent on retaining his US citizenship. His wish was granted: in 1952 President Harry S. Truman signed a law that guaranteed Horkheimer his continued citizenship despite his permanent residence in Germany. The Institute for Social Research was reestablished in 1950 with funding from the US military administration, the city of Frankfurt, private sponsors, and others. Having had his professorship at the University of Frankfurt restored, Horkheimer was elected dean of the faculty of philosophy. In 1951 he became the first unbaptized Jew in the country's history to be appointed a university rector. The same year, a new institute building was unveiled, though Horkheimer emphasized that it was by no means to be seen as reparation, "because nothing could make up for what the criminal National Socialist system in Germany had done to Jews."[21]

Horkheimer remained attached to his country of exile. He established an exchange program between the universities of Frankfurt and Chicago, sponsoring trips for students and lecturers to acquaint themselves with the democratic education system in the United States. Dismayed by the rise of the Soviet Union—"what happened under Stalin . . . is as bad . . . as what happened under Hitler"—Horkheimer no longer advocated social change by revolutionary means.[22] He supported German rearmament, the founding of the Bundeswehr, and even the Vietnam War, in stark contrast to Herbert Marcuse, who remained radically left-wing and denounced the United States' "brutal imperial world power."[23]

The writer Frank Thiess had remained in the Third Reich and now, after the war, stirred up media attention through his use of the term "inner emigration." In 1945 Thiess had attacked Thomas Mann in print, saying he had no right to comment on the subject of German guilt, as all actual emigrants had "watched the German tragedy" unfold from the "boxes and orchestra seats of foreign countries," the sentiment to which Ludwig Marcuse so strongly objected.[24] Thiess further pointed out that, "legally speaking," Mann was "no longer German," having become a US citizen on June 23, 1944.[25] As such, the bridges were burned between him and Germany. Mann left Pacific Palisades for good on June 24, 1952—mostly because the political climate in the United States had changed so drastically—and although he visited both East and West Germany, he decided to spend his twilight years in Switzerland.

Salka Viertel moved there too. Thomas Mann may have been the most famous German in the United States (and certainly Pacific Palisades), but within the exile community she undoubtedly held the most sway. Salka, who had become a US citizen in 1939, was targeted by the FBI early on as a founding member of the Anti-Nazi League and because of the "international" types who visited so frequently. In 1945 J. Edgar Hoover officially requested permission to monitor 165 Mabery Road: the mail was opened, phone lines bugged, neighbors questioned. In 1953, as Berthold lay dying in Vienna—they had divorced in 1948 after thirty years' marriage—Salka was refused a passport to go see him. In Washington the feds grilled the purported commie and cohort of Hanns Eisler's and Charlie Chaplin's. She enlisted an expensive lawyer to help, but, by the time she got her papers, Berthold's body was already in the ground.

Salka was a courageous woman in every respect. She had once taken in the Black director Carlton Moss and his wife, who was white, despite local residents collecting signatures against her "renting to Negroes."[26] In April 1953 she leased her house in Pacific Palisades to John Houseman, who bought it the following year. The director was born Jacques Haussmann in Bucharest in 1902, his father an Alsatian Jew and his mother a Brit. He produced the world premiere of Brecht's *Galileo* in 1947, directed by Joseph Losey and starring Charles Laughton in the title role.

Brecht had met Laughton at Salka's house, and the actor helped him revise the English version of the play. It must have rankled Brecht that when the gossip columnist Hedda Hopper wrote about Laughton's play in the *Los Angeles Times*, she never once mentioned the author's name. In attendance at the premiere at the Coronet Theatre in Hollywood, which seated only 260, were Ingrid Bergman, Charlie Chaplin, Gene Kelly, Billy Wilder, Frank Lloyd Wright, Igor Stravinsky, and Salka Viertel. She split her time between the United States and Europe and in 1960 settled down in Klosters, Switzerland. She spent the last eighteen years of her life there. Though the general public had largely forgotten about Salka, Greta Garbo had not: she visited her friend like clockwork until the very end.

IN 1952, on his way to the world premiere of his film *Limelight* in London, Charlie Chaplin was informed on the high seas that he would not be allowed to reenter the United States. The same year Feuchtwanger enjoyed his greatest commercial success with *Goya*, which was selected by the Book of the Month Club and translated into twenty-four languages. His final play, *The Devil in Boston*, was also performed in 1952 in front of audiences that included Thomas and Katia Mann, Aldous Huxley, and Christopher Isherwood. Arthur Miller would later adapt the piece, set in Salem in 1692, in his drama *The Crucible*.

The Devil in Boston was read as a topical critique of the House Un-American Activities Committee and its persecution of intellectuals and artists. HUAC had targeted Lion Feuchtwanger for years. On May 5, 1941, exactly twelve weeks after their arrival in Nogales, Arizona, the Feuchtwangers first submitted their petitions for naturalization. (Lion had been expatriated from Germany in 1933, Marta stripped of her German citizenship in 1936.) The decision was repeatedly delayed, while the FBI kept a close eye on Lion. Richard Nixon, then a senator, oversaw his file—he was hell-bent on preventing the alleged communist from becoming a US citizen. In 1957 and 1958, several "interviews" took place at the Feuchtwanger residence in Pacific Palisades, some of which went on for days—these were, of course, interrogations conducted by the Immigration and Naturalization Service, which coordinated closely with the FBI. Lion, who had recently undergone major surgery for cancer, was questioned one last time on October 20, 1958. Two months later he died at Mount Sinai Hospital in Los Angeles, after eighteen years of exile as a stateless person. Forty days later, on January 30, 1959, his widow Marta became a citizen.

PLAYERS, ALL: RONALD REAGAN ON SCREEN, HENRY MILLER IN THE BACKYARD, AND JAKOB GIMPEL ON PIANO

IN JULY 1952, a few days after Thomas Mann had turned his back on Pacific Palisades and the surveillance state Senator Joseph McCarthy had made of the United States, a B-movie actor pulled into town. He moved into a Cape Cod–style house at 1258 Amalfi Drive, less than a ten-minute walk from the Mann estate on San Remo Drive. Though a Democrat on paper, he had drifted to the right during the McCarthy era and is said to have ratted out at least six fellow actors to the FBI under the code name T-10 between 1947 and 1952, when Hollywood was being trawled for "anti-American activities." That man was Ronald Reagan. "[It] was to become more and more apparent to me [that] Joseph Stalin had set out to make Hollywood an instrument of propaganda for his program of Soviet expansionism aimed at communizing the world," Reagan recalled in his memoir, *An American Life*, published in 1990. "But I was to discover that a lot of 'liberals' just couldn't accept the notion that Moscow had bad intentions or wanted to take over Hollywood and many other American industries through subversion, or that Stalin was a murderous gangster. To them, fighting totalitarianism was 'witch hunting' and 'red baiting.'"[1]

Reagan was born in 1911 in Tampico, Illinois—population seven hundred. As a young man, this son of a shoe salesman worked as a lifeguard and radio sports commentator and in 1932 graduated college with a degree in economics and sociology. He made his way to Hollywood in 1937. Though he had no formal training, Warner Brothers took one look at this six-foot-tall, broad-shouldered, blue-eyed rookie blessed with a sonorous voice and furnished him with a seven-year contract. Reagan starred in a string of mediocre films and played the freshman halfback George Gipp in the football biopic *Knute Rockne: All American*. Otherwise he mostly made do with supporting roles. Reagan was called up for the air force but was not sent into combat because of his impaired vision; instead, he shot around four hundred army training reels.

In October 1947 the House Un-American Activities Committee summoned a number of people who worked in the film industry. The hearings were aimed at expelling all left-wing or even liberal-leaning filmmakers from Hollywood. First up was Walt Disney, whose racist and antisemitic leanings were common knowledge. (In 1938, despite a boycott initiated by the Hollywood Anti-Nazi League, Disney had hosted Leni Riefenstahl, a favorite of the Third Reich.) He told HUAC that communists posed a grave threat in the film industry and denounced several people who had worked for him. On October 25, 1947, five days before Bertolt Brecht's hearing, Reagan—who had been named president of the Screen Actors Guild that year—declared that a small cohort within SAG was employing communist tactics to steer union policies. He admitted he did not know if these members, whose names he concealed for the time being, were communists.

Disney and Reagan, like Robert Taylor and Gary Cooper, were among the "friendly" witnesses, as distinguished from "unfriendly" witnesses who refused to divulge their political views to HUAC, citing their First Amendment right to free speech. Over the course of these hearings, the "Hollywood Ten"—nine screenwriters and one director—were sentenced to prison for contempt of Congress. Many other film people were blacklisted for opaque reasons, including the actor Nancy Davis. She asked SAG president Reagan for help—it turned out that she was the victim of mistaken identity—and became his second wife on March 4, 1952. As Nancy later recalled, "Pacific Palisades . . . was an affordable and quiet neighborhood. . . . At the time, nobody could understand why we were moving way out there—'in the country,' as it was thought of then."[2]

In 1954 Ronald Reagan became a spokesperson for the General Electric Company (GE), though he would appear in another fifty-three films before his Hollywood career ended a decade later. He toured the country, gave speeches at GE offices and production facilities, and hosted the General Electric Theater television series, which aired every Sunday evening and featured screen adaptations of different novels, short stories, and plays. Notable guest stars included Fred Astaire, Bette Davis, James Dean, the Marx Brothers, James Stewart, and Reagan himself. The program would also discuss the future of electricity with audiences or report on the latest GE technology, such as jet engines. Promotional clips for the show were filmed at the General Electric Showcase House, located at 1669 San Onofre Drive in Pacific Palisades. Ronald and Nancy had moved their family into the 4,764-square-foot home in January 1957. The house was outfitted with all manner of GE appliances and the ninety circuits required to run them. There were so many "refrigerators, ovens, and fancy lights—not to mention a built-in garbage disposal—that they had to build a special panel on the side of the house for all the wiring and the switches," Nancy wrote.[3] Most innovative were the energy-saving controls for the air-conditioning, heating, and interior and exterior lighting, which made Reagan—of all people—a pioneer of eco-friendly living.

Ronald Reagan joined the Republican Party in 1962. Four years later, with endorsements from John Wayne, Walt Disney, and others, he was elected governor of the flower-power state of California. He won the November 4, 1980, presidential election in a landslide victory over incumbent Jimmy Carter. Reagan was sworn into office on January 20, 1981, as the fortieth—and, at age sixty-nine, the oldest—president of the United States. He was reelected in 1984. For almost three decades, Reagan was the most famous resident of Pacific Palisades, at least from an American point of view. A banner reading, "Welcome to Pacific Palisades—Home of our 40th President," was hoisted proudly in 1980, although the neighborhood is still considered a Democratic stronghold; in the 2024 presidential election, Kamala Harris took 71.17 percent of the vote.

The Reagans sold their house on San Onofre Drive in 1982. The subsequent fate of the property is typical of Pacific Palisades, which has risen—or perhaps fallen—to the status of bedroom community of the Hollywood elite: after changing hands for $5 million in 2013, it was transformed into a swanky, 12,000-square-foot manse called the Riviera White House and listed at $33 million. It featured a cashmere-lined home theater, bathroom decorated with twenty-five thousand peacock feathers, garage with an integrated bar, and wine cellar with space for two thousand bottles. It also came with an old shower door with a brass plaque that read, "On this spot, election night, November 4th, 1980, former California Governor Ronald Reagan was in the shower, his wife Nancy was taking a bath. The phone rang and Nancy answered. She handed the phone to her husband and, as water cascaded over him, he heard Jimmy Carter's voice, 'Mr. Reagan? Congratulations. You're President of The United States.'"[4]

BUT LET'S RETURN TO THE 1950S. The fact that Pacific Palisades, which had a population of around ten thousand at the time, remained an intellectual and artistic hub beyond its "Weimar" years was thanks in part to the Huntington Hartford Foundation. In 1923, at age twelve, George Huntington Hartford II had inherited $90 million, the equivalent of nearly $1.5 billion today. His family had come into their wealth through the Great Atlantic and Pacific Tea Company, better known as A&P, which at its height was the largest grocery chain in the world with upward of sixteen thousand branches. His inheritance enabled an extravagant lifestyle, and he dabbled in philanthropy, art collecting, and stage and film production. Hartford's tastes were not terribly sophisticated: he thought Mozart was overrated, Margaret Mitchell's *Gone with the Wind* the greatest American novel, and abstract painting a threat to humanity. He founded the Huntington Hartford Theater in Hollywood, a graphological institute, and an art museum in New York. He acquired a New York newspaper and tried his hand as a local reporter in a tux and Rolls-Royce. At one point he bought an island in the Bahamas and had several tons of sand flown to London, more than four thousand miles away, to decorate the Savoy Hotel ballroom for a charity event. In December 1948 he established the Huntington Hartford Foundation to promote creativity in the arts through scholarships, and in 1951 he set up an artist colony in Pacific Palisades for painters, sculptors, writers, and composers.

The retreat site in Rustic Canyon, originally surrounded by a chain-link fence topped with barbed wire, was shrouded in mystery. John Vincent, a former student of Arnold Schoenberg's who headed the Huntington Hartford

Foundation from 1953 to 1965, was probably behind the stories. According to legend, starting in 1933 the former owners Winona and Norman Stephens bowed to pressure from a Nazi spy named Schmidt (about whom nothing else is known) and invested $4 million to turn Murphy Ranch into a self-contained Nazi commune, where they ran paramilitary training exercises and held out hope for a German victory over the United States. The truth of the matter was this: Norman F. Stevens, a Pasadena-based engineer and son of a house painter from Maine, and his wife, Winona, daughter of the wealthy Chicago factory owner Arthur J. Bassett, had bought the fifty-acre property under the pseudonym "Jessie M. Murphy, widow" on August 28, 1933. They had a double-generator power plant built on-site, along with a 20,000-gallon fuel tank, 395,000-gallon water tank, air-raid shelter, and simple accommodations above a concrete garage. The contract to design a four-story manor house with a grand hall, dining rooms, parlors, and twenty-two bedrooms was awarded to the renowned American architect Paul R. Williams in 1939.

"They may have been Nazis, but they were Nazis with taste," local historian Randy Young commented on a television program exploring the compound seven decades later.[5] The Stevenses' plans were never carried out, though, because on December 8, 1941, one day after the Japanese attack on Pearl Harbor, local police are said to have raided the site and made multiple arrests, including the sinister Herr Schmidt, but no records can be found. As for the white swastika scrawled on the front door of the English writer and former rabbi Lewis Brown at 29 Latimer Road in Pacific Palisades in 1938, whether this vandalism was connected to Murphy Ranch has never been cleared up.

The Stevenses' land and an adjacent hundred-acre plot went to the Huntington Hartford Foundation. The architect Frank Lloyd Wright Jr.—son of the pioneer of organic architecture—designed about a dozen cottages spaced out around a central building with a dining hall and huge swimming pool. Christopher Isherwood was among the first guests, and the film producer and book publisher Frank E. Taylor asked him to join the foundation's board of trustees, along with writers Speed Lamkin and Robert Penn Warren. Isherwood soon became convinced that the selection of fellows was driven by gossip and personal preferences, and he chafed at the strict rules Hartford had implemented. Smoking was prohibited, as was the use of cars. Telephone calls were limited to three minutes, children were not allowed on premises, and no one was allowed overnight guests without prior approval. When one resident violated these rules in 1952 and lost his scholarship as a result, Isherwood stepped down from the board.

Over the years the four hundred or so fellows included the literary critic Mark Van Doren; the poets Byron Herbert Reece and Jean Starr Untermeyer; the sculptor Robert Cremean and the painter Bena Frank Mayer; Max Eastman, once a friend of Leon Trotsky's and his English translator, now a fervent supporter of Harry S. Truman; Van Wyck Brooks, who was awarded the Pulitzer Prize for History in 1937 for *The Flowering of New England*; and the painter George Biddle, a childhood friend of Franklin D. Roosevelt's whose murals and frescoes captured the president's New Deal visions for social reform. During a residency in 1957, Edward Hopper painted *Western Motel*, which depicts a woman waiting with packed bags in a sun-drenched motel room. The piece is thought to symbolize mobility and anonymity, the belief in progress and the melancholy of loneliness in modern American society.

The composer and onetime child prodigy Lukas Foss, born in Berlin in 1922, also found inspiration at the foundation. His father was the German Jewish philosopher Martin Fuchs. The family emigrated to France in 1933, then to the United States in 1937. Foss studied with Paul Hindemith at Yale University and in 1953 succeeded Arnold Schoenberg at the University of California, Los Angeles. The foundation hosted Ernst Toch no fewer than three times. While in residence, he worked on *Vanity of Vanities, All Is Vanity*, a cantata based on the Holocaust, and on his Symphony no. 3, which won the 1956 Pulitzer Prize. Eric Zeisl, who had emigrated from Vienna to Paris in 1938 and to the United States in September 1939, spent the summers of 1957 and 1958 at the foundation. "It was the happiest time of Eric's life," his widow, Gertrud, reflected.[6]

Zeisl met the composers Ingolf Dahl and Roy Harris at the artist colony. Dahl, born in Hamburg in 1912 to a German Jewish father and a Swedish mother, had emigrated to Switzerland in 1933 and to the United States in 1938. Harris was born in Oklahoma in 1898. His Symphony no. 3 from 1938 is an established part of the US classical repertoire. He had a personal connection to the exile community, as his closest collaborator for years was Walter Arlen, who had fled Vienna for the United States "on March 14, 1939—one day before my visa expired," Arlen recalled in a newspaper interview years later:

> It was lucky that I left. It's actually a miracle I'm alive. I saw myself as a representative of six million murdered Jews—as one who just happened not to have been murdered. . . . This tragedy has burdened my entire life—my father was in two concentration camps, my grandmother was murdered in Treblinka, my cousin later shot himself, and my mother committed suicide. During the war I had to stand guard over her because she might jump off the roof. . . . In 1947 I went to Santa Monica for the first time, because my grandfather, an uncle, and an aunt were already there. But from 1947 to '51 I traveled around like a gypsy as Roy Harris's assistant, through Colorado, Utah, and Tennessee. I was his travel companion. I wrote his scores. . . . A lot of things in America were very fortunate, of course, but that doesn't preclude misfortune. There hasn't been a minute since 1938 that I've been able to laugh freely. If you're not dead—which I'm not—you're still wounded, possessed by an inner despair. A nostalgia remains for what you have lost and for the life you could never live. That's all in my music.[7]

In 1965, a year after Roy Harris had moved to Pacific Palisades for good (he lived at 1200 Tellem Drive until his death in 1979), the Huntington Hartford Foundation closed its artist colony. The buildings were abandoned after the Great Mandeville Canyon Fire of October 1978, which destroyed thirty houses in Pacific Palisades and Brentwood.

California wildfires posed a constant danger, then as now. The Bel Air fire of November 1961 was one of the worst in LA history. Dry Santa Ana winds drove the blaze toward Pacific Palisades. The fire raged at the other end of Lucero Avenue and came close to destroying the Villa Aurora. Marta Feuchtwanger hosed down the hot ash landing on the roof, which was fortunately tile, not wood. A rattled university librarian, the Feuchtwangers' groundskeeper, and their secretary, Hilde Waldo, loaded Lion's most valuable books into a truck, which brought them to safety. All the neighboring properties had been evacuated and half of Pacific Palisades was in danger of being consumed by flames. Marta held out until the last moment, and, when she called the fire department to come rescue her, the wind changed. Five hundred villas in the surrounding area had burned down. The Villa Aurora had water damage from Marta's extinguishing efforts but had been spared from the flames.

ANOTHER MAJOR FIGURE in cultural history who called the Palisades home was the philosopher and anthropologist Gerald Heard, born in London in 1889. He had moved to the United States in 1937 with his friends Aldous and Maria Huxley and was himself a crime novelist in addition to his philosophical writings. In 1939 he met Swami Prabhavananda, a Ramakrishna monk and the founder of the Vedanta Society of Southern California. Heard began the study of Vedanta, a popular branch of Indian philosophy, with the swami and became something of a spiritual godfather to Aldous Huxley and Christopher Isherwood. In 1942 he founded Trabuco College, about seventy-five miles south of Los Angeles. The Vedanta Society of Southern California acquired the grounds in 1949 and eventually established the Ramakrishna Monastery there.

Until the early 1960s, Heard lived in Margaret Gage's guesthouse at 545 Spoleto Drive, two doors down from Felix Weil, the former benefactor of the Frankfurt Institute for Social Research. (Weil served as vice president of the California Riviera Home Owners Association, which ensured, among other things, that no ugly carports blighted the otherwise pristine residential neighborhood.) In 1955 Heard was one of the first to experiment with lysergic acid diethylamide, or LSD, which the Swiss chemist Albert Hofmann had synthesized in 1938. He and his friend Huxley became outspoken advocates of mind-expanding drugs. On November 22, 1963, at nearly the same moment as Lee Harvey Oswald shot President John F. Kennedy, Huxley's second wife, Laura, administered a different kind of shot: she injected her moribund husband with two doses of LSD, thus giving him "the most beautiful death."[8]

In 1949 the designer couple Charles and Ray Eames moved into Case Study House No. 8, the home they had designed at 205 Chautauqua Boulevard. Nestled into a wooded hillside, the geometric structure was made of black-lacquered double-T steel beams and glass panes interspersed with colored rectangles that immediately called Piet Mondrian to mind. The house was by no means coolly minimalistic, though: the inside revealed a profusion of textiles, stones, plants, toys, and folk art from around the world. The Eameses lived there until they died, Charles in 1978, Ray ten years later. Case Study House No. 8 is an icon, a masterpiece of modernism that has influenced the development of modern architecture as significantly as the couple's chair designs have shaped the world of furniture design. Their best-known chair today is probably the molded plastic chair, a one-piece, form-fitting shell made of fiberglass-reinforced polyester resin; in 1950 it became the first serially produced plastic chair in history to be launched on the market. Incidentally, the Eames lounge chair, which went into production in 1956 and remains a sitting-room standard of the moneyed class, was created at the suggestion of an Austrian emigrant—the director Billy Wilder, who was a close friend of the couple.

From 1953 until his death in 1973, Stanton Macdonald-Wright also lived and worked in the Castellammare area of Pacific Palisades. In 1912 the painter had cofounded the first-ever avant-garde art movement in the United States. Synchromism was based on the idea that colors in a painting could be arranged like notes in a score and evoke the same complex responses as symphonic music. Macdonald-Wright's "synchromies," among the first abstract paintings in US art, use rhythmic color forms with progressive and reductive shades. Born in Charlottesville, Virginia, in 1890, Macdonald-Wright studied in Paris, where he became friends with Pablo Picasso, Marc Chagall, and Henri Matisse. He showed his first synchromatic paintings in Munich in 1913, then in Paris and New York in 1914, and moved to Los Angeles in 1918. In 1942 he began teaching at the University of California, Los Angeles. Macdonald-Wright created murals for Los Angeles City Hall and the Santa Monica Library. He built a house inspired by Zen Buddhism and Far Eastern art in Pacific Palisades, where he completed the Synchrome Kaleidoscope, a device that projects colored light, which he had begun developing with Morgan Russell in 1913 and finished with help from the German emigrant Oskar Fischinger.

In 1963 one of the twentieth century's most controversial writers, the "King of Smut" Henry Miller, bought a two-story white villa with a heated swimming pool at 444 Ocampo Drive.[9] Born in New York in 1891 to German parents, the author of *Quiet Days in Clichy* and *The Rosy Crucifixion* trilogy was at the height of his career: in 1961 his sexually graphic, highly autobiographical novel, *Tropic of Cancer*, which Miller had written in 1934, was finally published in the United States. Besieged by hippie fans who lionized Miller and based their life philosophies on his output, the writer left his home in Big Sur and moved to Pacific Palisades, where he remained until his death in 1980. (His fifth and final marriage, to Hiroko "Hoki" Tokuda, a Japanese nightclub singer forty-six years his junior, lasted from 1966 to 1977.) *Tropic of Cancer* was initially classified as pornography and banned, but after several lawsuits the Supreme Court ruled in 1964 that Miller's work was not obscene and could return to bookshelves.

Not only did the writer advocate a life free of bourgeois constraints on paper, but he transgressed certain social boundaries in everyday life too. From today's perspective it seems pretty harmless that Miller's friends would gather in his backyard to play Ping-Pong, sunbathe, and swim, all in the nude, but, as one former neighbor, who was a young girl at the time, recalls, "[this] is where our weather-beaten swing set came in. If you settled into one of the cold metal seats and pumped your legs hard, you could soar above the fence line and catch a glimpse of [the nude sunbathers]. Occasionally we'd see Mr. Miller himself in the water—for the record he was never naked."[10]

Miller was familiar with a number of the emigrants. He had met Marta Feuchtwanger in 1941, when he was living in nearby Beverly Glen, at a party thrown by the pianist Jakob Gimpel. Miller said to her, "You know, I want to know more about you. You intrigue me. You have to tell me more about you." She ignored the overture—and the obscene remark he made when she refused to respond.[11] The two went on to become friends, however, and Marta described in her memoirs how much fun she had: spending time with him felt like Carnival, in Pacific Palisades. She also reported that Miller was surrounded by a steady stream of pretty, young women, often Asian, "and once he had a beautiful Greek young man."[12] In 1943 he met the screenwriter Renée Nell, who became an important friend for discussing and exchanging ideas. Nell, born Irmgard Auguste Beermann in Berlin in 1910, later became a prominent psychoanalyst whose patients included Leonard Bernstein.

One of Miller's closest friends in Pacific Palisades in the 1960s and 1970s was Jakob Gimpel, born in 1906 in what was then the Austrian city of Lemberg and is now Lviv, Ukraine. Gimpel trained with Alban Berg and emigrated to Los Angeles in 1938. He eked out a living at first by giving piano lessons and recording for film studios—in 1946 he played Franz Liszt's Hungarian Rhapsody no. 2 for the Bugs Bunny short *Rhapsody Rabbit*. The animated piano sequences were based on these sound recordings and film footage of Gimpel's hands moving across the keyboard. Celebrities who sought out Miller's company included the English writer Lawrence Durrell, Steve McQueen, Bob Dylan, Joan Baez, Norman Mailer, Warren Beatty, and the best-selling author Erica Jong. As for Miller, he made it his business to meet Hollywood starlets such as Ava Gardner, Kim Novak, and Elke Sommer.

Pacific Palisades has never wanted for celebrities. In recent years Dan Aykroyd and Hilary Swank have bought places (both on Paseo Miramar, not far from the Villa Aurora), as have Jennifer Garner, Ben Affleck, Matt Damon, Bradley Cooper, Rihanna, and *The Big Bang Theory* creator Chuck Lorre. The list of honorary mayors, elected for two-year terms, further illustrates the point. In 1953 it was Jerry Lewis, born Joseph Levitsch in New Jersey in 1926, the son of a singer and vaudeville performer who had emigrated from Russia. Lewis proved to be a master of physical comedy and in 1946 teamed up with Dean Martin. Martin and Lewis, as the comedy duo was known, specialized in improvised bits. In 1956 Lewis, regarded by many in Europe and beyond as the next Charlie Chaplin, embarked on a solo career. He lived at 1048 Amalfi Drive in Pacific Palisades, a street so many before him had called home: Vicki Baum, Mercedes de Acosta, Hanns Eisler, Douglas Fairbanks, Lion Feuchtwanger, Cary Grant, Aldous Huxley, Christopher Isherwood, Emil Ludwig, Thomas Mann, David Niven, Luise Rainer, David O. Selznick, Rose Stradner, and the father of classic Hollywood horror, James Whale. In later years this list would expand to include to Burt Bacharach, the songwriter behind "The Look of Love" and "Raindrops Keep Fallin' on My Head"; the actors James Caan, Harvey Fierstein, John Goodman, Whoopi Goldberg, Goldie Hawn, Rita Moreno, Kurt Russell, and Sylvester Stallone; and the director Steven Spielberg. Other honorary mayors have included Mel Blanc, who voiced Bugs Bunny and Daffy Duck, in 1959; Peter Graves in 1969; Walter Matthau in 1977;

Chevy Chase in 1986; Rita Moreno in 1988; Anthony Hopkins in 2000; Steve Guttenberg in 2002; Billy Crystal in 2018; and Eugene Levy in 2021.

IT'S NO COINCIDENCE that a striking number of prominent Palisadians are descended from Jewish immigrants from Germany, Austria, or Eastern Europe. A wave of second-generation immigrants moved from the East Coast and Midwest to Los Angeles after the war, increasing the Jewish population there from 130,000 in 1941 to 500,000 in 1980 and making Los Angeles the city with the third-largest Jewish population in the world, outside of Tel Aviv and New York. The demographic change was especially noticeable in Pacific Palisades, which—despite the refugee community there during World War II—had remained predominantly Methodist until the late 1960s and now saw its Jewish population burgeon. One sign of the times: the opening of Mort's Deli on the corner of Sunset Boulevard and Swarthmore Avenue, an institution until its closure in 2007.

A little farther west on Sunset Boulevard is Kehillat Israel, a Reconstructionist synagogue with a congregation of more than one thousand households. About 2 percent of Jews worldwide practice Reconstructionism, a progressive movement within Judaism; women have been allowed to be ordained since 1972, and its gender-equitable liturgy does not refer to God exclusively with male attributes. Just south of where Paseo Miramar branches off Sunset Boulevard is the Chabad Jewish Community Center of Pacific Palisades, whose membership is about four hundred families strong. Chabad is a group within Orthodox Judaism that emphasizes contemplative prayer and the systematic study of Hasidic teachings. Overall, about 30 percent of Palisadians today identify as Jewish, compared to less than 2 percent in the United States as a whole.

The levels of wealth and education are also above average among Pacific Palisades' current population of around twenty-nine thousand: 48.7 percent of Palisadians hold a bachelor's degree or higher, which beats out 99.0 percent of all US neighborhoods, and the median income there is higher than in 96.0 percent of all US neighborhoods.[13] Nevertheless, a well-known slogan that one often sees on T-shirts reads, "If you're rich, you live in Beverly Hills. If you're famous, you live in Malibu. If you're lucky, you live in Pacific Palisades."[14]

THE LEGACY OF EXILE

AS THE SOLE HEIR to Lion Feuchtwanger's estate after he died in in 1958, Marta Feuchtwanger reached an agreement the following year with the University of Southern California (USC): the villa and library would become university property, while she retained the right to live there. She even collected a small salary as "curator" of the villa, which gradually filled with copies of Lion's work and correspondence. Marta was an imposing, distinctive figure in LA public life, ultimately a symbolic figure of exile, a living legend. She had a regal air about her, attending concerts, exhibitions, and readings dressed in sleeveless Chinese tunics of gold-and-silver–embellished brocade, black silk capes, or the occasional Indian sari, her hair pulled back in a tight bun. She accepted her first invitation to Germany in 1969 with some hesitation but confessed afterward, "The events proved my good feelings right. It's wonderful that I was able to behold this transformation in Germany."[1]

When Marta died in 1987, at the age of ninety-six in a nursing home in Santa Monica, Lion's biographer, Volker Skierka, enlisted people in politics, journalism, and the arts to help campaign for the preservation of Villa Aurora, the "last remaining cultural monument to German exile literature."[2] Fritz J. Raddatz, who ran the feuilleton desk at *Die Zeit*, pitched the idea of a "Villa Massimo on the American West Coast"—a reference to the storied German cultural institution in Rome—which won the support of Freimut Duve, chair of the Bundestag Committee of Cultural and Media Affairs; and Michael Naumann, the head of Rowohlt.[3] Others joined the cause, including Richard von Weizsäcker, Willy Brandt, Hans-Dietrich Genscher, Hans-Jochen Vogel, LA mayor Tom Bradley, US ambassador to Germany Richard Burt, writers from Günter Grass to Jurek Becker, and *Süddeutsche Zeitung* correspondent Marianne Heuwagen.

In 1988 the nonprofit Friends of Villa Aurora was founded in Berlin, along with its sister organization in Los Angeles, the Foundation for European-American Relations. The German Class Lottery Foundation and the German Federal Foreign Office helped the Friends of Villa Aurora purchase the villa from USC in 1990. Eight thousand invaluable volumes were transferred to the university library, while the remaining twenty-two thousand books remained at Villa Aurora on permanent loan from USC. Frank Dimster, an architecture professor at USC with German Romanian roots, oversaw the renovation, made possible through a grant from the German Federal Foreign Office and more than six million D-marks earmarked by the Lottery Foundation for the project. A new foundation was built, supported by twenty-three concrete pillars; asbestos was removed, plumbing and sanitary facilities renewed, and a security system and air conditioning installed.

Since the completion of the renovation work in 1995, Villa Aurora has awarded up to twelve scholarships each year for a three-month residency in the fields of visual arts, composition, film, literature, and performance. Over the years more than four hundred residents have enlivened the spirit of the place and found inspiration in US culture. Villa Aurora also awards the annual Feuchtwanger Fellowship to writers committed to defending human rights in their countries or whose freedom of expression is restricted—the term "writer in exile" is avoided so as not to suggest that residents are being smuggled in who will then never leave the country.

Today Villa Aurora serves not only as a place for international encounters but as a monument to those who sought refuge from Nazi persecution, many of whom had a tremendous influence on American culture. Remembering the Exiles is a series of readings, lectures, concerts, and film screenings to commemorate the people who found a new home in Southern California. Nevertheless, antisemitic prejudice or an aversion to "Feuchtwanger the communist" has kept some potential donors from supporting Villa Aurora; at one point other patrons were deterred by a misunderstanding that the villa was named after the Russian battleship *Aurora*.

There are another two actors, long based in Pacific Palisades, whose commitment to the villa again highlights the interconnected worlds of exile and Hollywood. The first is Eric Braeden, known in his native Germany primarily for his role as John Jacob Astor in *Titanic* but best known among American daytime-TV viewers as Victor Newman on *The Young and the Restless*, a character he has played since 1980. Braeden, born Hans-Jörg Gudegast outside Kiel in 1941, emigrated to the United States in 1959 with about fifty dollars in his pocket, and he has proven to be deeply dedicated to fostering German American relations and German Jewish dialogue. To promote a more positive image of his old homeland, in 1989 Braeden founded the German American Cultural Society, for which he was awarded a Cross of the Order of Merit of the Federal Republic of Germany in 1992 and a Commander's Cross of the Order of Merit in 2005 at Villa Aurora. In 2007 he became the first German actor after Marlene Dietrich to receive a star on the Hollywood Walk of Fame. Braeden even played Lion Feuchtwanger once, at a staged reading at Villa Aurora.

The second Villa devotee is Armin Mueller-Stahl, probably the only actor to have known success in East Germany, West Germany, and Hollywood. He was brilliant as Thomas Mann in the three-part miniseries *Die Manns: Ein Jahrhundertroman* (*The Manns: Novel of a Century*), first broadcast in 2001. Although scenes set at Mann's house in Pacific Palisades were shot not on location but in a studio in Cologne, the interviews with Mann's secretary, Hilde Kahn, and Katia Mann's nephew Klaus Pringsheim Jr. were recorded there.

WHEN THOMAS MANN'S FORMER RESIDENCE at 1550 San Remo Drive was listed for sale in 2016, there was no indication that it was the former home of a world-famous writer. Joyce Rey, the luxury real estate agent handling the sale, seemed to think the land itself was the greatest draw for potential buyers—and not the two-story house that Marta Feuchtwanger's dear friends Chet and Jon Lappen had lived in for decades. The couple had bought the house from Mann for $50,000 on August 26, 1953. After Chet died, his wife moved to a retirement home. Their house was listed as a rental property in 2012 and used at times as an Airbnb. Demolition now seemed inevitable, to make way for a more lucrative new construction.

The German novelist Herta Müller, a Nobel laureate herself; then foreign minister Frank-Walter Steinmeier; then commissioner for culture and the media Monika Grütters; and others spoke out in favor of preserving the property—known as Seven Palms, though only three of the original trees still stood—and establishing it as a memorial site. It would house a residency program that facilitated exchange between intellectuals, academics, and artists on the major issues of our time. The German Federal Foreign Office purchased the property in November 2016 for around $13 million with the express aim of creating a hub for energetic transatlantic debate. The inaugural Thomas Mann Fellows in 2018 were Heinrich Detering, professor of modern German literature and comparative literature at the University of Göttingen; Jutta Allmendinger, director of the Berlin Social Science Center; and Yiannos Manoli, who holds the Fritz Hüttinger chair of microelectronics at the University of Freiburg and directs the Hahn-Schickard Institute for Microelectronics and Information Technology.

In September 2019 Frido Mann returned to his grandparents' house for its grand opening. German president Frank-Walter Steinmeier delivered opening remarks:

> This evening, the attention of our transatlantic community is on a different "White House." And indeed, this house was not only a family home, a place of thinking and writing, a center of "Weimar on the Pacific," a hub of literature, music, and art. No, it was also a political "White House," and Thomas Mann's study was, in many ways, the Oval Office of the émigré opposition to Hitler's reign of terror in Berlin.
>
> Frido Mann told me about one of his earliest childhood memories, and this image really stuck with me. Standing in the sunlit house shortly before his fourth birthday, the little boy was feeling anxious because of the frantic telephone calls, hushed visitors, and general sense of agitation all around him. It was July 21, 1944. The attempt on Hitler's life had failed. But as news of the previous day trickled in, the family did not feel disappointment or resignation, but rather a newfound hope that this must finally be the beginning of the end of the detested dictator. . . .
>
> To all of the new fellows, I want to say that your work here will be important. You are going on this transatlantic journey at a time of po-

litical turbulence on both sides of the Atlantic, but also of turbulence between the two sides.

. . . May the Fellows fill this house with the spirit of democracy and debates that build bridges between our continents. . . . I am certain that Thomas Mann would be proud that his beloved home on San Remo Drive has a transatlantic future.[4]

ACKNOWLEDGMENTS

MANY THANKS GO TO my agent, Marc Koralnik, at Liepman Literary Agency in Zurich, for his tireless commitment; to my publisher, Felicitas von Lovenberg, and nonfiction director, Anne Stadler, at Piper Verlag in Munich, for the trust they put in my project; and to Charlyne Bieniek and Esther Feustel, for their careful editing. I would also like to thank Sue Berger Ramin at Brandeis University Press, who was daring enough to take on a US edition, and Elisabeth Lauffer, who accepted the challenge of translation.

This book would not exist were it not for my time as writer-in-residence at Villa Aurora in Pacific Palisades. In addition to the Villa Aurora staff—Joachim Bernauer and Claudia Suhr Gordon, in particular, who opened countless doors for me, and Betty Herrera, whose warmth was astonishing—those who contributed to the success of my stay include Walter Arlen†, Don Bachardy, Barbara Bain, Ned Bellamy, Nathan Birnbaum, Karin Blubacher†, Mechthild Borries-Knopp, Tom Bower†, Eric Braeden, Nicole Brunnhuber, Red Buttons†, Doug Cooney, Bill Cusack, Corina Danckwerts, Maia Danziger, Angie Dickinson, Frank Dimster, Deborah Dixon, Norbert Dobeleit, Eugene Elman†, Leonhard M. Fiedler, Frances Fisher, Rhonda Fleming†, Florian Flicker†, Guido Föhrweißer, Achim Freyer, Ron Gilbert, Anthony Goldschmidt†, Bruce Goldsmith, Joanne Gordon, Melanie Griffith†, Barbara Gross, Petra Haffter, Donna Hansen, Jamilia Jazylbekova, Yvonne Jurmann†, Konrad Kellen†, Lyle Kessler, Udo Kier, Bruno Kirby†, Ute Kirchhelle†, Peggy Moran Koster†, Martin Landau†, Sonia Laszlo, Charlie Laughton†, Christian Lebano, Thierry Leduc, Janet Leigh†, Joanne Linville†, Elaine Madsen, Karl Malden†, Art Manke, Jeff McCracken, Ralf Moeller, Terry Moore, Kate Mulligan, Patricia Netzer†, Uschi Obermaier, Ngozi Ola, Susan Peretz†, Jacqueline de Rothschild Piatigorsky†, John Pommer†, Jürgen Prochnow, Rosemarie Reisch, Patricia Riekel, Tim Robbins, Mickey Rooney†, Mark Rydell, Leonora Schildkraut†, Cornelius Schnauber†, Barbara Zeisl Schoenberg, Ronald Schoenberg, Frances Schoenberger, Edwin G. Schuck, Marje Schuetze-Coburn, Dolores J. Sloan, Ann Sommer†, Michael Sommer†, Veronika Vis Sommer, Birgit Stein†, Jamieson Stern, Dick Van Dyke, Richard Walter, Hans Jürgen Wendler, and Randy Young.

For our many talks, messages, and tips, my thanks go to Katja Andy (New York)†, Leon Askin (Vienna)†, Wayan Astra (Ubud), Senta Berger (Grünwald), Carl Christoph Bernoulli (Basel)†, Peter Daniel Bernoulli (Kilchberg)†, Robert-Alexander Bohnke (Tübingen)†, Gisela Braun-Fischer (Zurich)†, Peter Michael Braunwarth (Vienna), Juan Alberto Cedillo (Mexico City), Diana Landshoff Celenza (Durham)†, Mari-Claire Charba (New York), Meta Cordy (New York)†, Peter Crane (Seattle), Charles Dearmond (New York), Neil Derrick (New York)†, Stephan Dörschel (Berlin), Magie Dominic (New York), Eva-Maria Duhan (Basel)†, Kenward G. Elmslie (New York)†, Walter Fähnders (Osnabrück), Konrad Feilchenfeldt (Munich), Anat Feinberg (Stuttgart), Edward Field (New York), Manfred Flügge (Berlin), Jean-Pierre Fonda (Geneva), Paul Foster (New York)†, Gray Foy (New York)†, Stephen Fry (London), Edda Fuhrich (Vienna), Elisabeth Furtwängler (Clarens)†, Gero Gandert (Berlin)†, Gail Curtis Gatterburg (Retz)†, John Gilman (New York), James Gossage (New York), Monika Graves (Key Largo), Jonathan Bryan Guinness, 3rd Baron Moyne (Cirencester), Maria Zuckmayer Guttenbrunner (Raabs an der Thaya), Robert Heide (New York), Ruth Hellberg (Munich)†, Guidotto Graf Henckel Fürst von Donnersmarck (Rottach-Egern), Michael Herzog (Munich), Hanne Brecht Hiob (Munich)†, William M. Hoffman (New York)†, Marianne Hoppe (Berlin)†, Jan-Christopher Horak (Pasadena), Eugene Istomin (New York)†, Jean-Claude van Itallie (New York), Wolfgang Jacobsen (Berlin), Grace Jeszenszky (Kammer), Susan Kagan (New York), Maximilian Kempner (Lexington)†, Hermann Kesten (Riehen)†, Helmut Kindler (Küsnacht)†, Georg Kreisler (Salzburg)†, Fredric Kroll (Freiburg im Breisgau), Andreas Landshoff (Amsterdam)†, Christian Graf von Ledebur-Wicheln (Värmdö)†, John F. Ledebur (Schwertberg), Frank Lenart (Munich), Andreas F. Lowenfeld (New York)†, Michael Matzigkeit (Düsseldorf), Michael McGrinder (New York), Diana McLellan (Washington)†, Angelika von Mendelssohn-Siebeck

(Berlin)†, Bernhard Minetti (Berlin)†, Melissa Müller (Munich), Rosaleen Mulji (Andover), Marcel Ophüls (Lucq-de-Béarn), Ron Padgett (New York), Manfred Paletta (Frankfurt am Main), Stephan Pascal (New York), Robert Patrick (Los Angeles)†, Christine Pendl (Vienna), Vita Petersen (New York)†, Glenn Plaskin (New York), Howard Pollack (Houston), Tully Potter (Billericay), Michael Warren Powell (New York)†, Hans Helmut Prinzler (Berlin)†, Gisela Prossnitz (Salzburg), Jo Alma Révy-Staub (Zug)†, Peter Riva (Wassaic), Joseph J. Roddy (Croton-on-Hudson)†, Eva Römer (Munich), Michael Roloff (Seattle)†, Padraig Rooney (Cerbère), Harvey Sachs (New York), Rachel Salamander (Munich), David Sandberg (Berlin), Elisabeth Sandmann (Munich), Martin Sattler (Heidelberg), Allan Schiller (New York), Julius H. Schoeps (Berlin), Claudia Schoppmann (Berlin), Bärbel Schrader (Berlin), Tonio Selwart (New York)†, Itai Shoffman (New York), Alexander Stephan (Columbus), Jonathan Sternberg (NewYork)†, Tjokorda Putra Sukawati (Ubud), Frithjof Trapp (Hamburg), Peter Viertel (Klosters)†, Dagmar Walach (Berlin), Dagmar Wünsche (Berlin), and David Christian Yorck (San Diego).

I would also like to thank the staff at the following institutions. *Basel*: Paul Sacher Foundation; State Archive; Basel University Library. *Berlin*: Federal Archives; Deutsche Kinemathek, Museum für Film und Fernsehen; Freie Universität, Institute for Theater Studies, Walter Unruh Collection; Berlin State Archive; Leo and Walter Spies Archive; Berlin State Library, Manuscripts and Early Printed Books; Berlin State Library, Music Department, Mendelssohn Archive; the Archives of the Academy of Arts; New Synagogue Berlin, Centrum Judaicum; Stiftung Stadtmuseum Berlin, Department of Theater and Documenta Artistica. *Bern*: Swiss Archive of the Performing Arts; Swiss National Library; Swiss Federal Archives; Swiss Literary Archives. *Beverly Hills*: Margaret Herrick Library, Academy of Motion Pictures Arts and Sciences. *Binghampton*: University of Binghampton, Special Collections. *Boston*: Boston University, Howard Gotlieb Archival Research Center. *Düsseldorf*: Bundeszentralkartei der Entschädigungsverfahren nach dem Bundesentschädigungsgesetz; Theatermuseum der Landeshauptstadt, Dumont-Lindemann Archive. *Essen*: Zentrum für Musik in der Emigration der Folkwang Hochschule. *Frank-*

furt am Main: German Library; German Film Institute; German Broadcasting Archive. *Graz*: Archives for the History of Sociology in Austria. *Cologne*: Theater Research Collection at the University of Cologne. *Los Angeles*: Screen Actors Guild; University of California, Film and Television Archive; University of Southern California, Marta Mierendorff Collection; University of Southern California, Max Kade Center. *Marbach*: German Literature Archive. *Munich*: Leibniz Institute for Contemporary History; Monacensia Library and Literary Archive. *New Hampshire*: University of New Hampshire Library, Milne Special Collections and Archives. *New Orleans*: Loyola University, College of Music. *New York*: Columbia University Libraries, Butler Library; Kurt Weill Foundation; Leo Baeck Institute; New York Public Library, Special Collections, Manuscripts and Archives Division; New York Public Library of the Performing Arts, Billy Rose Theatre Division; New York University, Fales Library and Special Collections. *Paris*: Bibliothèque Mitterand; Bibliothèque Nationale. *Philadelphia*: University of Pennsylvania, Annenberg Rare Book and Manuscript Library. *Potsdam*: Film Museum. *Salzburg*: Salzburg Festival Archive. *San Diego*: University of California, Special Collections. *Santa Monica*: Public Library. *Urbana*: University of Illinois Archives. *Washington*: National Archives. *Vienna*: Department for Restitution Affairs of the Jewish Community Vienna (IKG Wien); Austrian National Library, Department of Manuscripts, Autographs, and Literary Legacies; Austrian Theatermuseum; Arnold Schönberg Center; Theater in der Josefstadt; Vienna City Library, Department of Manuscripts. *Winchester*: FBI, Record/Information Dissemination Section. *Zurich*: Swiss Social Archives; City Archives.

May the following represent those whose support, encouragement, and cheer; restorative romps; employment; and other good deeds lifted my spirits: Dieter Blubacher (Rheinfelden)†, Bernhard Bodmer (Basel), Martin Bopp (Basel)†, Charles Brauer and Lilot Hegi (Böckten), Thomas Gierl (Basel), Simone Gojan (Rüti), Elisabeth Graf (Baden), Maiķ Günther (Oldenburg), Monika Häckermann (Ritzerau), Michael Heltau (Vienna), Sandra Huck (Stuttgart), Tobias Lange-Rüb (Frankfurt am Main), Claudia Lege (Emmendingen), Antonia Merkel (Rheinfelden), Jürgen Neff (Hamburg), Ilse

Nickel (Berlin), Liane Pollermann (Wangen), Anton Rey (Zurich), Barbara Schmidt (Cologne), Oliver Schmidt (Wismar), Angela Schwartz (Basel) and Eleonora Wenner (Winterthur). And may the many who go unmentioned be so kind as to forgive me.

And, last but not least, I would like to thank Romeo Meyer (Zurich).

NOTES

PREFACE

1. Quoted in Sarah Hucal, "LA Wildfires Threaten German Cultural Sites," *Deutsche Welle*, January 9, 2025.

"A REAL CASTLE ON THE SEA"

1. T. Mann, *Autobiographisches*, 402; Hermann Kesten to Franz Schoenberner, January 8, 1947, in *Deutsche Literatur im Exil*, 295–96.

2. Alfred Döblin to Hermann Kesten, January 10, 1943, in Kesten, *Deutsche Literatur im Exil*, 228.

3. Konrad Kellen, conversation with author, Pacific Palisades, February 2, 2002, as for all following Kellen quotations.

4. [Translator's note:] This offensive term was ubiquitous in German and English during the ages of colonialism and empire. In German likening an experience to "life among the Hottentots" (*wie bei den Hottentotten*) is similar to the English expression "it's like a zoo in here."

5. Hanak, Haas, and Wagner, *Endstation Schein-Heiligenstadt*, 7. [Translator's note: The term *scheinheilig* means "hypocritical" or "duplicitous." Furthermore, when used as a standalone prefix, *Schein-* qualifies the term that follows as being a sham: in Zeisl's opinion Hollywood was a phony Heiligenstadt, a neighborhood in Vienna's nineteenth district of Döbling. Although a proper noun, the name evokes the construction *heilige Stadt*, or "holy city"—and to the ears of German speakers, "Hollywood" sounded a whole lot like "Holy-Wood."]

6. The composer was born Schönberg but changed the spelling of his surname, swapping out the umlauted ö for *oe*, upon reaching the United States.

7. Ann Sommer, conversation with author, Pacific Palisades, February 25, 2007.

8. Sommer, conversation, January 26, 2002.

9. Sommer, conversation, February 25, 2007, as for all following quotations.

10. Declaration of enrollment in Reichsfachschaft Film, September 25, 1933, Reich Chamber of Culture: Sommer, Hans, German Federal Archives, Berlin (formerly Berlin Document Center, BDC)

11. President of Reich Chamber of Music to Hans Sommer, January 4, 1938, German Federal Archives.

12. Reich Chamber of Film, newsletter, July 6, 1938, German Federal Archives.

13. Quoted in Corngold, *Weimar in Princeton*, 74.

FRITZ DIVES OFF A CLIFF, THE LAKOTA DANCE, AND CHRIST RETURNS TO EARTH

1. See Davis, *William Hart*.

2. See Taves, *Thomas Ince*.

3. Cerra and Wanamaker, *Movie Studios*, 8.

4. Thomas H. Ince, "In the 'Movies' Yesterday and Today: History and Development of the Motion Picture Screen," *Nevada State Journal*, March 2, 1924.

5. Harry Carr, "Impressions of the Cyclonic Personality of Thomas Ince: How He Rose to Power," *Los Angeles Times*, November 23, 1924, morning edition, 1.

6. "Dance to Run the Fog Away," *Los Angeles Daily Times*, February 14, 1916, morning edition, sec. 2, p. 2.

7. Edwin Schallert, "A Ghost Town of the Films," *Los Angeles Times*, May 29, 1921, morning edition, sec. 3, pp. 1, 10.

8. The literature often mentions a fire on July 4, 1922, which I was unable to verify in other documents or newspaper articles

METHODISTS CAMP OUT, AND A LONESOME SWABIAN CONSTRUCTS A JAPANESE PALACE

1. "Pacific Palisades to Be Shown in Motion Pictures," *Bulletin*, April 11, 1923, sec. 2, p. 1.

2. Henry Christeen Warnack, "Violates Good Taste," *Los Angeles Daily Times*, April 18, 1916, sec. 2, p. 6.

3. The neighborhood was officially expanded to include the area directly west of Santa Monica, which includes Mabery Road (made famous by Salka Viertel's salon), as part of the "Santa Monica Canyon Add" on April 28, 1925.

4. "Sunday Service to Draw Easter Throngs," *Los Angeles Times*, April 11, 1922, morning edition, sec. 2, p.7.

5. Advertisement, *Los Angeles Daily Times*, July 11, 1922, morning edition, sec. 1, p. 6.

6. Advertisement, *Los Angeles Daily Times*, July 16, 1922, morning edition, sec. 3, p. 34.

7. "Master Home Permit Issued," *Los Angeles Times*, September 4, 1927, 8.

8. Ed Ainsworth, "Auctioneer Hammer to End Famed Oriental Art Dream," *Los Angeles Times*, September 3, 1951, morning edition, 2.

"GIVE IN TO THEIR 'TAKE IT EASY'"

1. Mann and Mann, *Rundherum*, 31.

2. S. Viertel, *Kindness of Strangers*, 134

3. Ibid., 135.

4. Francesco von Mendelssohn to Salka Viertel, August 1928, German Literature Archive, Marbach.

5. Mendelssohn to Viertel, July 1929, German Literature Archive.

6. Zinnemann, *Life in the Movies*, 24.

7. Berthold Viertel to Salka Viertel, June 28, 1940, German Literature Archive.

8. Goebbels, *Tagebücher, 1924–1945*, German Literature Archive, 758.

9. Quoted in Kreimeier, *Ufa Story*, 210.

10. Baum, *Quite Different*, 336.

11. Ibid., 345.

12. Quoted in Nottelmann, *Karrieren*, 209.

13. T. Mann, *Tagebücher, 1937–1939*, 204.

14. Baum, *Quite Different*, 336.

15. M., "Goldberg's Longtime L.A. Home."

16. Hauptmann, "Systematische Vernichtung," 163.

"WHAT WATCH?" "TEN WATCH." "SUCH MUCH?"

1. Nürnberg, "Amerika-Erlebnisse."

2. Quoted in Heilbut, *Exiled in Paradise*, 236.

3. Burlingame, *TV's Biggest Hits*, 89.

4. Kreisler, *Lola und das Blaue*, 15.

5. Polgar, "Leben am Pacific," 21.

6. T. Mann, *Tagebücher, 1946–1948*, 108.

7. Adorno, *Minima Moralia*, 29. [Translator's note:] The *Freischütz* is a figure from German folklore, a marksman who makes a pact with the devil in exchange for magic bullets that will hit whatever target he chooses. The tale is recounted in the 1821 opera by the German romantic composer Carl Maria von Weber.

8. "Der Skandal im 'Deutschen' Theater: Schupo muß jüdische Sudeleien beschützen," *Der Angriff*, December 29, 1933.

9. Kortner, *Aller Tage Abend*, 423.

10. Brecht, *Arbeitsjournal, 1942–1955*, 490.

11. Albert Bassermann to Paul Kohner, May 8, 1939, in Klapdor, *Unheilbarer Europäer*, 177.

12. Fürst, "Ein Taxi-Chauffeur," 13.

13. Quoted in Hecht, *Helene Weigel*, 190, 191.

14. Quoted in Hecht, *Brecht Chronik*, 743.

15. S. Viertel, *Kindness of Strangers*, 282.

16. Lotte Andor, "Ich war nie ein Bernhardiner," 1983, LBI Memoir Collection ME 412, Leo Baeck Archive, New York, 11.

17. Like those on Mabery Road, plots on the west side of Adelaide Drive use the zip code for Santa Monica, though they belong to the neighborhood of Pacific Palisades (Los Angeles City Council District 11). Houses on the east side, including Lorre's, are part of Santa Monica.

18. Hanns-Georg Rodek, "Letzter Flüchtling in Hollywood," *Die Welt*, December 11, 2004.

19. [Translator's note: The Kulturbund Deutscher Juden (Cultural Federation of German Jews) employed Jewish actors, artists, and musicians after the 1933 Law for the Restoration of the Professional Civil Service was passed, which barred Jews and political opponents of the Nazis from the civil service and other public institutions. National Socialist authorities later forced the organization to rename itself the Jüdischer Kulturbund (Jewish Cultural Federation), thereby removing the association between "German" and "Jew."]

20. Brecht, *Arbeitsjournal, 1938–1942*, 359, 405.

21. Thomas Mann to Agnes E. Meyer, October 25, 1946, in T. Mann, *Tagebücher, 1946–1948*, 465–66.

22. Capote, *Breakfast at Tiffany's*, 33.

23. Kutner, "Miss Rainer Regrets," *Modern Screen*, February 1937, 47, 106.

24. Rainer, "God."

25. Brecht, *Arbeitsjournal, 1938–1942*, 494, 469.

26. Brecht, *Arbeitsjournal, 1942–1955*, 509.

27. Brecht, *Werke*, 27:50.

28. Brecht, *Arbeitsjournal, 1938–1942*, 362, 303, 313.

29. Brecht, *Collected Poems* 876.

30. Quoted in Asper, "Etwas Besseres," 426.

31. Lyon, "Broadway," 118; Rainer, "God."

32. Erskine Johnson, "He's Really a Nice Fellow!" *Pittsburgh Press*, December 20, 1942, 23.

33. Klaus Mann to Erika Mann, [January 1927?], in Kroll and Täubert, *Klaus-Mann-Schriftenreihe*, 166.

34. Ewald André Dupont, press release, n.d., Marta Mierendorff Collection, University of Southern California, Los Angeles.

35. Tonio Selwart, conversation with author, New York, February 20, 2002.

"YOU LOSE YOUR HOME AND THERE'S NO FINDING A NEW ONE"

1. Slonimsky, "Ernst Toch," 499.

2. Ernst Toch to Ernst and Johanna Bass, January 30, 1934, in Hanak, Haas, and Wagner, *Endstation Schein-Heiligenstadt*, 60.

3. Quoted in Traber and Weingarten, *Verdrängte Musik*, 114.

4. Quoted in Weschler, "My Grandfather's Last Tale."

5. Quoted in Albert, *Das schwierige Handwerk*, 50.

6. Quoted in Kosfeld, "Todestag des Komponisten."

7. Gertrud Zenzes to Gottfried Benn, April 5, 1953, in Hof and Kraft, *Gottfried Benn*, 216

8. Kellen, conversation, February 12, 2002.

9. Francesco von Mendelssohn to Christoph Bernoulli, n.d., Mendelssohn Archive, Berlin State Library.

10. Eleonora von Mendelssohn to Berthold and Salka Viertel, n.d., German Literature Archive.

11. Klaus Mann, *Tagebücher, 1940–1943*, 12.

12. B. Viertel, *Studienausgabe*, 227, 228.

13. Francesco von Mendelssohn to Alice Bernoulli, July 4, 1946, Mendelssohn Archive, Berlin State Library.

14. Vita Petersen, conversation with author, New York, January 9, 2002.

15. Dieter Sattlers, unpublished diaries, April 25, 1965, privately owned.

16. Grautoff, *Göttin*, 112.

17. Klaus Mann to Ruth Landshoff, February 4, 1939, German Literature Archive.

18. Quoted in *Time Magazine*, May 22, 1939.

19. Quoted in G. Reinhardt, *Liebhaber*, 277.

20. *Völkischer Beobachter*, March 3, 1933.

21. Quoted in Wulf, *Theater und Film*, 266.

22. Max Reinhardt to Eleonora von Mendelssohn, late August 1937, box 3, Eleonora von Mendelssohn Papers, New York Public Library Manuscripts and Archives Division.

23. Thimig-Reinhardt, *Wie Max Reinhardt lebte*, 186.

24. Hollaender, *Von Kopf bis Fuß*, 327.

25. Klaus Mann, *Tagebücher, 1936–1937*, 98.

26. Lion Feuchtwanger to Bertolt Brecht, February 16, 1936, in Feuchtwanger, "Briefe an die Freunde," 12. [Translator's note: In calling Reinhardt's production a "Jewish-American Oberammergau," Feuchtwanger is referencing the Oberammergau passion play, which has been performed regularly in the Bavarian village of Oberammergau since 1634.]

27. Zuckmayer, *Als wär's ein Stück*, 72.

28. Quoted in Novak, *Salzburg hört Hitler atmen*, 105.

29. Max Reinhardt to Francesco von Mendelssohn, draft letter, August 1943, sign. 2.2.2.13, partial papers of Max Reinhardt, Manuscript Department, Vienna City Library.

30. Thimig-Reinhardt, *Wie Max Reinhardt lebte*, 209.

31. Max Reinhardt to Helene Thimig, August 25, 1942, sign. 2.2.1.388, Vienna City Library.

32. Thimig-Reinhardt, *Wie Max Reinhardt lebte*, 231, 203.

33. [Translator's note: *Volljüdin* means "full Jew," a Nazi term for someone with at least three Jewish grandparents.]

34. Helene Thimig to Max Reinhardt, 1941, sign. 2.1.1.79, Vienna City Library.

35. Thimig to Reinhardt, July 15, 1943, sign. 2.1.1.166, Vienna City Library.

36. Thimig-Reinhardt, *Wie Max Reinhardt lebte*, 236–37.

37. Quoted in G. Reinhardt, *Liebhaber*, 278; Brecht, *Arbeitsjournal, 1938–1942*, 445.

38. Kortner, *Aller Tage Abend*, 393.

39. Max Reinhardt to Einar Nilson, November 18, 1934, in Fiedler, *Max Reinhardt*, 122; Max Reinhardt to Friedrich von Ledebur, July 1940, in M. Reinhardt, *Leben für das Theater*, 317.

40. Quoted in G. Reinhardt, *Liebhaber*, 278.

41. Thimig to Reinhardt, August 8, 1942, sign. 2.1.1.127, Vienna City Library.

42. Thimig to Reinhardt, September 7, 1942, sign. 2.1.1.131, Vienna City Library.

43. Quoted in Fuhrich-Leisler and Prossnitz, *Max Reinhardt in Amerika*, 406.

44. Gottfried Reinhardt to Salka Viertel, October 22, 1943, German Literature Archive.

45. Quoted in Pascal, *Grand Surprise*, 543.

46. Quoted in Fuhrich-Leisler and Prossnitz, *Max Reinhardt in Amerika*, 409.

PAYING HOMAGE TO GOETHE IN HOLLYWOOD

1. Marcuse, *Mein zwanzigstes Jahrhundert*, 289; Bahr, "Der Schriftstellerkongress 1943," 43.

2. Thomas Mann, "Freund Feuchtwanger," *Die Weltwoche*, July 2, 1954; T. Mann, *Tagebücher, 1940–1943*, 661.

3. T. Mann, *Tagebücher, 1933–1934*, 93, 30, 71.

4. "Mann Finds U.S. Sole Peace Hope," *New York Times*, February 22, 1938.

5. T. Mann, *Tagebücher, 1938–1940*, 387.

6. Dietrich, *Nehmt nur mein Leben*, 278–81.

7. Quoted in G. Reinhardt, *Liebhaber*, 270.

8. Claire Lehmkuhl to Erich Maria Remarque, in Gilbert, *Erich Maria Remarque*, 334.

9. Quoted in Schad, *Frauen gegen Hitler*, 135.

10. T. Mann, *Tagebücher, 1940–1943*, 112.

11. T. Mann to Meyer, July 8, 1940, in Vaget, *Thomas Mann*, 211.

12. T. Mann, *Tagebücher, 1940–1943*, 116–17, 129, 130.

13. Ibid., 429–30, 478, 491, 560; T. Mann, *Tagebücher, 1944–1946*, 23.

14. Katia Mann, *Unwritten Memories*, 119.

15. T. Mann, *Briefe, 1937–1947*, 250.

16. Katia Mann, *Unwritten Memories*, 120.

17. Quoted in Vaget, *Amerikaner*, 361.

18. George Tabori, conversation with Inge Jens, October 15, 1987, in T. Mann, *Tagebücher, 1946–1948*, 714.

THE KING OF PACIFIC PALISADES HELPS DISPOSE OF THE DEAD MICE

1. Quoted in Young, "Exile in Paradise," 16.
2. "Ideal Dwelling Ceremony Set," *Los Angeles Times*, August 21, 1927, sec. 5, p. 6.
3. Feuchtwanger and Weschler, *Émigré Life*, 3:1147.
4. Ibid., 3:1153, 3:1155.
5. Ibid., 3:1158–59.
6. Quoted in Flügge, *Die vier Leben*, 335.
7. Ibid., 9.
8. Quoted in Skierka, *Lion Feuchtwanger*, 37.
9. Quoted in Flügge, *Die vier Leben*, 162.
10. Ibid., 163.
11. Skierka, *Lion Feuchtwanger*, 330.
12. Feuchtwanger and Weschler, *Émigré Life*, 3:1135.
13. Lion Feuchtwanger to Arnold Zweig, July 9, 1941, in Skierka, *Lion Feuchtwanger*, 214.
14. Marcuse, *Mein zwanzigstes Jahrhundert*, 281.
15. Tabori, *Unterammergau*, 15–16.
16. Marcuse, *Mein zwanzigstes Jahrhundert*, 280.

"AND THAT SUBSTANCE IS OUR WORK"

1. Quoted in Jungk, *Franz Werfel*, 289.
2. Max Horkheimer to Theodor Adorno, August 28, 1941, in Horkheimer, *Briefwechsel*, 144.
3. Adorno, *Letters to His Parents*, 71.
4. Horkheimer, *Vorträge und Aufzeichnungen*, 443.
5. See Rosen, *Max Horkheimer*, 27.
6. Ibid., 38.
7. Max Horkheimer to Friedrich Pollock, April 27, 1941, in Horkheimer, *Briefwechsel*, 27.
8. T. Mann, *Tagebücher, 1940–1943*, 293.

9. Max Horkheimer to Leo Löwenthal, June 18, 1941, in Horkheimer, *Briefwechsel*, 70.

10. Horkheimer to Pollock, October 4, 1941, in Horkheimer, *Briefwechsel*, 187.

11. Theodor Adorno to Max Horkheimer, September 28, 1942, in Horkheimer, *Briefwechsel*, 334.

12. T. Mann, *Tagebücher, 1946–1948*, 189.

13. T. Mann, *Gesammelte Werke*, 296; T. Mann, *Tagebücher, 1946–1948*, 189.

14. Max Horkheimer to Clara and Siegfried Kander, August 13, 1945, in Horkheimer, *Briefwechsel*, 643.

15. Mann and Mann, *Escape to Life*, 277.

16. Thomas Mann, *Tagebücher, 1940–1943*, 655.

17. Max Horkheimer to Margot Weil, May 6, 1942, in Horkheimer, *Briefwechsel*, 277–78.

18. Quoted in Henke, *Arnold Schönberg*, 154.

19. Max Horkheimer to Felix Weil, March 10, 1942, in Horkheimer, *Briefwechsel*, 274.

SALKA VIERTEL SERVES SAUSAGE SOUP, AND ALFRED DÖBLIN SEARCHES FOR GOD

1. Marcuse, *Mein zwanzigstes Jahrhundert*, 276.

2. Richard Révy to Manfred George, September 20, 1943, in Horak, *Fluchtpunkt Hollywood*, 33.

3. Goetz and Martens, *Memoiren*, 306.

4. S. Viertel, *Kindness of Strangers*, 207–8.

5. Ibid., 208.

6. Quoted in Carroll, "Exil im Paradies," 110, 111.

7. Frank, *Links*, 201–4.

8. Quoted in Moore, "Exil in Hollywood," 29.

9. Brecht, *Arbeitsjournal, 1938–1942*, 304.

10. Ibid., 325.

11. Lion Feuchtwanger to Franz Carl Weiskopf, March 3, 1942, in Feuchtwanger, *Briefwechsel*, 62.

12. Quoted in Gilbert, *Erich Maria Remarque*, 323.

13. T. Mann, *Tagebücher, 1944–1946*, 54.

14. Kortner, *Aller Tage Abend*, 423.

15. Grautoff, *Göttin*, 111–12.

16. Quoted in Prager, *"Gone Hollywood,"* 117.

17. Quoted in Grautoff, *Göttin*, 113.

18. T. Mann, *Tagebücher, 1944–1946*, 13; T. Mann, *Tagebücher, 1946–1948*, 43.

19. Brün-Kortner and Asper, "Erinnerungen," 33.

20. Katia Mann, *Unwritten Memories*, 123.

21. Quoted in Révy, *Apokalyptischer Zeit*, 46.

22. Joseph, *Portraits I*, 290.

23. B. Viertel, "Ansprache an Alfred Döblin," 17.

24. S. Viertel, *Kindness of Strangers*, 251.

25. T. Mann, *Tagebücher, 1940–1943*, 253, 406, 412. [Translator's note: An old-fashioned word for "wife," *das Weib* is also a denigrating term for women more generally.]

26. Katia Mann to Klaus Mann, April 20, 1942, in Jüngling, *"Ich bin doch nicht,"* 146.

27. Heinrich Mann to Berthold Fles, April 19, 1944, in Jüngling, *"Ich bin doch nicht,"* 159.

28. Jüngling, *"Ich bin doch nicht,"* 166.

29. T. Mann, *Tagebücher, 1944–1946*, 137.

30. Brecht, *Arbeitsjournal, 1942–1955*, 605.

31. Ibid., 621, 694.

32. Brecht, *Arbeitsjournal, 1938–1942*, 295.

33. Brecht, *Arbeitsjournal, 1942–1955*, 664, 696.

34. Katia Mann, *Unwritten Memories*, 124, 123.

35. T. Mann, *Tagebücher, 1940–1943*, 566.

36. Ibid., 146.

37. Ludwig, *Im Urteil der Weltpresse*, 6.

38. Tucholsky, *Gesammelte Werke*, 48.

39. Quoted in Berger, *In jenen Tagen*, 287.

40. Goebbels, *Tagebücher von Joseph Goebbels*.

41. Joseph, *Tisch bei Romanoff's*, 204.

42. Brecht, *Arbeitsjournal, 1938–1942*, 366.

"TERRIBLY DISTURBED BY THE DWINDLING SENSE OF JUSTICE IN THIS COUNTRY"

1. T. Mann, *Tagebücher, 1946–1948*, 164.

2. Lehnert, "Bert Brecht," 68.

3. T. Mann, *Tagebücher, 1944–1946*, 313.

4. Quoted in Vaget, *Amerikaner*, 125.

5. T. Mann, *Tagebücher, 1940–1943*, 561.

6. T. Mann, *Deutsche Hörer!* 59.

7. T. Mann, *Tagebücher, 1944–1946*, 78.

8. Vansittart, *Black Record*, book jacket.

9. Quoted in Taylor, *Strangers in Paradise*, 170.

10. T. Mann to Meyer, in Vaget, *Thomas Mann*, 504.

11. Brecht, *Collected Poems*, 881–83.

12. T. Mann, *Tagebücher, 1944–1946*, 200–201.

13. Ibid., 235–36, 286; Heine and Schommer, *Thomas Mann Chronik*, 420.

14. Marcuse, *Mein zwanzigstes Jahrhundert*, 273.

15. Frank, *Links*, 213.

16. Federal Bureau of Investigation, report, June 18, 1942, in Stephan, *Im Visier des FBI*, 165.

17. *Public Law 601: Hearings Regarding Hanns Eisler before the Committee on Un-American Activities*, 80th Cong. (September 24–26, 1947).

18. Quoted in Schebera, *Hanns Eisler im USA-Exil*, 73.

19. Lou Eisler to Alan Bush, August 27, 1947, in Schebera, *Hanns Eisler im USA-Exil*, 165.

20. T. Mann, *Tagebücher, 1946–1948*, 165.

21. Quoted in Rosen, *Max Horkheimer*, 48.

22. Ibid., 52.

23. Herbert Marcuse to Max Horkheimer, June 17, 1967, ibid., 53.

24. Frank Thiess, "Die innere Emigration," *Münchner Zeitung*, August 18, 1945.

25. Quoted in Vaget, *Amerikaner*, 492.

26. Prager, "*Gone Hollywood,*" 258.

PLAYERS, ALL: RONALD REAGAN ON SCREEN, HENRY MILLER IN THE BACKYARD, AND JAKOB GIMPEL ON PIANO

1. R. Reagan, *American Life*, 110.

2. N. Reagan, *My Turn*, 124–25.

3. Ibid., 128.

4. Foo, "Other Former White House."

5. Quoted in Almendrala, "Hitler Bunker."

6. Quoted in Wagner, *Fremd bin ich ausgezogen*, 247.
7. Arlen, "Musik ist das Beste."
8. Florian Kugel, "Aldous Huxleys letzter Trip," *Der Spiegel*, September 15, 2020.
9. Dearborn, *Happiest Man Alive*, 279.
10. Bozhkov, "Iconoclast Next Door."
11. Flügge, *Die vier Leben*, 337.
12. Feuchtwanger and Weschler, *Émigré Life*, 4:1641.
13. "Los Angeles."
14. *Palisadian Post*, November 13, 2008.

THE LEGACY OF EXILE

1. Flügge, *Die vier Leben*, 378.
2. "Ein wahres Schloß am Meer," *Der Spiegel*, December 20, 1987.
3. Flügge, *Die vier Leben*, 405.
4. Steinmeier, "Address at the Opening."

BIBLIOGRAPHY

WORKS CITED IN TEXT AND NOTES

Adorno, Theodor W. *Letters to His Parents, 1939–1951*. Edited by Christoph Gödde and Henri Lonitz. Translated by Wieland Hoban. Cambridge, MA: Polity, 2006.

———. *Minima Moralia*. Translated by Edmund F. N. Jephcott. London: Verso, 2005.

Albert, Claudia. *Das schwierige Handwerk des Hoffens: Hanns Eislers "Hollywooder Liederbuch" (1942/43)*. Stuttgart: Metzler, 1991.

Almendrala, Anna. "Hitler Bunker in Los Angeles: Murphy Ranch Reveals an Alternate Universe." Huffington Post. March 19, 2012. www.huffpost.com.

Arlen, Walter. "Musik ist das Beste was mir passiert ist." Wiener Zeitung. Accessed December 13, 2021. www.wienerzeitung.at.

Asper, Helmut G. *"Etwas Besseres als den Tod . . .": Filmexil in Hollywood: Porträts, Filme, Dokumente*. Marburg: Schüren, 2002.

Bahr, Ehrhard. "Der Schriftstellerkongress 1943 an der Universität von Kalifornien." In *Deutsche Exilliteratur seit 1933*. Vol. 1, *Kalifornien*, edited by John M. Spalek and Joseph Strelka, 40–61. Bern: De Gruyter, 1976.

Baum, Vicki. *It Was All Quite Different: The Memoirs of Vicki Baum*. New York: Funk and Wagnalls, 1964.

Berger, Friedemann. *In jenen Tagen . . . Schriftsteller zwischen Reichstagsbrand und Bücherverbrennung*. Leipzig: Kiepenheuer, 1983.

Bozhkov, Jill Sharer. "The Iconoclast Next Door." *Los Angeles Magazine*, January 3, 2016. https://lamag.com.

Brecht, Bertolt. *Arbeitsjournal, 1938–1942*. Edited by Werner Hecht. Frankfurt: Suhrkamp, 1973.

———. *Arbeitsjournal, 1942–1955*. Edited by Werner Hecht. Frankfurt: Suhrkamp, 1973.

———. *The Collected Poems of Bertolt Brecht*. Translated by Tom Kuhn and David Constantine. New York: Liveright, 2018.

———. *Werke: Große kommentierte Berliner und Frankfurter Ausgabe*. Vols. 27–29. Frankfurt: Suhrkamp, 1995.

Brün-Kortner, Marianne, and Helmut G. Asper. "Erinnerungen an Berthold Viertel: Ein Gespräch." In *Traum von der Realität: Berthold Viertel*, edited by Siglinde Bolbecher, Konstantin Kaiser, and Peter Roessler. Vienna: Döcker, 1998.

Burlingame, Jon. *TV's Biggest Hits: The Story of Television Themes from "Dragnet" to "Friends."* New York: Schirmer Books, 1996.

Capote, Truman. *Breakfast at Tiffany's*. London: Penguin Books, 1961.

Carroll, Brendan G. "Exil im Paradies: Europäische Emigranten und der Traum von Hollywood." In Hanak, Haas, and Wagner, *Endstation Schein-Heiligenstadt*.

Cerra, Julia Lugo, and Marc Wanamaker. *Movie Studios of Culver City*. Charleston, SC: Arcadia, 2011.

Corngold, Stanley. *Weimar in Princeton: Thomas Mann and the Kahler Circle*. New York: Bloomsbury Academic, 2022.

Davis, Ronald L. *William Hart: Projecting the American West*. Norman: University of Oklahoma Press, 2003.

Dearborn, Mary V. *The Happiest Man Alive: A Biography of Henry Miller*. New York: Touchstone, 1991.

Dietrich, Marlene. *Nehmt nur mein Leben*. Munich: Bertelsmann, 1979.

Feuchtwanger, Lion. "Briefe an die Freunde." *Sinn und Form*, no. 1 (1959): 12–19. https://sinn-und-form.de.

———. *Briefwechsel mit Freunden, 1933–1958*. Vol. 2. Berlin: Aufbau, 1991.

Feuchtwanger, Marta, and Lawrence M. Weschler. *An Émigré Life: Munich, Berlin, Sanary, Pacific Palisades*. Vols. 3–4. Los Angeles: Oral History Program, University of California, 1976.

Fiedler, Leonhard. *Max Reinhardt*. Reinbek: Rowohlt, 1975.

Flügge, Manfred. *Die vier Leben der Marta Feuchtwanger*. Berlin: Aufbau, 2010.

Foo, Mei Anne. "Ronald Reagan's Other Former White House for Sale." Jaman Properties. July 1, 2016. https://jamanproperties.com.

Frank, Leonhard. *Links, wo das Herz ist*. Berlin: Aufbau, 2009.

Fuhrich-Leisler, Edda, and Gisela Prossnitz. *Max Reinhardt in Amerika*. Salzburg: Müller, 1976.

Fürst, Manfred. "Ein Taxi-Chauffeur in Hollywood." *Aufbau* 9, no. 28 (July 9, 1943).

Gilbert, Julie. *Erich Maria Remarque und Paulette Goddard: Biographie einer Liebe*. Munich: List, 1997.

Goebbels, Joseph. *Tagebücher, 1924–1945*. Vol. 2, *1930–1934*, edited by Ralf Georg Reuth. Munich: Piper, 1999.

———. *Die Tagebücher von Joseph Goebbels*. Vol. 1, *Aufzeichnungen, 1923–1941*, edited by Elke Fröhlich. Munich: Saur, 1987.

Goetz, Curt, and Valérie von Martens. *Memoiren*. Stuttgart: Bastei Lübbe, 1969.

Grautoff, Christiane. *Die Göttin und ihr Sozialist: Christiane Grautoffs Autobiographie; Ihr Leben mit Ernst Toller*. Edited by Werner Fuld and Albert Ostermaier. Bonn: Wallstein, 1996.

Hanak, Werner, Michael Haas, and Karin Wagner, eds. *Endstation Schein-Heiligenstadt: Eric Zeisls Flucht Nach Hollywood*. Vienna: Jüdisches Museum Wien, 2006.

Hauptmann, Hans. "Die systematische Vernichtung der arischen Kulturgüter." In *Der Jud ist schuld... ? Diskussionsbuch über die Judenfrage*, 151–65. Basel: Zinnen, 1932.

Hecht, Werner. *Brecht Chronik, 1898–1956*. Frankfurt: Suhrkamp, 1997.

———. *Helene Weigel: Eine große Frau des 20. Jahrhunderts*. Frankfurt: Suhrkamp, 2000.

Heilbut, Anthony. *Exiled in Paradise: German Refugee Artists and Intellectuals in America, from the 1930s to the Present*. New York: Viking, 1983.

Heine, Gert, and Paul Schommer. *Thomas Mann Chronik*. Frankfurt: Fischer, 2004.

Henke, Matthias. *Arnold Schönberg*. Munich: dtv Verlagsgesellschaft, 2001.

Hof, Holger, and Stephan Kraft, eds. *Gottfried Benn, Getrud Zenzes: Briefwechsel, 1921–1956*. Göttingen: Wallstein, 2021.

Hollaender, Friedrich. *Von Kopf bis Fuß: Mein Leben mit Text und Musik*. Munich: Kindler, 1965.

Horak, Jan-Christopher. *Fluchtpunkt Hollywood: Eine Dokumentation zur Filmemigration nach 1933*. Münster: MAkS, 1984.

Horkheimer, Max. *Briefwechsel, 1941–1948*. Vol. 17 of *Gesammelte Schriften*. Frankfurt: Fischer, 1996.

———. *Vorträge und Aufzeichnungen, 1949–1973*. Vol. 7 of *Gesammelte Schriften*. Frankfurt: Fischer, 1985.

Joseph, Albrecht. *Portraits I: Carl Zuckmayer, Bruno Frank*. Translated by Rüdiger Völckers. Aachen: Weidle, 1993.

———. *Ein Tisch bei Romanoff's: Erinnerungen*. Mönchengladbach: Juni, 1991.

Jungk, Peter Stephan. *Franz Werfel: Eine Lebensgeschichte*. Frankfurt: Fischer, 2006.

Jüngling, Kerstin. "*Ich bin doch nicht nur schlecht*": *Nelly Mann*. Berlin: Propyläen, 2009.

Kesten, Hermann, ed. *Deutsche Literatur im Exil: Briefe europäischer Autoren*. Vienna: Desch, 1964.

Klapdor, Heike, ed. *Ich bin ein unheilbarer Europäer: Briefe aus dem Exil*. Berlin: Aufbau, 2007.

Kortner, Fritz. *Aller Tage Abend: Autobiographie*. Munich: Kindler, 1979.

Kosfeld, Christian. "Todestag des Komponisten Ernst Koch." *ZeitZeichen*. WDR 5. October 1, 2019. www1.wdr.de.

Kreimeier, Klaus. *The Ufa Story: A History of Germany's Greatest Film Company, 1918–1945*. Translated by Robert Rita Kimber. Berkeley: University of California Press, 1999.

Kreisler, Georg. *Lola und das Blaue vom Himmel: Eine Erinnerung*. Edited by Thomas B. Schumann. Hürth: Memoria, 2002.

Kroll, Fredric, and Klaus Täubert. *Klaus-Mann-Schriftenreihe*. Vol. 2, *1906–1927: Unordnung und früher Ruhm*. Wiesbaden: Blahak, 1977.

Lehnert, Herbert. "Bert Brecht und Thomas Mann." In *Deutsche Exilliteratur seit 1933*. Vol. 1, *Kalifornien*, edited by John M. Spalek and Joseph Strelka, 62–88. Bern: De Gruyter, 1976.

"Los Angeles, CA (Pacific Palisades)." Neighborhood Scout. Accessed July 17, 2024. www.neighborhoodscout.com.

Ludwig, Emil. *Im Urteil der Weltpresse*. Berlin: Rowohlt, 1928.

Lyon, James K. "Broadway und 'Der kaukasische Kreidekreis.'" In *Brechts Kaukasischer Kreidekreis*, edited by Werner Hecht, 117–26. Frankfurt: Suhrkamp, 1985.

M., Kathryn. "Whoopi Goldberg's Longtime L.A. Home Seeks to Trade Hands for $9.6M." Dwell. Accessed June 13, 2024. www.dwell.com.

Mann, Erika, and Klaus Mann. *Escape to Life: Deutsche Kultur im Exil*. Reinbek: Rowohlt, 1996.

———. *Rundherum: Abenteuer einer Weltreise*. Reinbek: Rowohlt, 1999.

Mann, Katia. *Unwritten Memories*. Edited by Elisabeth Plessen and Michael Mann. Translated by Hunter and Hildegard Hannum. New York: Knopf, 1975.

Mann, Klaus. *Tagebücher, 1936–1937*. Reinbek: Rowohlt, 1995.

———. *Tagebücher, 1940–1943*. Reinbek: Rowohlt, 1995.

Mann, Thomas. *Autobiographisches*. Frankfurt: Fischer, 1968.

———. *Briefe, 1937–1947*. Edited by Erika Mann. Frankfurt: Fischer, 1963.

———. *Deutsche Hörer! Radiosendungen nach Deutschland aus den Jahren, 1940–1945*. Frankfurt: Fischer, 1987.

———. *Gesammelte Werke*. Vol. 11. Frankfurt: Fischer, 1960.

———. *Tagebücher, 1933–1934*. Edited by Peter de Mendelssohn. Frankfurt: Fischer, 1977.

———. *Tagebücher, 1937–1939*. Edited by Peter de Mendelssohn. Frankfurt: Fischer, 2003.

———. *Tagebücher, 1938–1940*. Edited by Peter de Mendelssohn. Frankfurt: Fischer, 2003.

———. *Tagebücher, 1940–1943*. Edited by Peter de Mendelssohn. Frankfurt: Fischer, 2003.

———. *Tagebücher, 1944–1946*. Edited by Inge Jens. Frankfurt: Fischer, 2003.

———. *Tagebücher, 1946–1948*. Edited by Inge Jens. Frankfurt: Fischer, 2003.

Marcuse, Ludwig. *Mein zwanzigstes Jahrhundert: Auf dem Weg zu einer Autobiographie*. Zurich: Diogenes, 1975.

Moore, Erna M. "Exil in Hollywood." In *Deutsche Exilliteratur seit 1933*. Vol. 1, *Kalifornien*, edited by John M. Spalek and Joseph Strelka, 21–39. Bern: De Gruyter, 1976.

Nottelmann, Nicole. *Die Karrieren der Vicki Baum*. Cologne: Kiepenheuer und Witsch, 2007.

Novak, Andreas. *Salzburg hört Hitler atmen*. Munich: Anstalt, 2005.

Nürnberg, Rolf. "Amerika-Erlebnisse: Rolf Nürnberg erzählt über seine Eindrücke." *Film-Kurier*, no. 208 (September 3, 1932).

Pascal, Stephen, ed. *The Grand Surprise: The Journals of Leo Lerman*. New York: Knopf, 2007.

Polgar, Alfred. "Leben am Pacific." *Aufbau* 8, no. 36 (September 4, 1942).

Prager, Katharina. *"Ich bin nicht gone Hollywood!": Salka Viertel; Ein Leben in Theater und Film*. Vienna: Braumüller, 2007.

Rainer, Luise. "God, or Whoever It Is, Gave So Much into My Cradle and I Have Not Lived Up to It." *Scotsman*, January 4, 2010. https://web.archive.org.

Reagan, Nancy. *My Turn: The Memoirs of Nancy Reagan*. With William Novak. Thorndike, ME: Thorndike, 1990.

Reagan, Ronald. *An American Life*. New York: Simon and Schuster, 1990.

Reinhardt, Gottfried. *Der Liebhaber: Erinnerungen seines Sohnes Gottfried Reinhardt an Max Reinhardt*. Zurich: Droemer Knaur, 1974.

Reinhardt, Max. *Leben für das Theater: Briefe, Reden, Aufsätze, Interviews, Gespräche, Auszüge aus Regiebüchern*. Edited by Hugo von Fetting. Berlin: Argon, 1989.

Révy, Richard. *Ich lebte in apokalyptischer Zeit: Aus Schriften und Tagebüchern*. Müggendorf: Kontinuum, 1996.

Rosen, Zvi. *Max Horkheimer*. Munich: Beck, 1995.

Schad, Martha. *Frauen gegen Hitler: Schicksale im Nationalsozialismus*. Munich: Heyne, 2001.

Schebera, Jürgen. *Hanns Eisler im USA-Exil*. Meisenheim: Hain, 1978.

Skierka, Volker. *Lion Feuchtwanger*. Berlin: Quadriga, 1984.

Slonimsky, Nicolas. "Ernst Toch (1887–1976 [*sic*])." *Neue Zeitschrift für Musik* 128, no. 12 (1967): 499–501.

Steinmeier, Frank-Walter, "Address at the Opening of the Thomas Mann House in Pacific Palisades, U.S." Bundespräsidialamt. June 19, 2018. https://bundespraesident.de.

Stephan, Alexander. *Im Visier des FBI: Deutsche Exilschriftsteller in den Akten amerikanischer Geheimdienste*. Stuttgart: Aufbau, 1995.

Tabori, George. *Unterammergau oder die guten Deutschen*. Frankfurt: Suhrkamp, 1983.

Taves, Brian. *Thomas Ince: Hollywood's Independent Pioneer*. Lexington: University Press of Kentucky, 2012.

Taylor, John Russell. *Strangers in Paradise: The Hollywood Émigrés, 1933–1950*. New York: Holt, Rinehart and Winston, 1983.

Thimig-Reinhardt, Helene. *Wie Max Reinhardt lebte . . . Eine Handbreit über dem Boden*. Frankfurt: Fischer, 1975.

Traber, Habakuk, and Elmar Weingarten, eds. *Verdrängte Musik: Berliner Komponisten im Exil*. Berlin: Argon, 1987.

Tucholsky, Kurt. *Gesammelte Werke*. Vol. 10. Reinbek: Rowohlt, 1975.

Vaget, Hans Rudolf, ed. *Thomas Mann, Agnes E. Meyer: Briefwechsel, 1937–1955*. Frankfurt: Fischer, 1992.

———. *Thomas Mann, der Amerikaner*. Frankfurt: Fischer, 2011.

Vansittart, Sir Robert Gilbert. *Black Record: Germans Past and Present*. London: Hamish Hamilton, 1941.

Viertel, Berthold. "Ansprache an Alfred Döblin." *Aufbau* 9, no. 34 (August 20, 1943).

———. *Studienausgabe in vier Bänden*. Vol. 2, *Kindheit eines Cherub*, edited by Siglinde Bolbecher and Konstantin Kaiser. Vienna: Gesellschaftskritik, 1991.

Viertel, Salka. *The Kindness of Strangers*. New York: Holt, Rinehart and Winston, 1969.

Wagner, Karin. *Fremd bin ich ausgezogen: Eric Zeisl*. Vienna: Czernin, 2005.

Weschler, Lawrence M. "My Grandfather's Last Tale." *Atlantic*, December 1996. www.theatlantic.com.

Wulf, Joseph. *Theater und Film im Dritten Reich*. Frankfurt: Ullstein, 1983.

Young, Randy. "Exile in Paradise: The Feuchtwangers in Pacific Palisades." In *10 Years Villa Aurora: 1995–2005*, edited by Mechthild Borries-Knopp, Anna Kindler, Gisela Lehmeier, Signe Rossbach, and Nicole Stangl, 12–21. Ebenhausen: Dölling und Galitz, 2005.

Zinnemann, Fred. *A Life in the Movies: An Autobiography*. New York: Scribner's Sons, 1992.

Zuckmayer, Carl. *Als wär's ein Stück von mir: Horen der Freundschaft*. Frankfurt: Fischer, 1966.

RECOMMENDATIONS FOR FURTHER READING

Bach, Steven. *Marlene Dietrich: Life and Legend*. Minneapolis: University of Minnesota Press, 2011.

Bachardy, Don. *Stars in My Eyes*. Madison: University of Wisconsin Press, 2000.

Bahr, Ehrhard. *Weimar on the Pacific: German Exile Culture in Los Angeles and the Crisis of Modernism*. Berkeley: University of California Press, 2008.

Barron, Stephanie, ed. *Exiles + Emigrés: The Flight of European Artists from Hitler*. Los Angeles: Los Angeles County Museum of Art, 1997.

Bartley, Margaret. *Grisha: The Dramatic Story of Cellist Gregor Piatigorsky*. New Russia, NY: Otis Mountain, 2004.

Barton, Ruth. *Hedy Lamarr: The Most Beautiful Woman in Film*. Lexington: University Press of Kentucky, 2010.

Bedford, Sybille. *Aldous Huxley: A Biography*. New York: Knopf/Harper and Row, 1974.

Braeden, Eric, and Lindsay Harrison. *I'll Be Damned: How My Young and Restless Life Led Me to America's #1 Daytime Drama*. New York: Dey Street Books, 2017.

Brinkmann, Reinhold, and Christian Wolff. *Driven into Paradise: The Musical Migration from Nazi Germany to the United States*. Berkeley: University of California Press, 1999.

Brunas, Michael, John Brunas, and Tom Weaver. *Universal Horrors: The Studio's Classic Films, 1931–1946*. Jefferson, NC: McFarland, 2007.

Callow, Simon. *Charles Laughton: A Difficult Actor*. New York: Fromm International, 1997.

Chaplin, Charles. *My Autobiography*. London: Bodley Head, 1964.

Crawford, Dorothy Lamb. *A Windfall of Musicians: Hitler's Émigrés and Exiles in Southern California*. New Haven, CT: Yale University Press, 2011.

Dawes, Amy. *Sunset Boulevard: Cruising the Heart of Los Angeles*. Los Angeles: Los Angeles Times Books, 2002.

De Acosta, Mercedes. *Here Lies the Heart*. New York: Arno, 1960.

Doherty, Thomas. *Hollywood and Hitler, 1933–1950*. New York: Columbia University Press, 2013.

Gemünden, Gerd. *Continental Strangers: German Exile Cinema, 1933–1951*. New York: Columbia University Press, 2014.

Goldberg, Whoopi. *Book*. New York: Morrow, 1998.

Henreid, Paul. *Ladies' Man: An Autobiography*. New York: St. Martin's Press, 1984.

Hirsch, Foster. *A Method to Their Madness: The History of the Actors Studio*. New York: Norton, 1984.

Horowitz, Joseph. *Artists in Exile: How Refugees from Twentieth-Century War and Revolution Transformed the American Performing Arts*. New York: HarperCollins, 2008.

Isherwood, Christopher. *Diaries*. Vol. 1, *1939–1960*. Edited by Katherine Bucknell. New York: HarperCollins, 1997.

Jezic, Diane. *The Musical Migration and Ernst Toch*. Ames: Iowa State University Press, 1989.

Kirkham, Pat. *Charles and Ray Eames: Designers of the Twentieth Century*. Cambridge, MA: MIT Press, 1998.

Loomis, Jan. *Pacific Palisades*. Charleston, SC: Arcadia, 2009.

Palmier, Jean-Michel. *Weimar in Exile: Exile in Europe, Exile in America*. New York: Verso, 2006.

Paris, Barry. *Garbo: A Biography*. New York: Knopf, 1995.

Piatigorsky, Gregor. *Cellist*. New York: Da Capo, 1965.

Piatigorsky, Jacqueline. *Jump the Waves: A Memoir*. New York: St. Martin's Press, 1988.

Preminger, Otto. *Preminger: An Autobiography*. New York: Bantam Books, 1977.

Rifkind, Donna. *The Sun and Her Stars: Salka Viertel and Hitler's Exiles in the Golden Age of Hollywood*. New York: Other Press, 2021.

Rooney, Mickey. *Life Is Too Short*. New York: Ballantine Books, 1992.

Schanke, Robert A., ed. *"That Furious Lesbian": The Story of Mercedes de Acosta*. Carbondale: Southern Illinois University Press, 2003.

Schenderlein, Anne C. *Germany on Their Minds: German Jewish Refugees in the United States and Their Relationships with Germany, 1938–1988*. New York: Berghahn Books, 2020.

Starr, Kevin. *The Dream Endures: California Enters the 1940s*. Oxford: Oxford University Press, 2002.

Stephan, Alexander. *"Communazis": FBI Surveillance of German Emigré Writers*. Translated by Jan van Heurck. New Haven, CT: Yale University Press, 2000.

Viertel, Peter. *The Canyon*. New York: Harcourt, Brace, 1940.

Wallace, David. *Exiles in Hollywood*. Pompton Plains, NJ: Limelight, 2006.

Williams, Tom. *A Mysterious Something in the Light: The Life of Raymond Chandler*. London: Aurum, 2012.

Young, Betty Lou, and Randy Young. *Pacific Palisades: Where the Mountains Meet the Sea*. Pacific Palisades, CA: Pacific Palisades Historical Society Press, 1983.

INDEX OF NAMES

de Acosta, Mercedes: *740 Amalfi Drive* 38
Adorno, Theodor W.: *316 South Kenter Avenue* 63
Baum, Vicki: *1461 Amalfi Drive* 44
Berlau, Ruth: *165 Mabery Road* 24
Brecht, Bertolt and Helene Weigel: *817 25th Street* 58, *1063 26th Street* 62
Cage, John: *545 Swarthmore Avenue* 15
Eames, Charles and Ray: *Chautauqua Boulevard 205* 21
Eisler, Hanns: *689 Amalfi Drive* 35, *1650 Amalfi Drive* 46
Fairbanks, Douglas: *1525 Amalfi Drive* 44
Feuchtwanger, Lion and Marta: *1650 Amalfi Drive* 46, *1744 Mandeville Canyon Road* 53, *13827 Sunset Boulevard* 42, *520 Paseo Miramar (Villa Aurora)* 6
Getty, J. Paul: *17985 Pacific Coast Highway* 2
Goldberg, Whoopi: *1525 Amalfi Drive* 44
Gould, Ernest: *269 Bellino Drive* 3
Grant, Cary and Barbara Hutton: *1525 Amalfi Drive* 44
Hardt, Ludwig: *418 Mount Holyoke Avenue* 12
Harris, Roy: *Tellem Drive 1200* 8
Heard, Gerald: *545 Spoleto Drive* 29
Henreid, Paul: *18068 Blue Sail Drive* 1
Herrmann, Eva: *15000 Corona del Mar* 16, *533 Spoleto Drive* 27, *790 Latimer Road* 34
Homolka, Oskar and Florence: *914 Corsica Drive* 39
Horkheimer, Max: *13542 D'Este Drive* 49
Horner, Harry: *728 Brooktree Road* 28
Huldschinsky, Paul: *370 Via Florence* 4, *317 Mesa Road* 25
Huxley, Aldous: *701 Amalfi Drive* 32
Isherwood, Christopher: *165 Mabery Road* 24, *145 Adelaide Drive* 31
Kaus, Gina: *262 South Carmelina Avenue* 60
Kellen, Konrad: *540 Paseo Miramar* 5
Kortner, Fritz and Johanna Hofer: *120 Homewood Road* 59
Kosleck, Martin: *17310 Sunset Boulevard (Santa Ynez Inn)* 7
Landi, Elissa and Caroline Zenardi: *1525 Amalfi Drive* 44
Lang, Fritz: *2141 La Mesa Drive* 50